COWBOYS & ALIENS®

PROLOGUE

Writer
Andrew Foley

Art and Colors
Dennis Calero

GRAPHIC NOVEL

Writers
Fred Van Lente & Andrew Foley

Penciller
Luciano Lima and Magic Eye Studios

Inkers
J. Wilson
Silvio Spotti
Luciano Kars
Magic Eye Studios

Colors
Andrew Elder

Letters
Scott O. Brown

Title & Book Design
Zachary Pennington

COWBOYS & ALIENS®
created by Scott Mitchell Rosenberg

PLATINUM STUDIOS COMICS

PLATINUM STUDIOS®, INC. • LOS ANGELES, CALIFORNIA • 2006

Published by Platinum Studios Comics
an imprint of Platinum Studios™, Inc.

Scott Mitchell Rosenberg ✳ Chairman and Chief Executive Officer

Brian Altounian ✳ President and Chief Operating Officer

William L. Widmaier ✳ Senior Vice President, Head of New Media Group

Georges Elias ✳ Senior Vice President, Head of Mobile Group

Randy Greenberg ✳ Executive Vice President, Worldwide Marketing

Helene Pretsky ✳ Executive Vice President, Business Affairs and General Counsel

Aaron Severson ✳ VP, Story Development

Zachary Pennington ✳ VP Creative, New Media Group

Richard Marincic ✳ Director of Development, Filmed Entertainment

Adam Rosenblum ✳ Manager, Intellectual Property Assets

Dan Forcey ✳ Manager, Corporate Communications

Jina Jones ✳ Assistant to Director of Film/TV Development

Lee Nordling ✳ Editor

Meredith Berg ✳ Story Editor

Kalilah Robinson ✳ Editorial Assistant

Carly Wagner and Sid Davis ✳ Editorial Assistant

Platinum Studios, Inc.
11400 Olympic Bl. 14th Floor
Los Angeles, CA 90064

First Edition, December 2006

Retail Edition ISBN: 1-934220-00-0
Retailer Variant A Edition ISBN: 1-934220-01-9
Retailer Variant B Edition ISBN: 1-934220-02-7
Retailer Variant C Edition ISBN: 1-934220-03-5
Retailer Variant D Edition ISBN: 1-934220-04-3
Gold Edition ISBN: 1-934220-05-1
Classic Edition ISBN: 1-934220-06-X

10 9 8 7 6 5 4 3 2 1
Printed in Canada

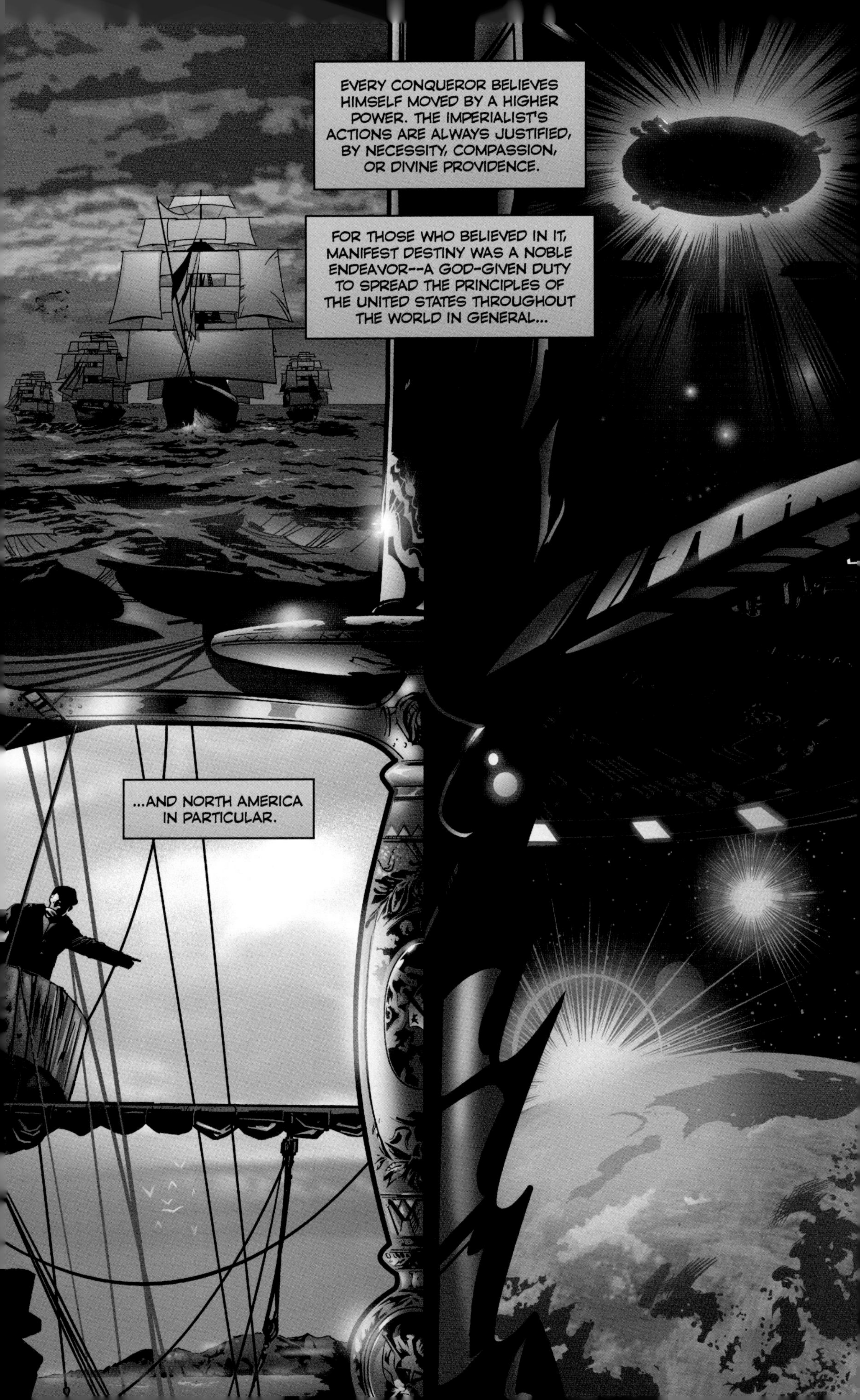
EVERY CONQUEROR BELIEVES HIMSELF MOVED BY A HIGHER POWER. THE IMPERIALIST'S ACTIONS ARE ALWAYS JUSTIFIED, BY NECESSITY, COMPASSION, OR DIVINE PROVIDENCE.
FOR THOSE WHO BELIEVED IN IT, MANIFEST DESTINY WAS A NOBLE ENDEAVOR--A GOD-GIVEN DUTY TO SPREAD THE PRINCIPLES OF THE UNITED STATES THROUGHOUT THE WORLD IN GENERAL...
...AND NORTH AMERICA IN PARTICULAR.

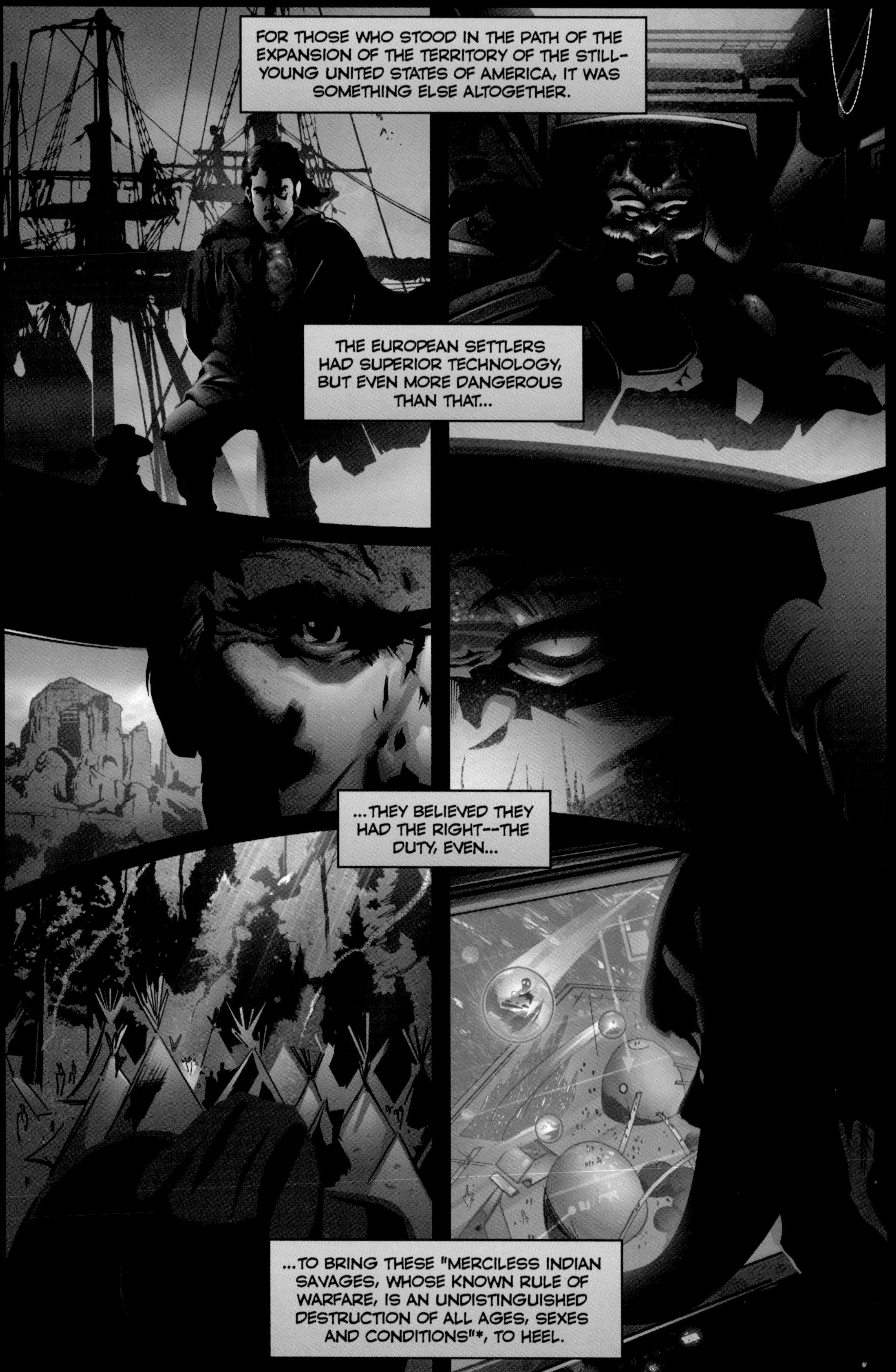
FOR THOSE WHO STOOD IN THE PATH OF THE EXPANSION OF THE TERRITORY OF THE STILL-YOUNG UNITED STATES OF AMERICA, IT WAS SOMETHING ELSE ALTOGETHER.
THE EUROPEAN SETTLERS HAD SUPERIOR TECHNOLOGY, BUT EVEN MORE DANGEROUS THAN THAT...
...THEY BELIEVED THEY HAD THE RIGHT--THE DUTY, EVEN...
...TO BRING THESE "MERCILESS INDIAN SAVAGES, WHOSE KNOWN RULE OF WARFARE, IS AN UNDISTINGUISHED DESTRUCTION OF ALL AGES, SEXES AND CONDITIONS"*, TO HEEL.

*QUOTE FROM THE DECLARATION OF INDEPENDENCE OF THE UNITED STATES OF AMERICA

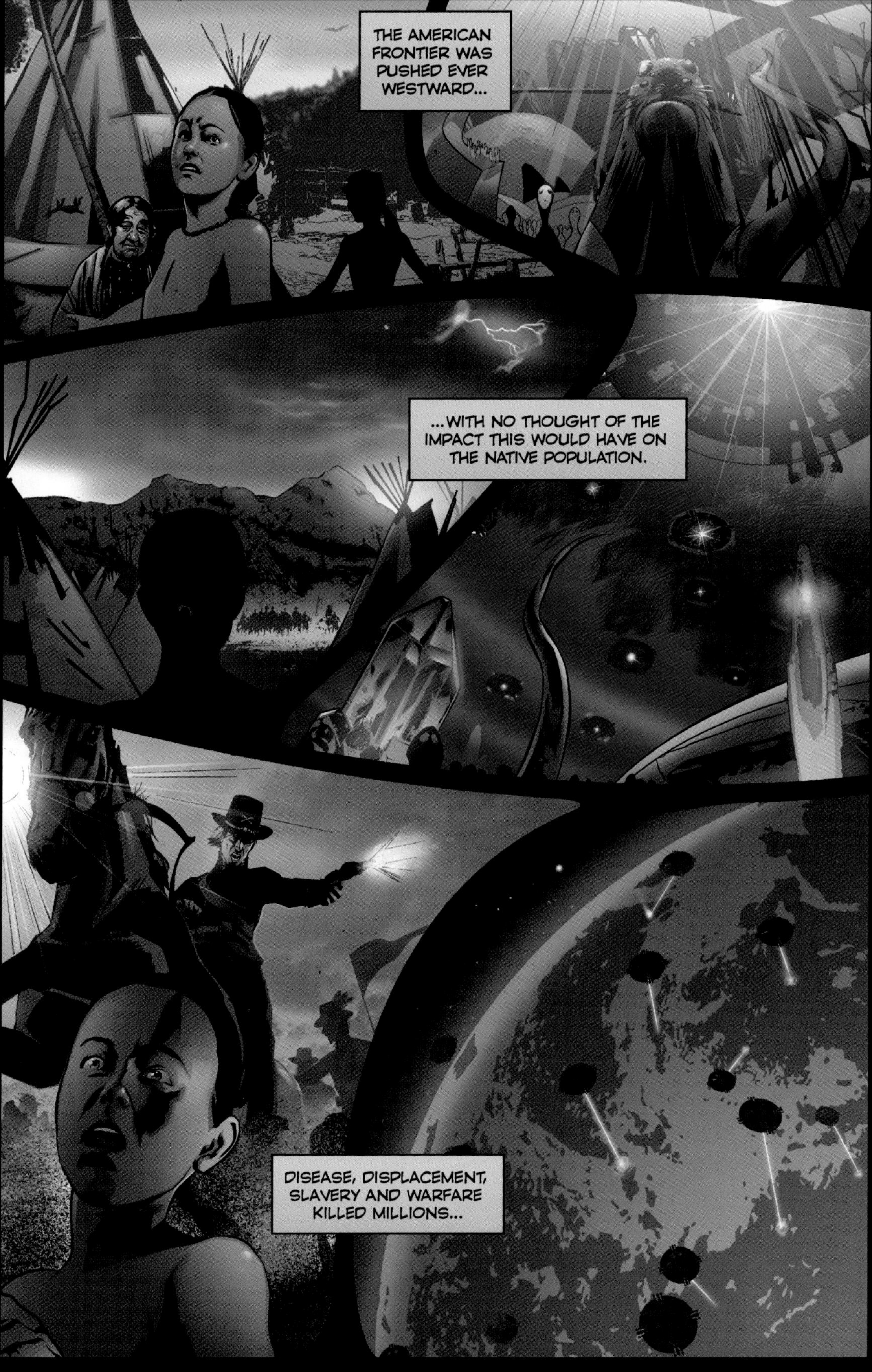
THE AMERICAN FRONTIER WAS PUSHED EVER WESTWARD...
...WITH NO THOUGHT OF THE IMPACT THIS WOULD HAVE ON THE NATIVE POPULATION.
DISEASE, DISPLACEMENT, SLAVERY AND WARFARE KILLED MILLIONS...

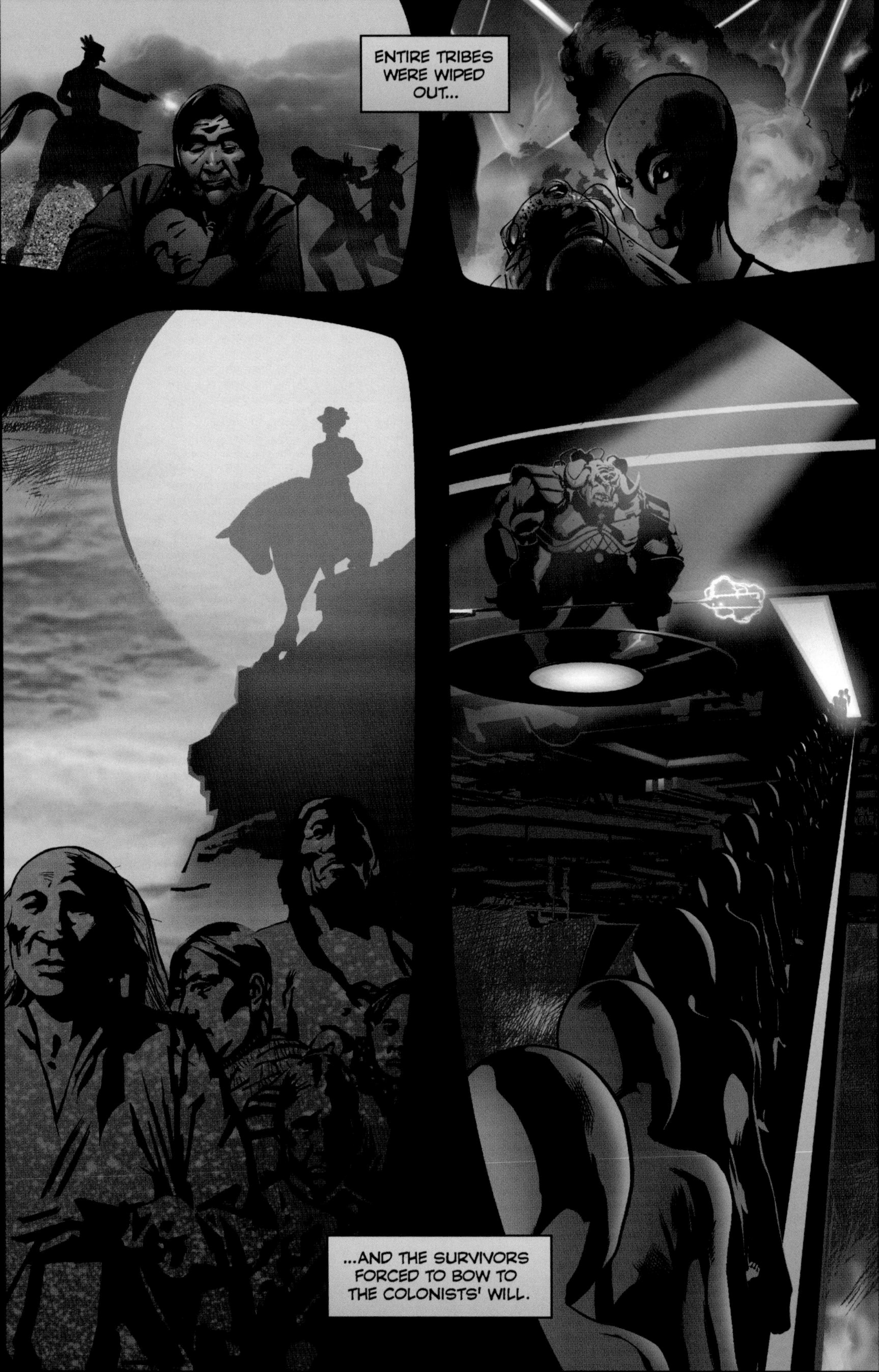
ENTIRE TRIBES WERE WIPED OUT...
...AND THE SURVIVORS FORCED TO BOW TO THE COLONISTS' WILL.

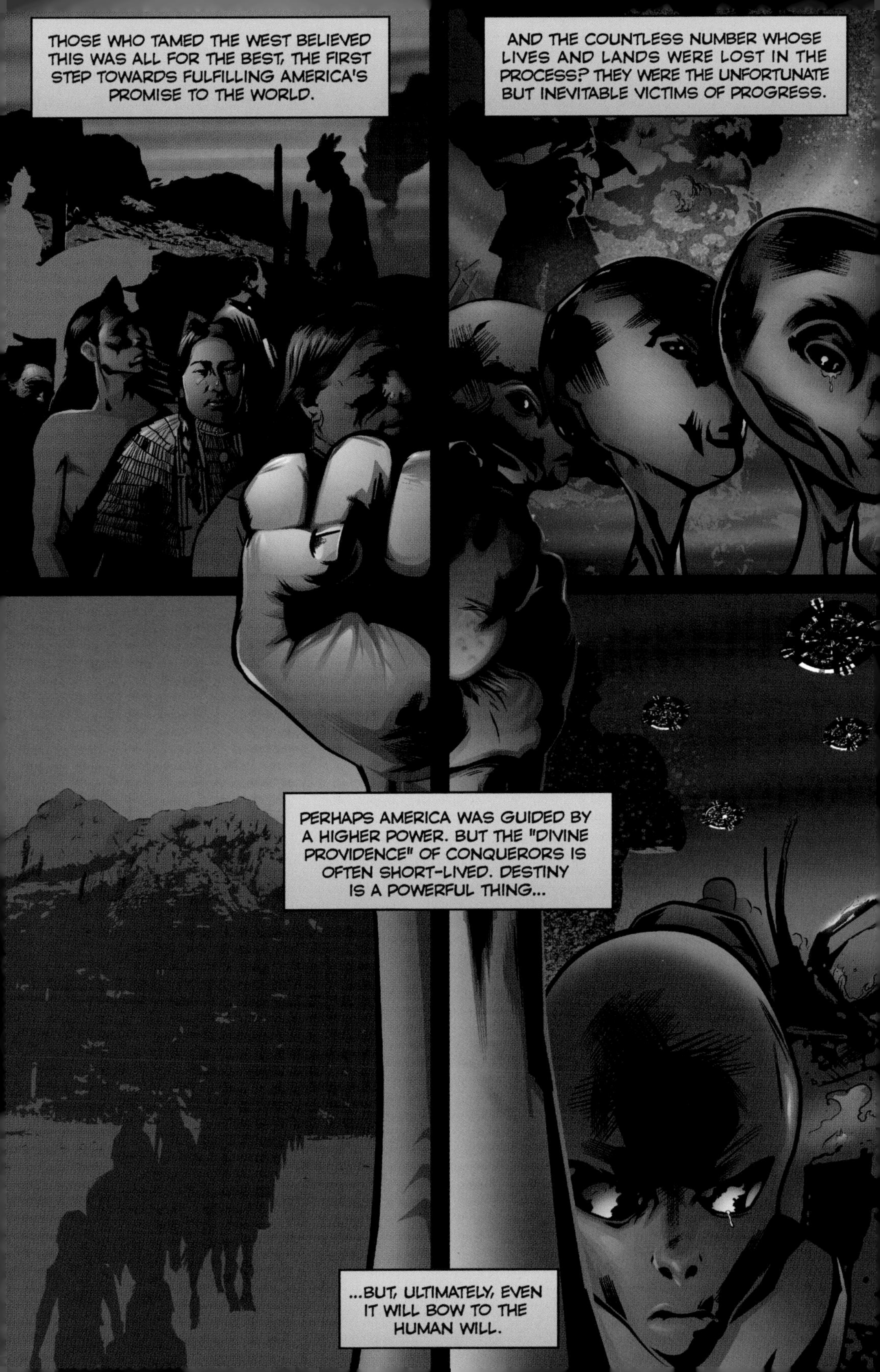
THOSE WHO TAMED THE WEST BELIEVED THIS WAS ALL FOR THE BEST, THE FIRST STEP TOWARDS FULFILLING AMERICA'S PROMISE TO THE WORLD.
AND THE COUNTLESS NUMBER WHOSE LIVES AND LANDS WERE LOST IN THE PROCESS? THEY WERE THE UNFORTUNATE BUT INEVITABLE VICTIMS OF PROGRESS.
PERHAPS AMERICA WAS GUIDED BY A HIGHER POWER. BUT THE "DIVINE PROVIDENCE" OF CONQUERORS IS OFTEN SHORT-LIVED. DESTINY IS A POWERFUL THING...
...BUT, ULTIMATELY, EVEN IT WILL BOW TO THE HUMAN WILL.

The Old West
1873

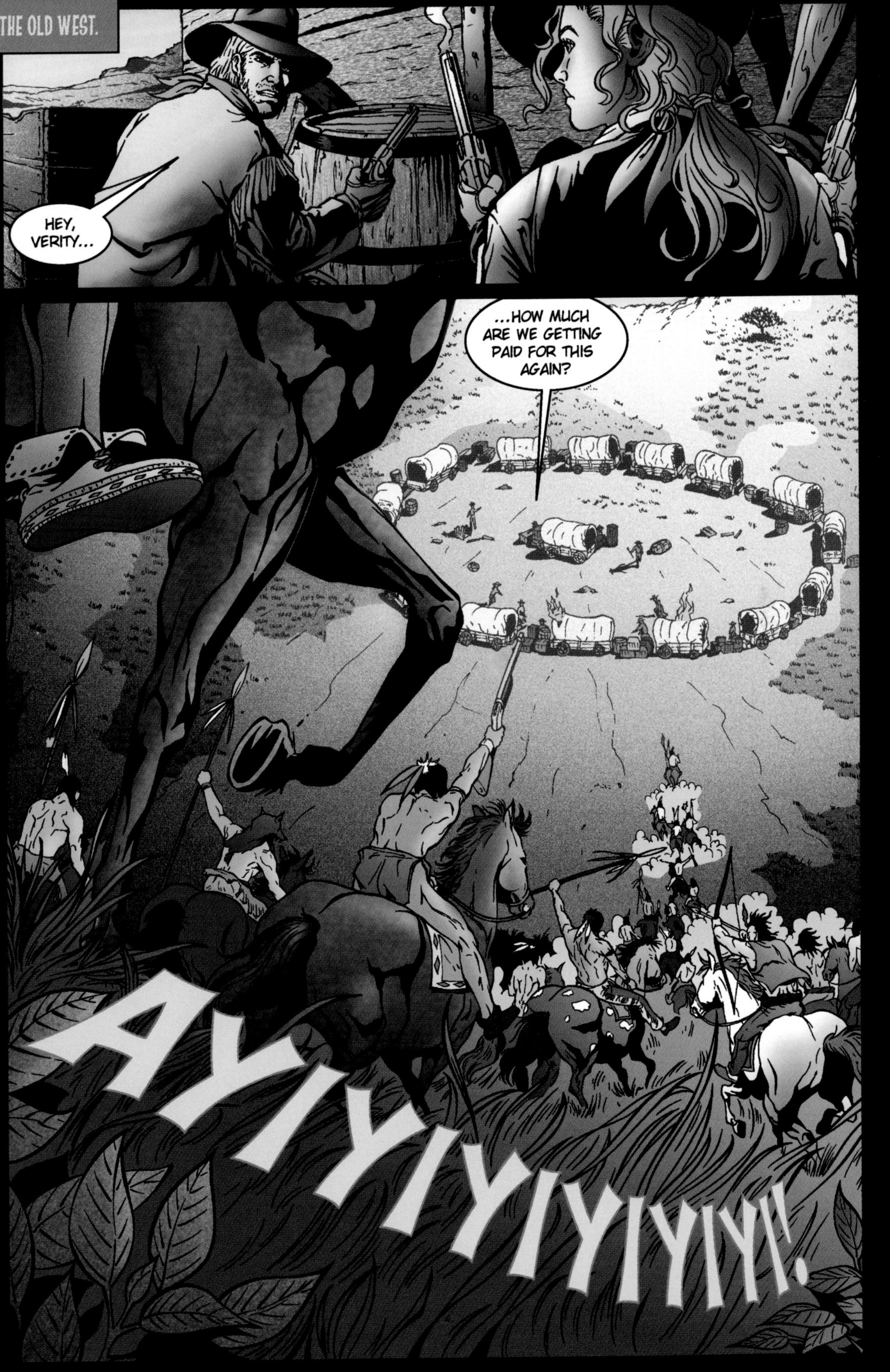
THE OLD WEST.
HEY, VERITY...
...HOW MUCH ARE WE GETTING PAID FOR THIS AGAIN?
AYIYIYIYIYIYI!

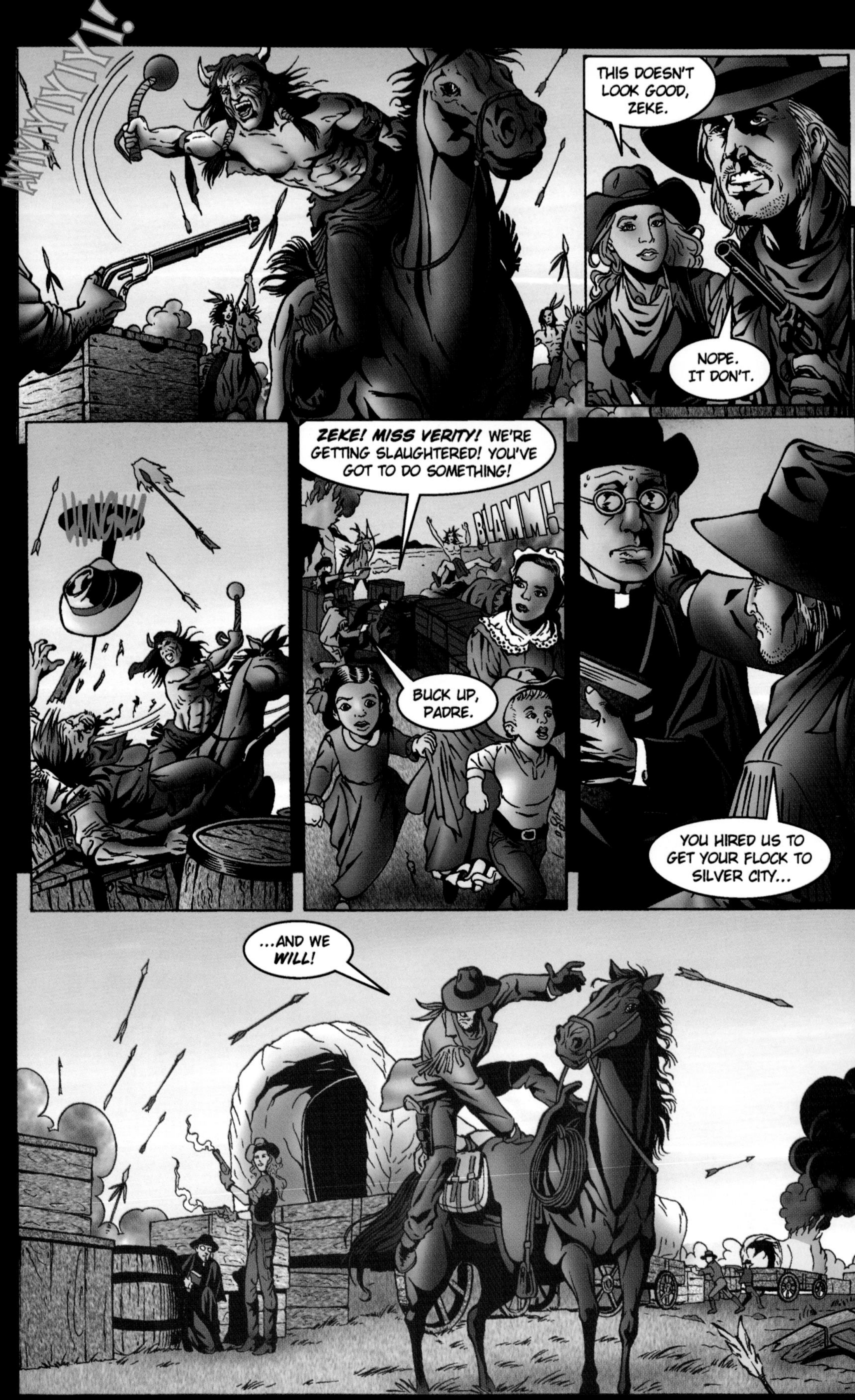
THIS DOESN'T LOOK GOOD, ZEKE.
NOPE. IT DON'T.
ZEKE! MISS VERITY! WE'RE GETTING SLAUGHTERED! YOU'VE GOT TO DO SOMETHING!
BUCK UP, PADRE.
YOU HIRED US TO GET YOUR FLOCK TO SILVER CITY...
...AND WE WILL!

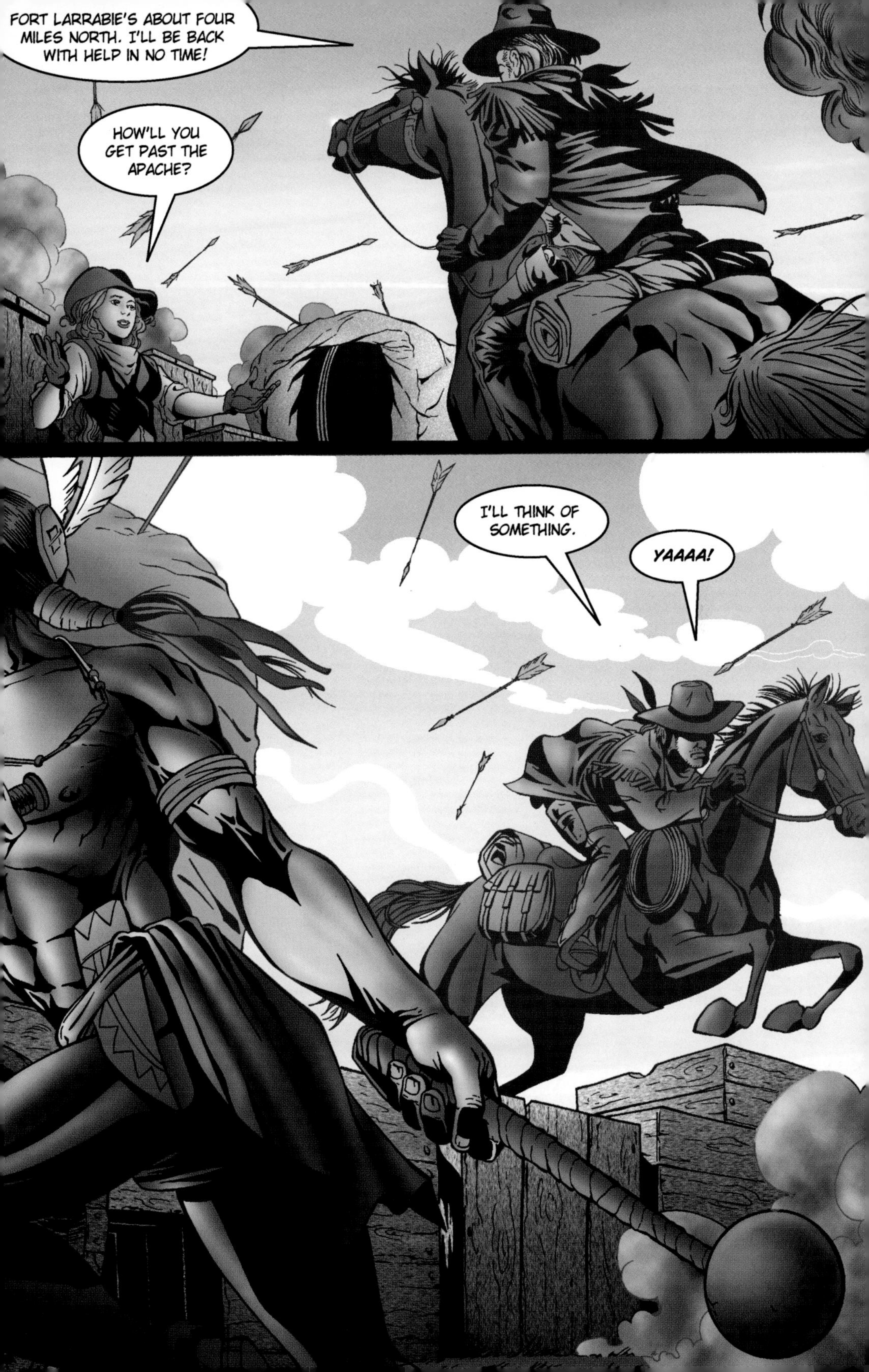
FORT LARRABIE'S ABOUT FOUR MILES NORTH. I'LL BE BACK WITH HELP IN NO TIME!
HOW'LL YOU GET PAST THE APACHE?
I'LL THINK OF SOMETHING.
YAAAA!

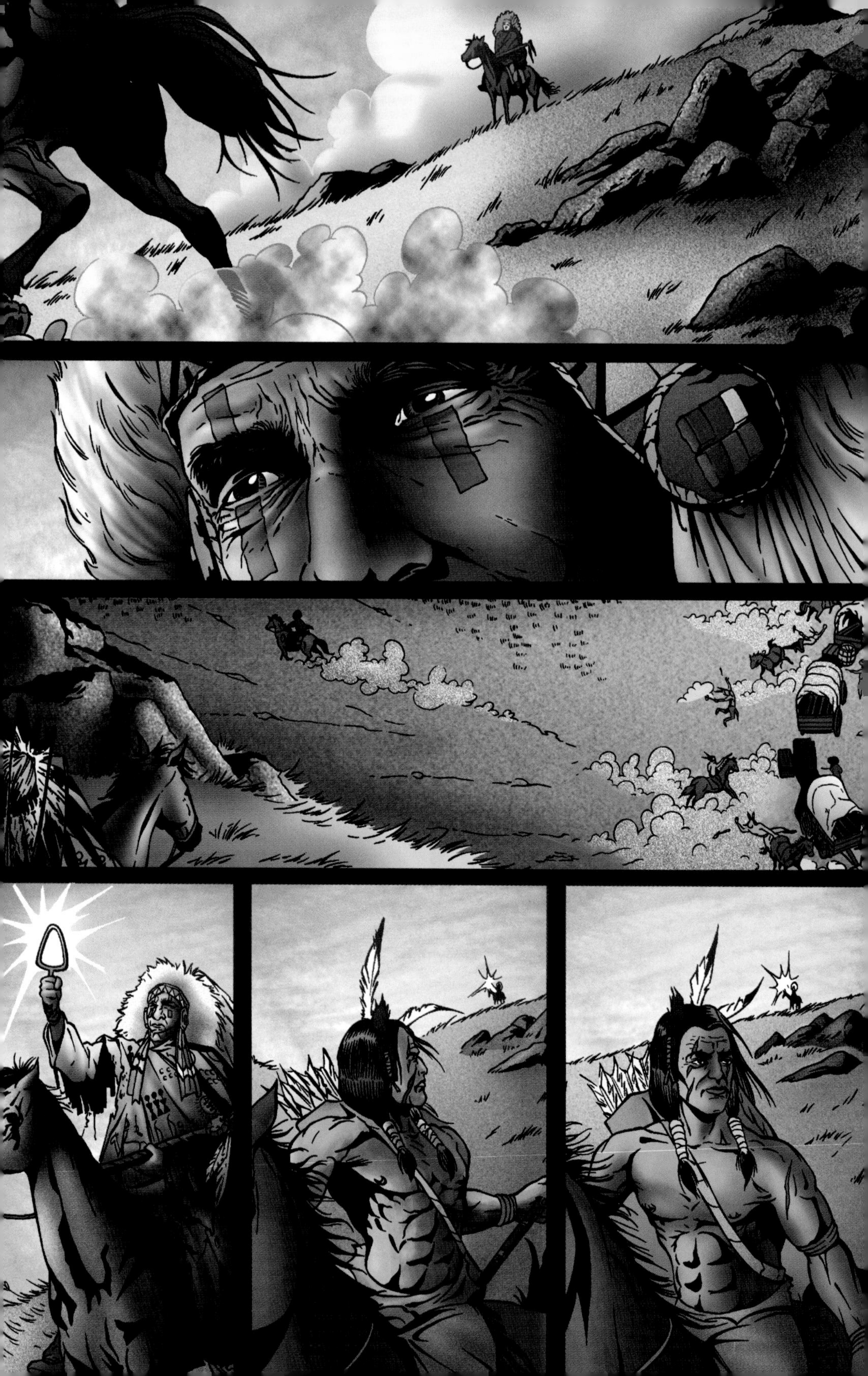

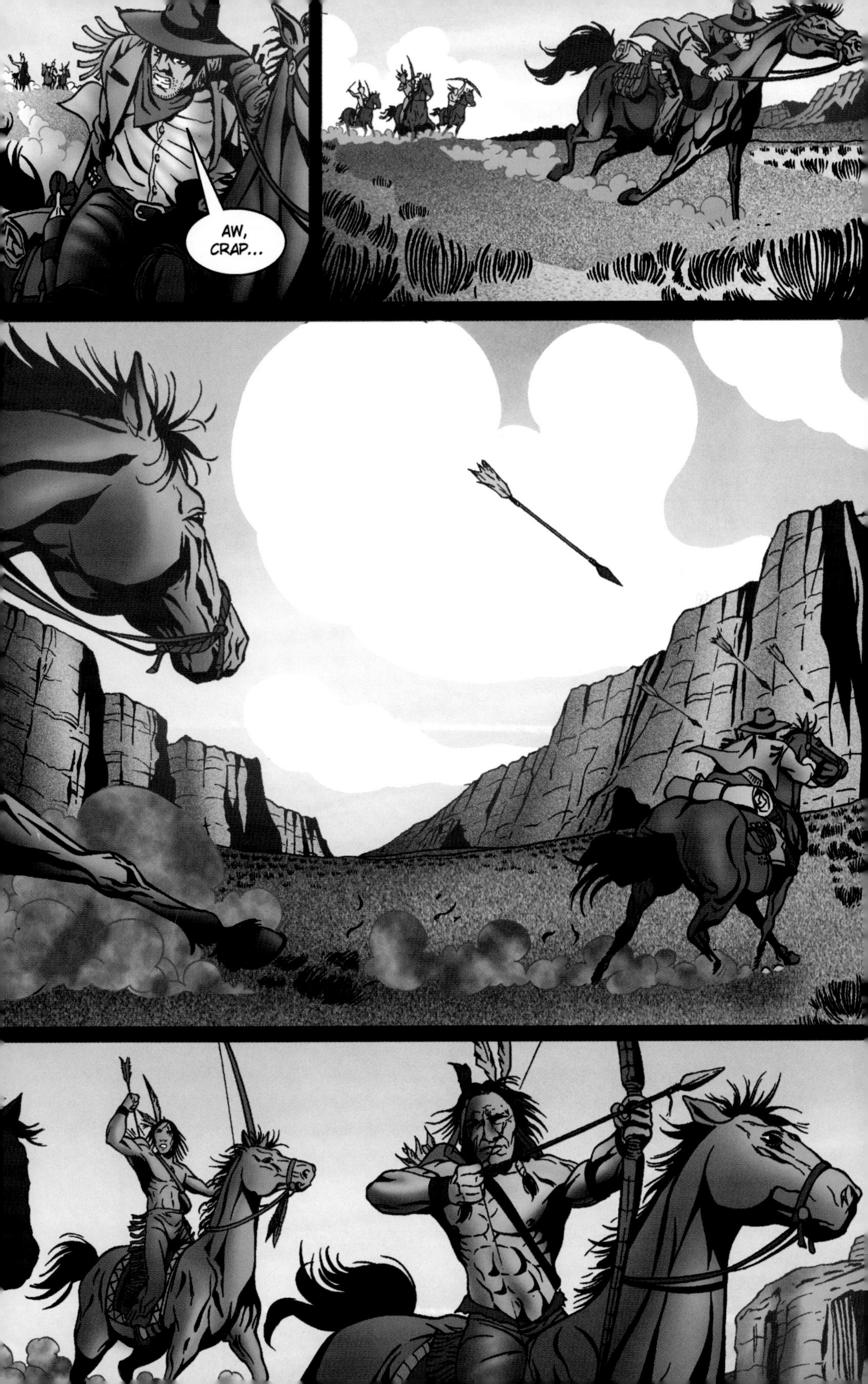
AW, CRAP...

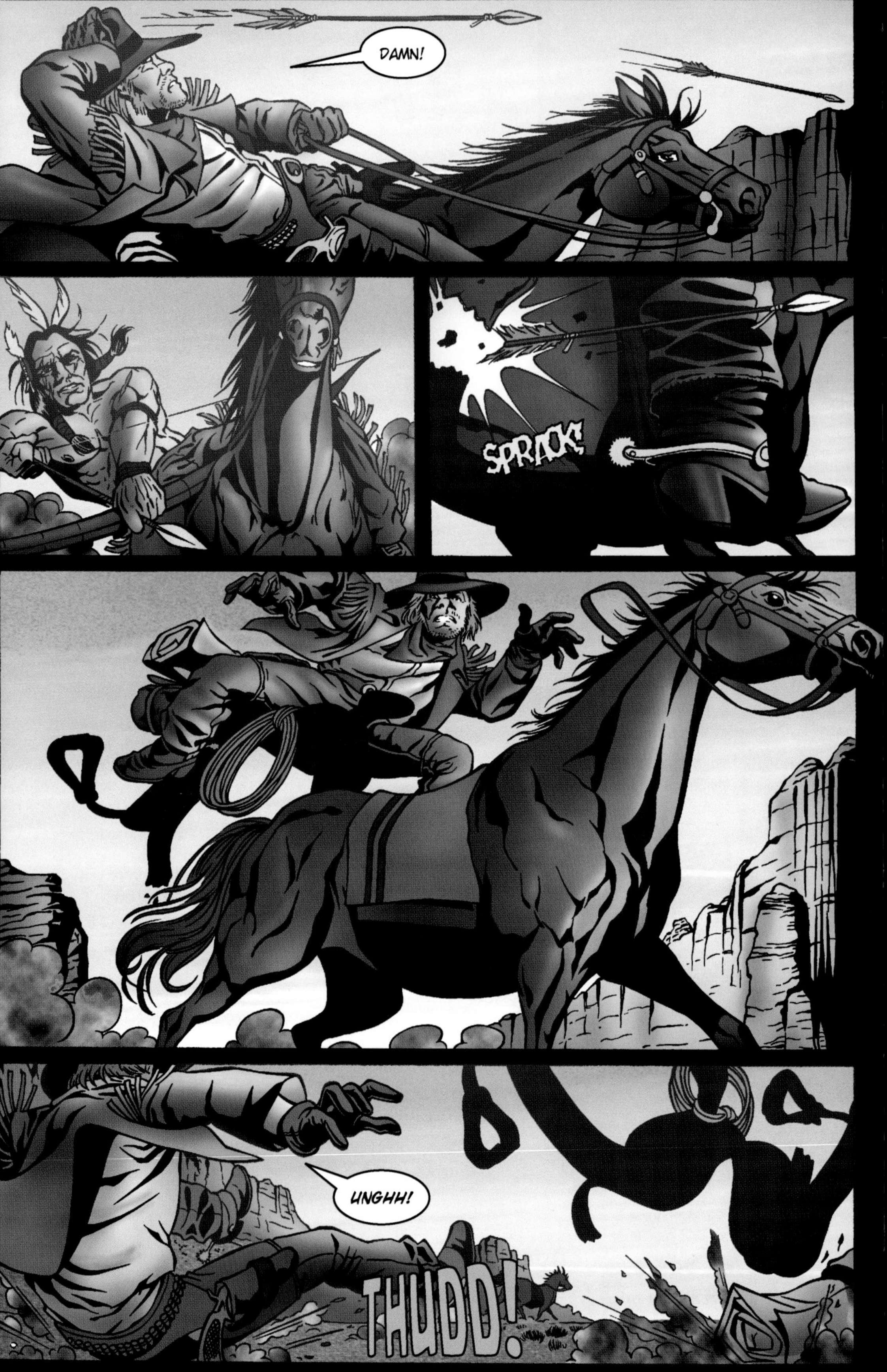
DAMN!
SPRACK!
UNGHH!
THUDD!

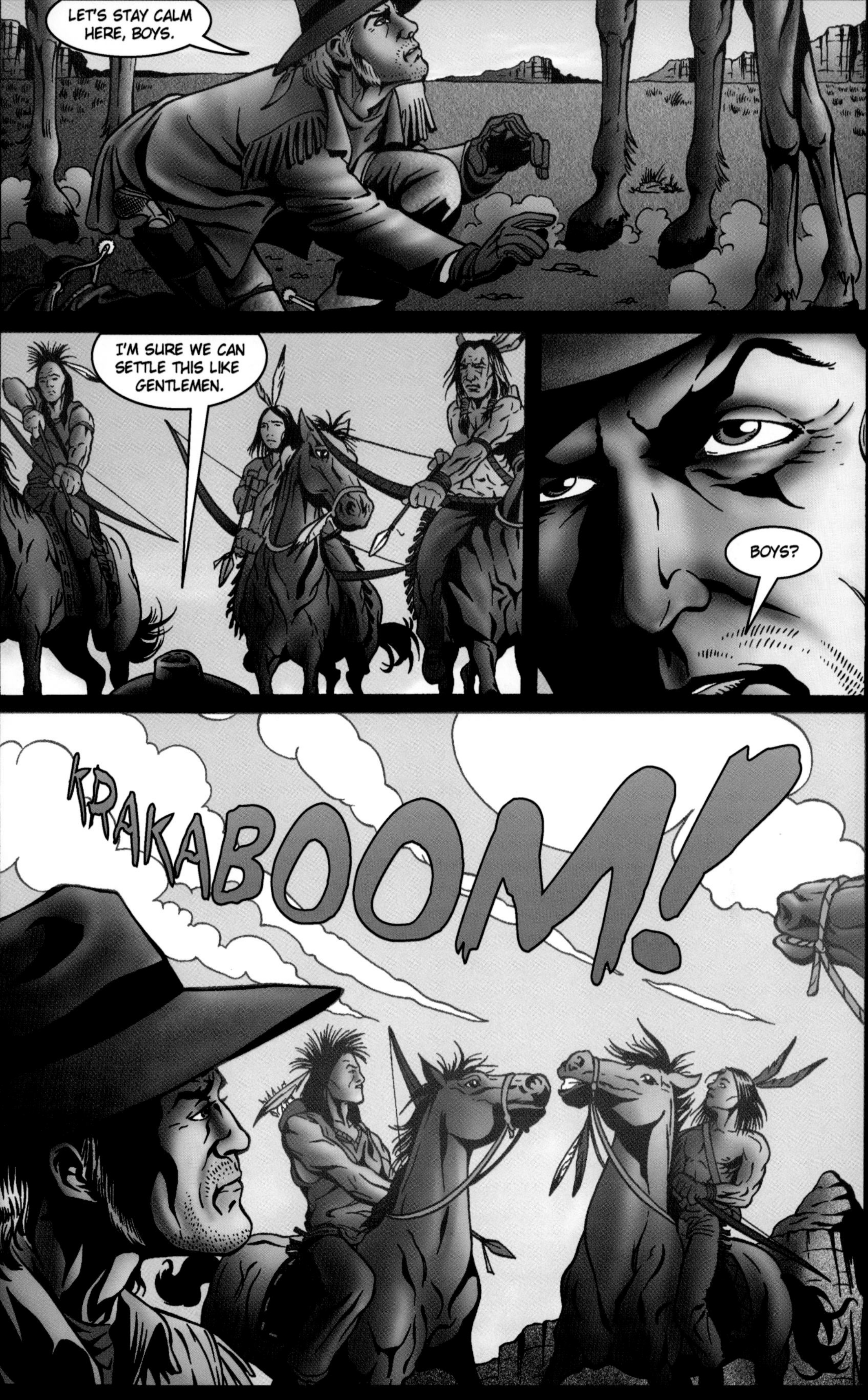
LET'S STAY CALM HERE, BOYS.
I'M SURE WE CAN SETTLE THIS LIKE GENTLEMEN.
BOYS?
KRAKABOOM!

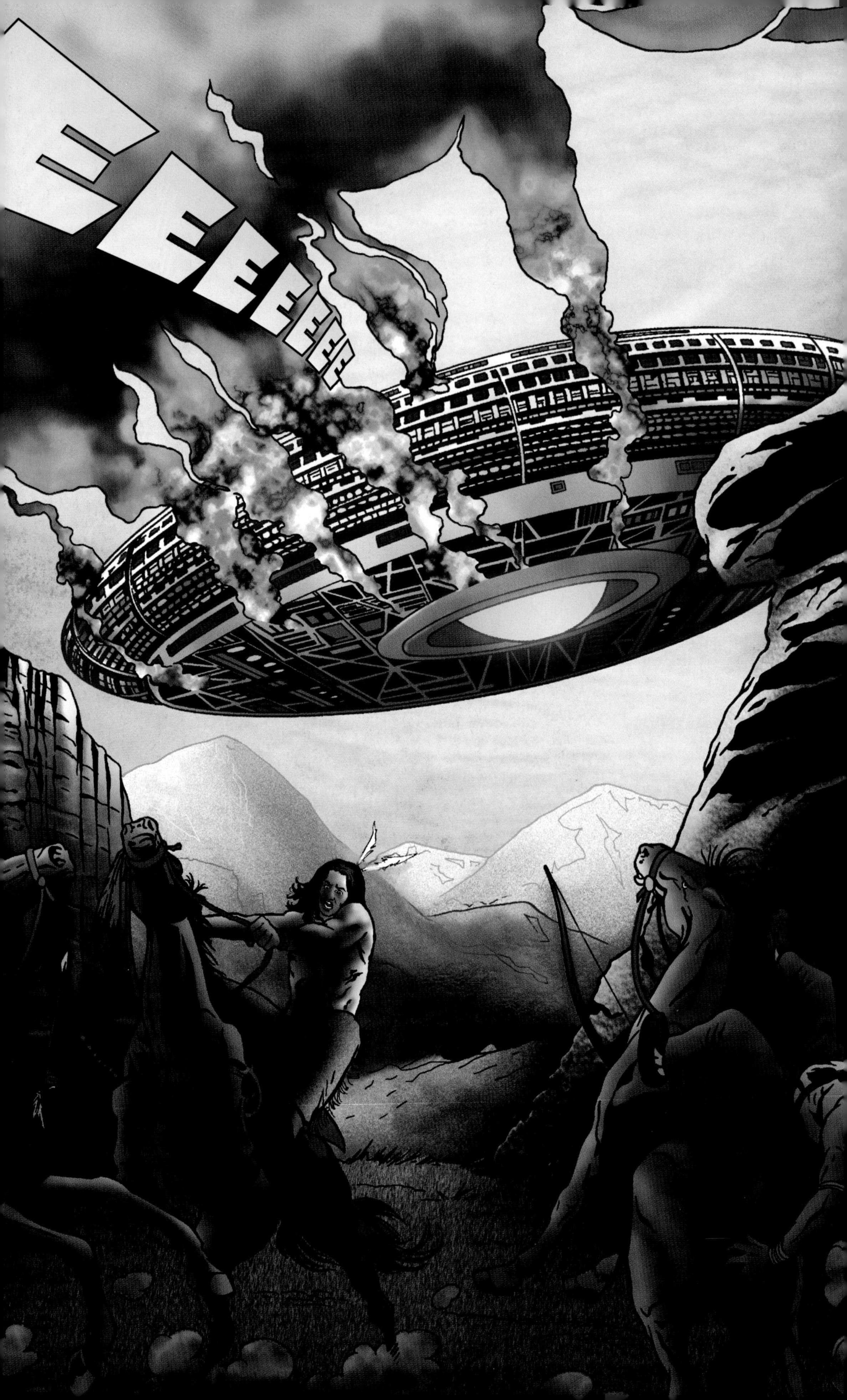

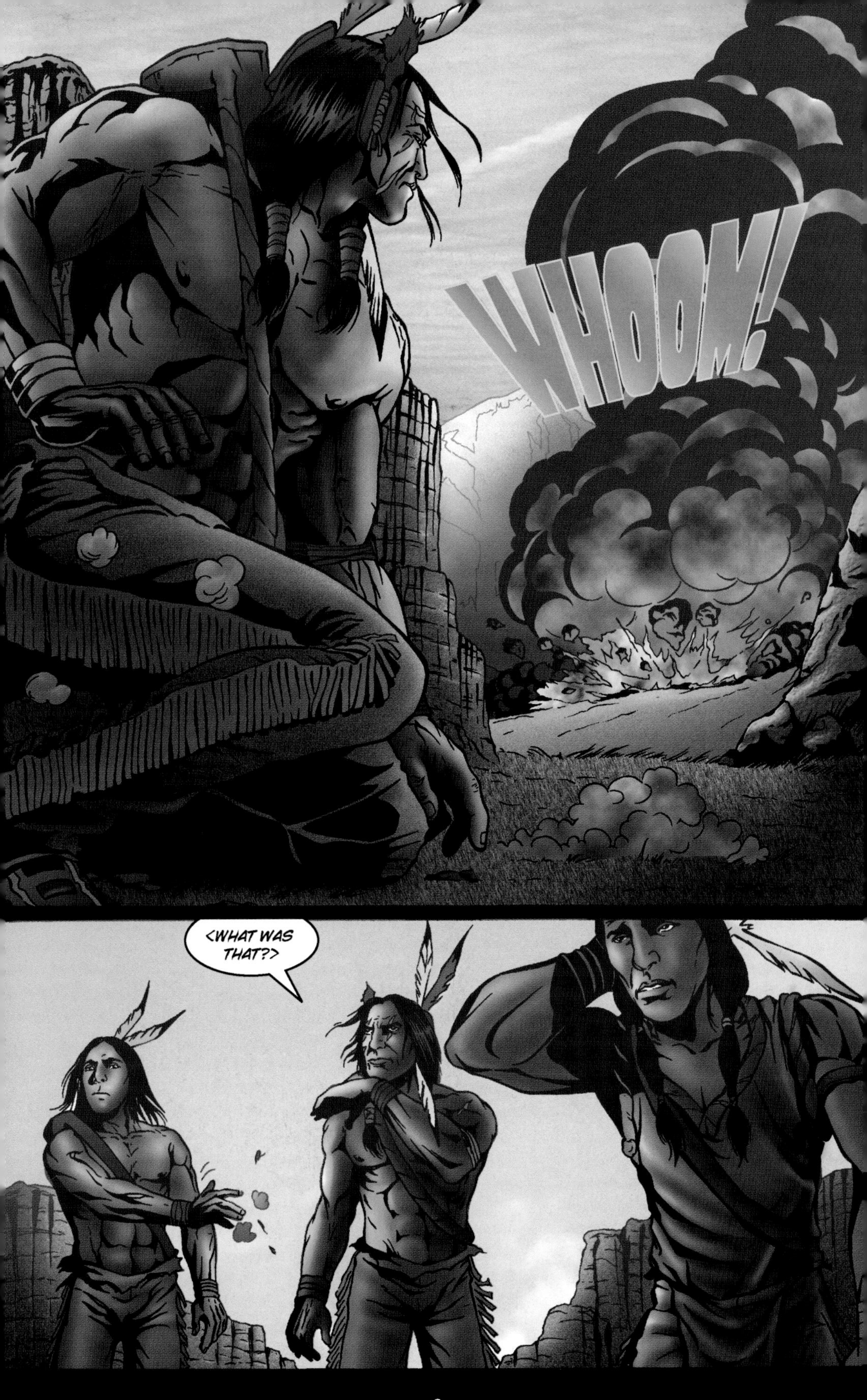
WHOOM!
<WHAT WAS THAT?>

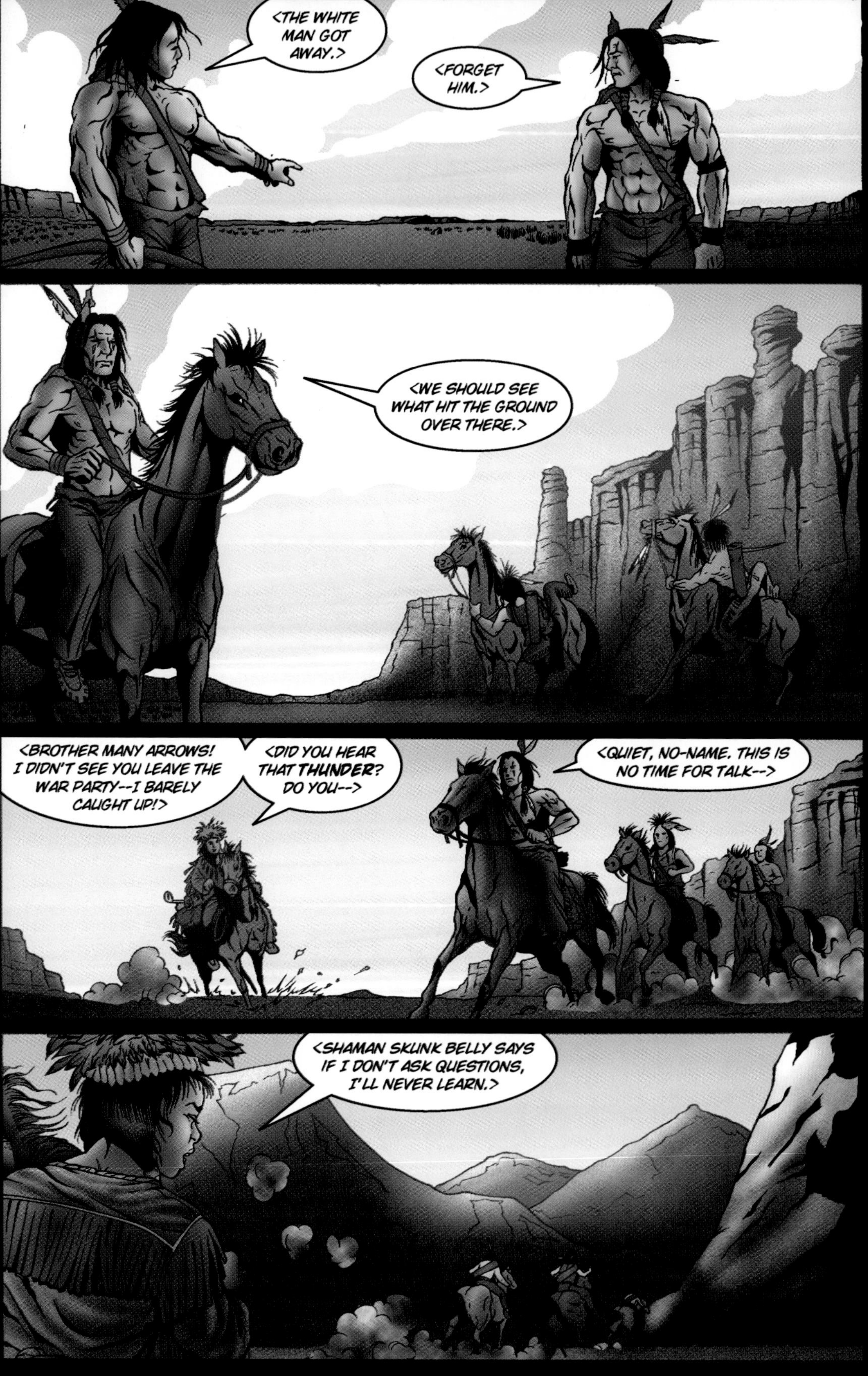
<THE WHITE MAN GOT AWAY.>
<FORGET HIM.>
<WE SHOULD SEE WHAT HIT THE GROUND OVER THERE.>
<BROTHER MANY ARROWS! I DIDN'T SEE YOU LEAVE THE WAR PARTY--I BARELY CAUGHT UP!>
<DID YOU HEAR THAT **THUNDER**? DO YOU-->
<QUIET, NO-NAME. THIS IS NO TIME FOR TALK-->
<SHAMAN SKUNK BELLY SAYS IF I DON'T ASK QUESTIONS, I'LL NEVER LEARN.>

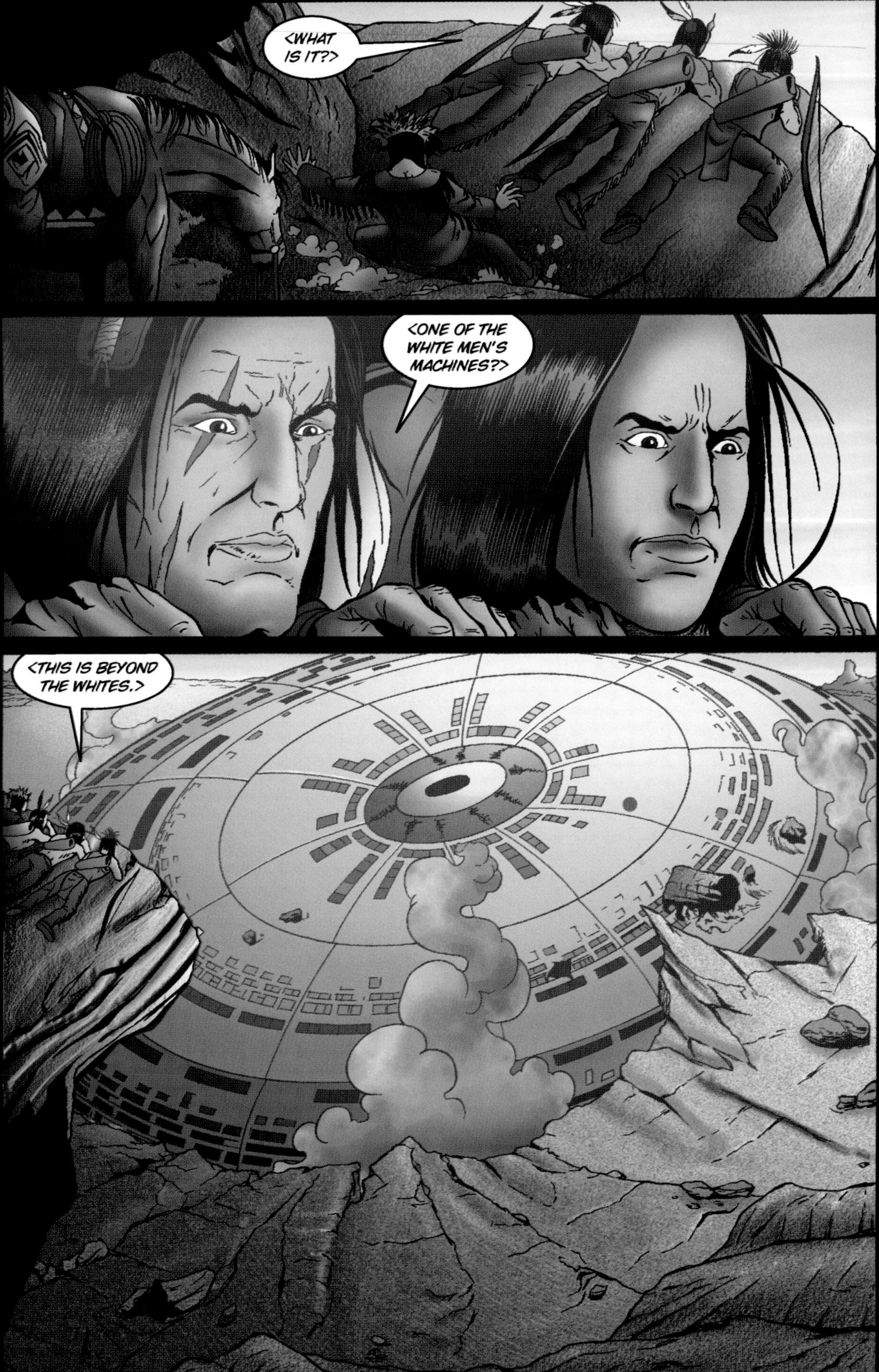
<WHAT IS IT?>
<ONE OF THE WHITE MEN'S MACHINES?>
<THIS IS BEYOND THE WHITES.>

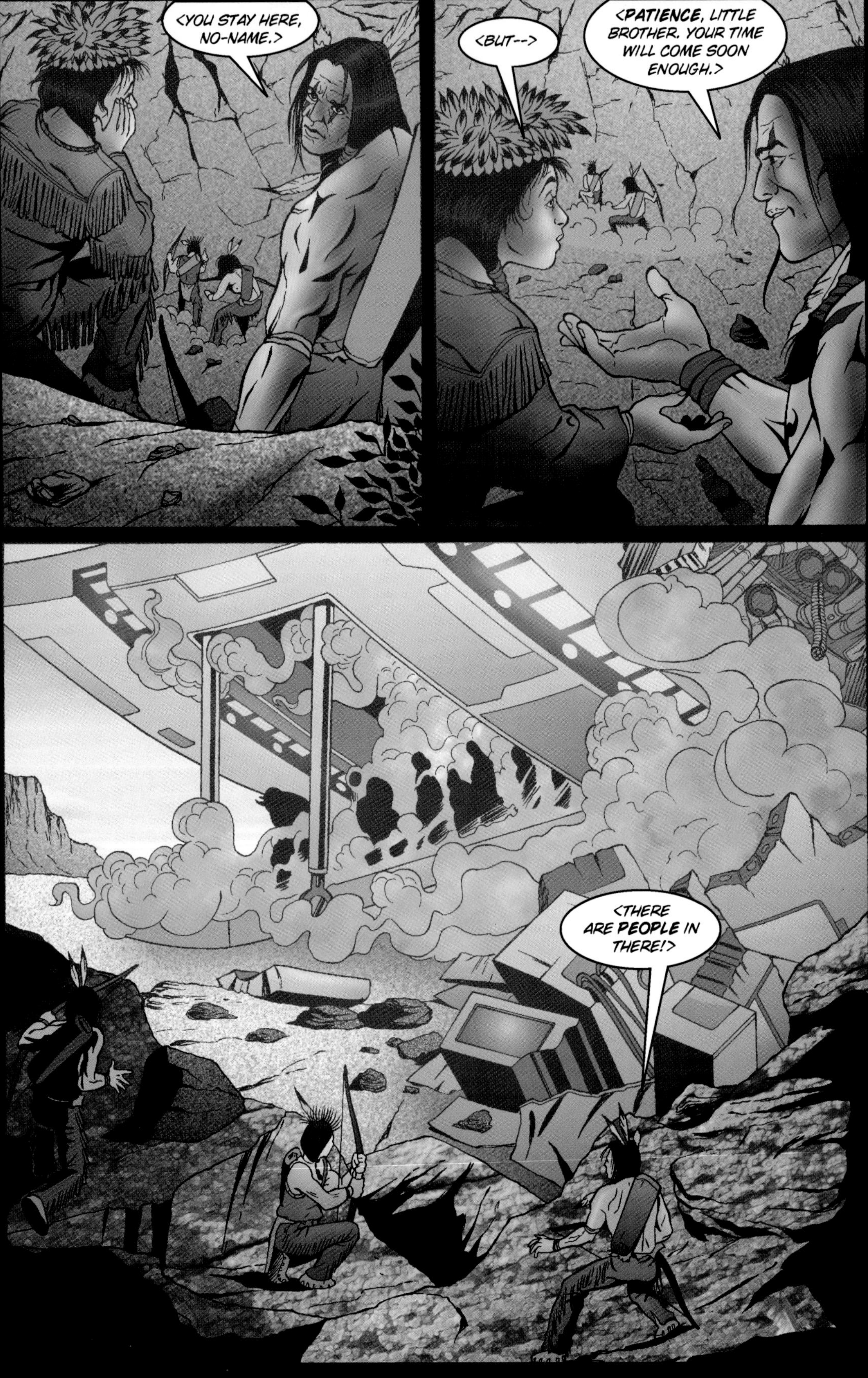
<YOU STAY HERE, NO-NAME.>
<BUT-->
<PATIENCE, LITTLE BROTHER. YOUR TIME WILL COME SOON ENOUGH.>
<THERE ARE PEOPLE IN THERE!>

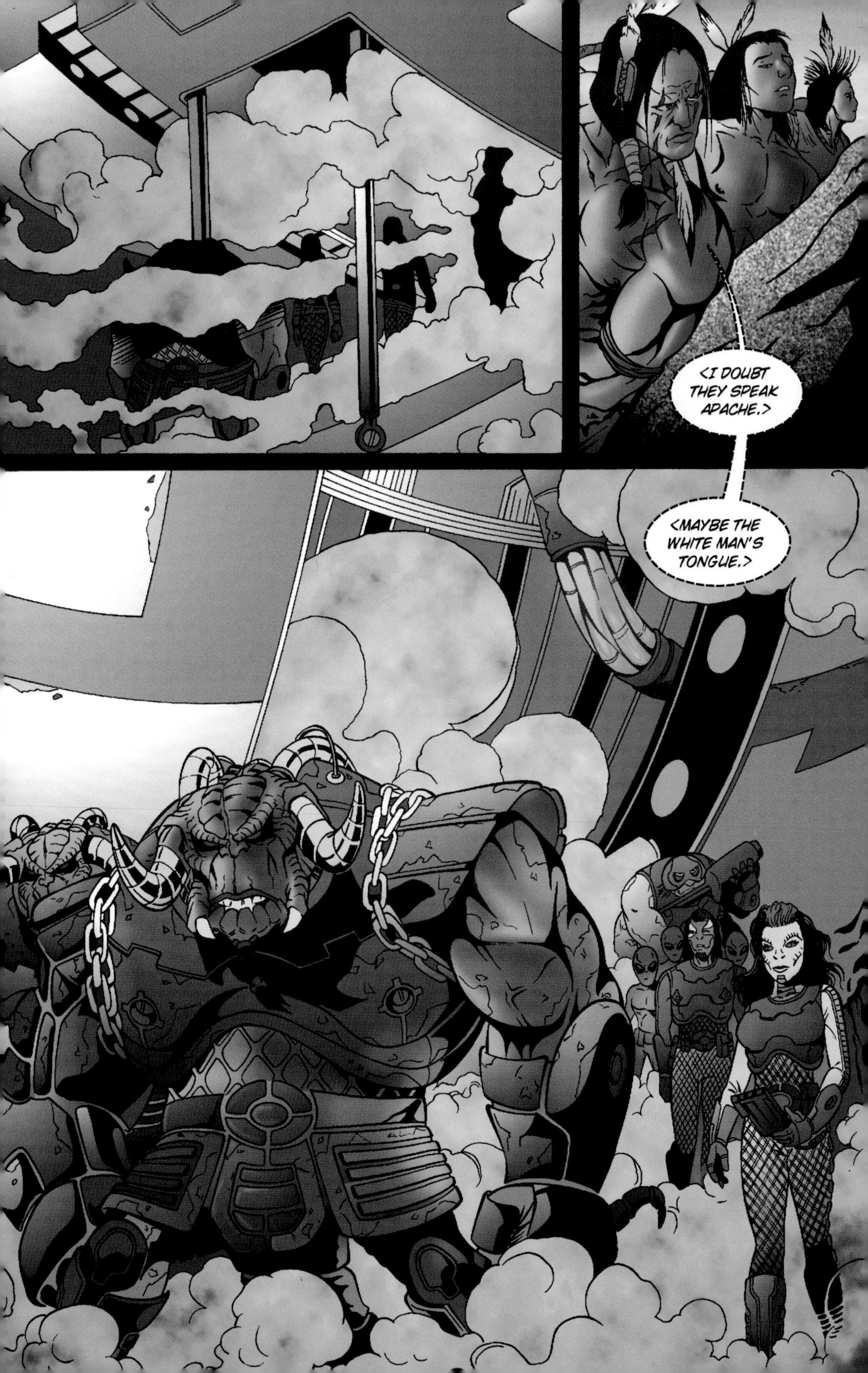
<I DOUBT THEY SPEAK APACHE.>
<MAYBE THE WHITE MAN'S TONGUE.>

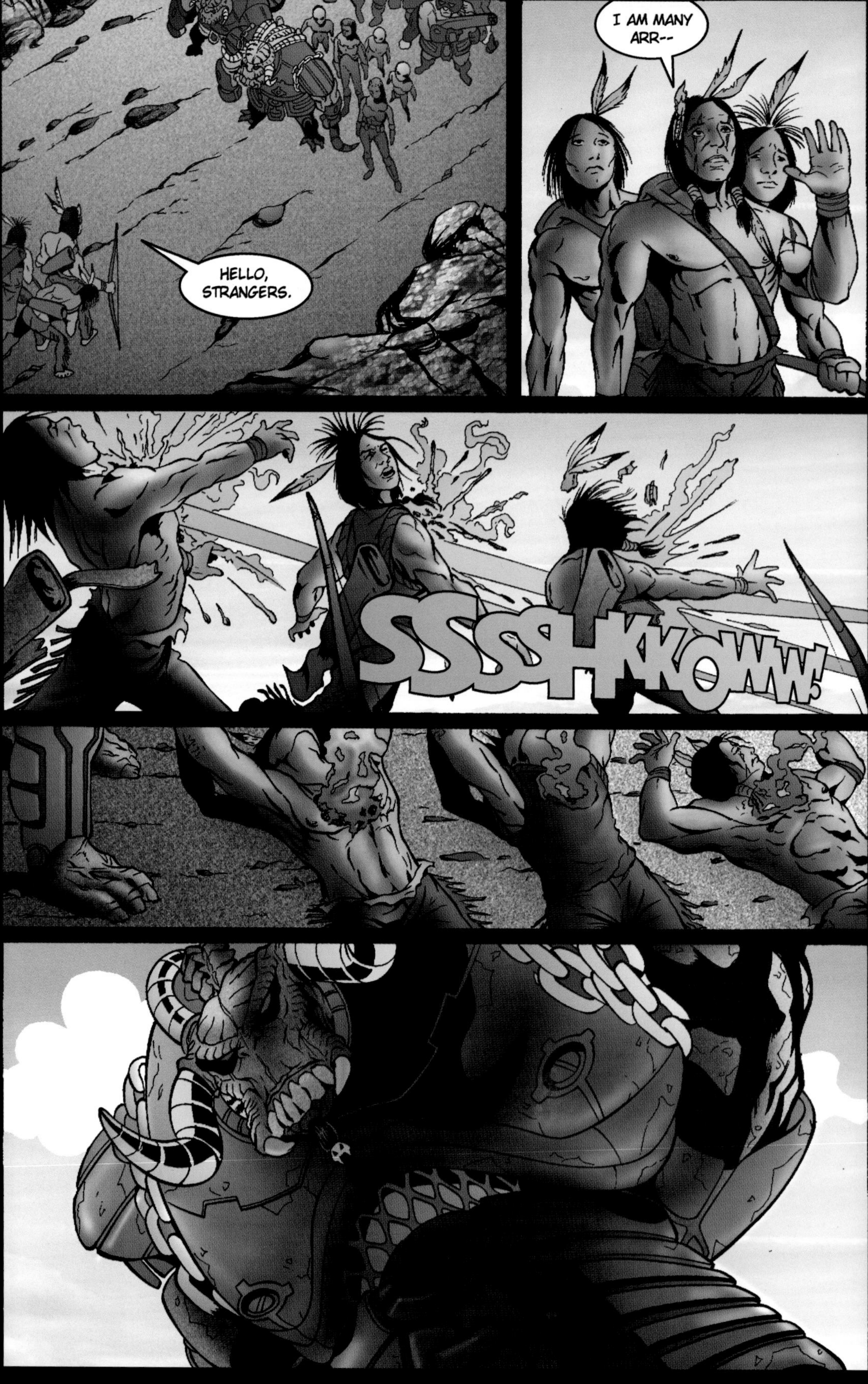
HELLO, STRANGERS.
I AM MANY ARR--
SSSSHKKOWW!

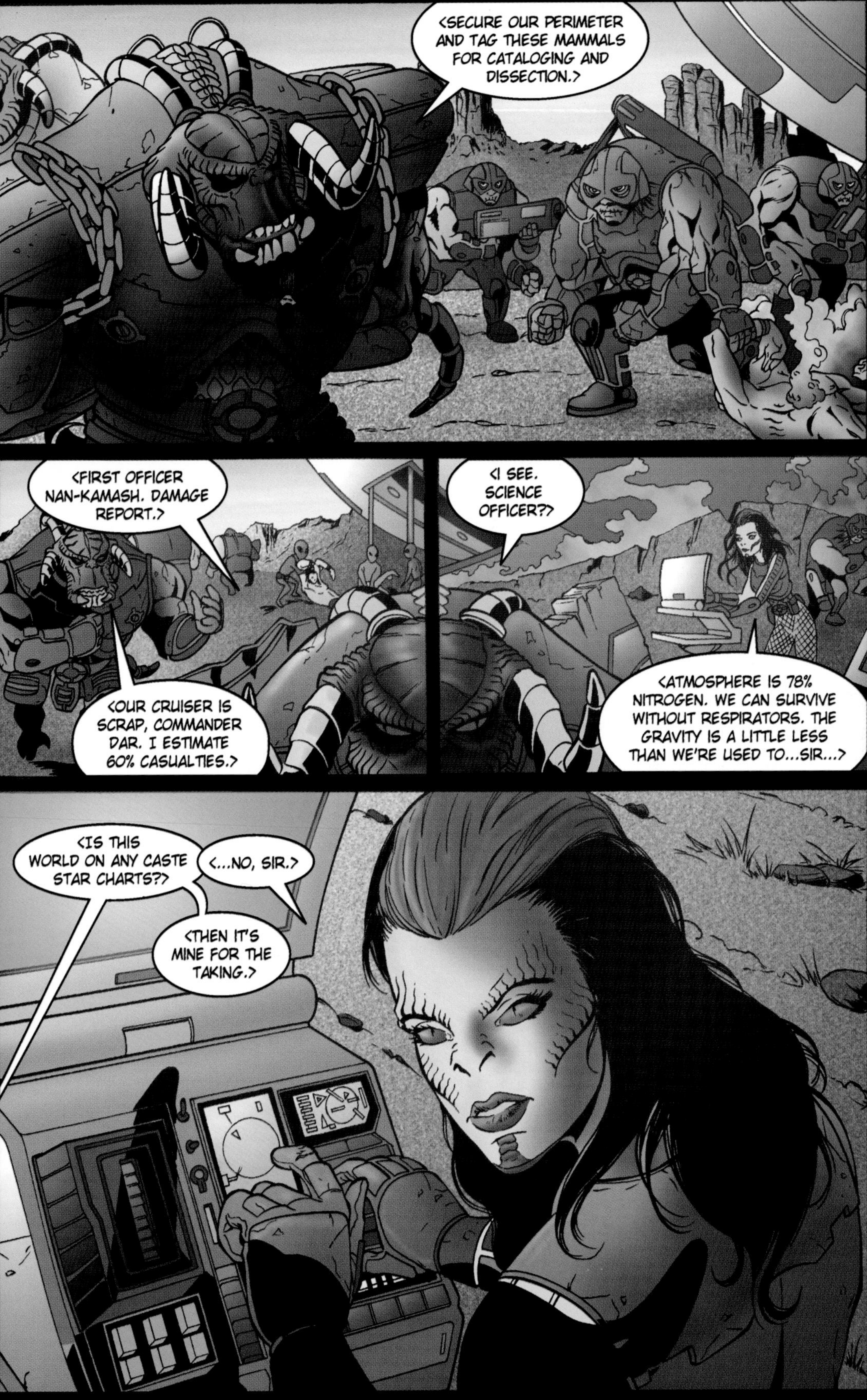
<SECURE OUR PERIMETER AND TAG THESE MAMMALS FOR CATALOGING AND DISSECTION.>
<FIRST OFFICER NAN-KAMASH. DAMAGE REPORT.>
<OUR CRUISER IS SCRAP, COMMANDER DAR. I ESTIMATE 60% CASUALTIES.>
<I SEE. SCIENCE OFFICER?>
<ATMOSPHERE IS 78% NITROGEN. WE CAN SURVIVE WITHOUT RESPIRATORS. THE GRAVITY IS A LITTLE LESS THAN WE'RE USED TO...SIR...>
<IS THIS WORLD ON ANY CASTE STAR CHARTS?>
<...NO, SIR.>
<THEN IT'S MINE FOR THE TAKING.>

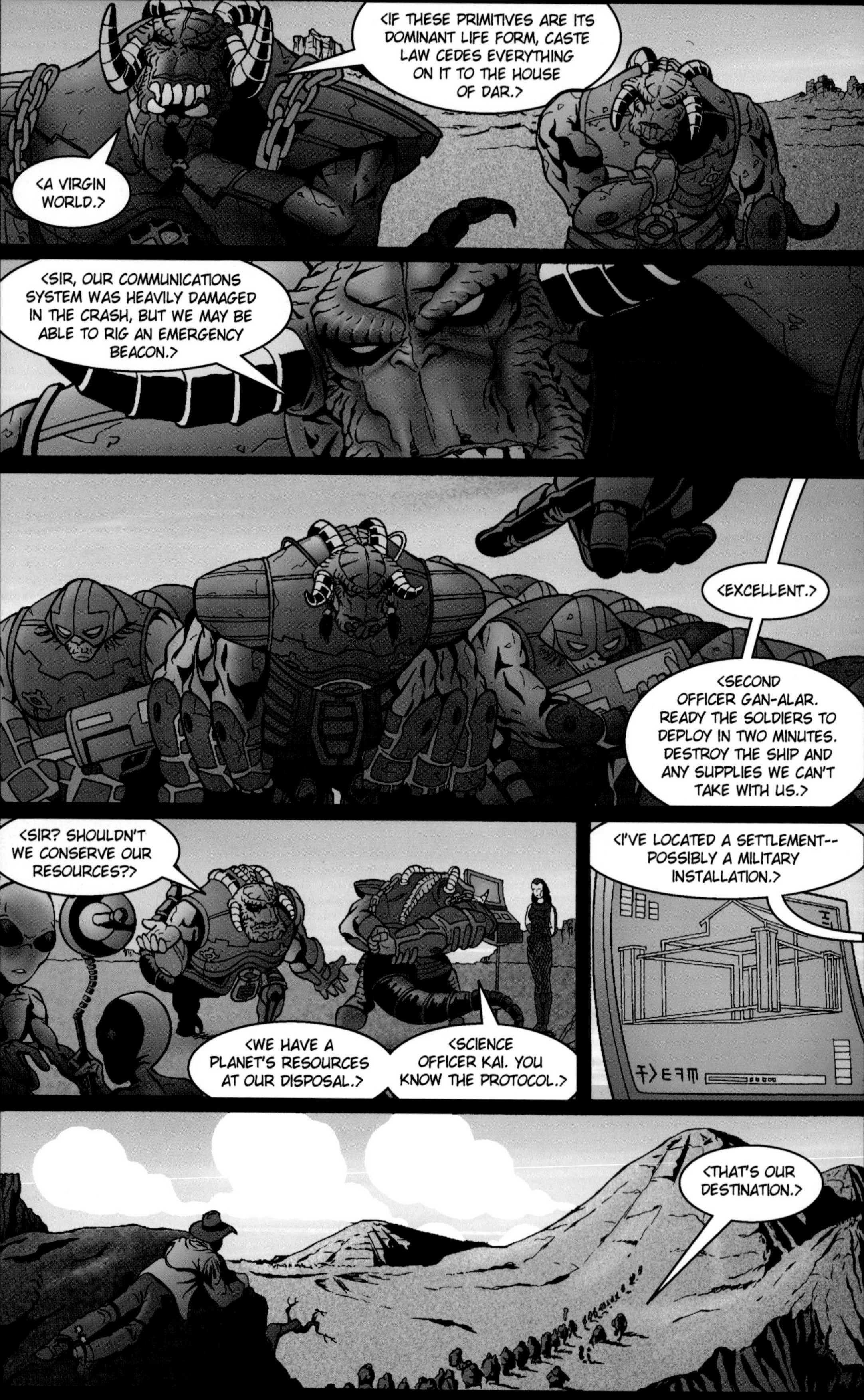
<IF THESE PRIMITIVES ARE ITS DOMINANT LIFE FORM, CASTE LAW CEDES EVERYTHING ON IT TO THE HOUSE OF DAR.>
<A VIRGIN WORLD.>
<SIR, OUR COMMUNICATIONS SYSTEM WAS HEAVILY DAMAGED IN THE CRASH, BUT WE MAY BE ABLE TO RIG AN EMERGENCY BEACON.>
<EXCELLENT.>
<SECOND OFFICER GAN-ALAR. READY THE SOLDIERS TO DEPLOY IN TWO MINUTES. DESTROY THE SHIP AND ANY SUPPLIES WE CAN'T TAKE WITH US.>
<SIR? SHOULDN'T WE CONSERVE OUR RESOURCES?>
<WE HAVE A PLANET'S RESOURCES AT OUR DISPOSAL.>
<SCIENCE OFFICER KAI. YOU KNOW THE PROTOCOL.>
<I'VE LOCATED A SETTLEMENT-- POSSIBLY A MILITARY INSTALLATION.>
<THAT'S OUR DESTINATION.>

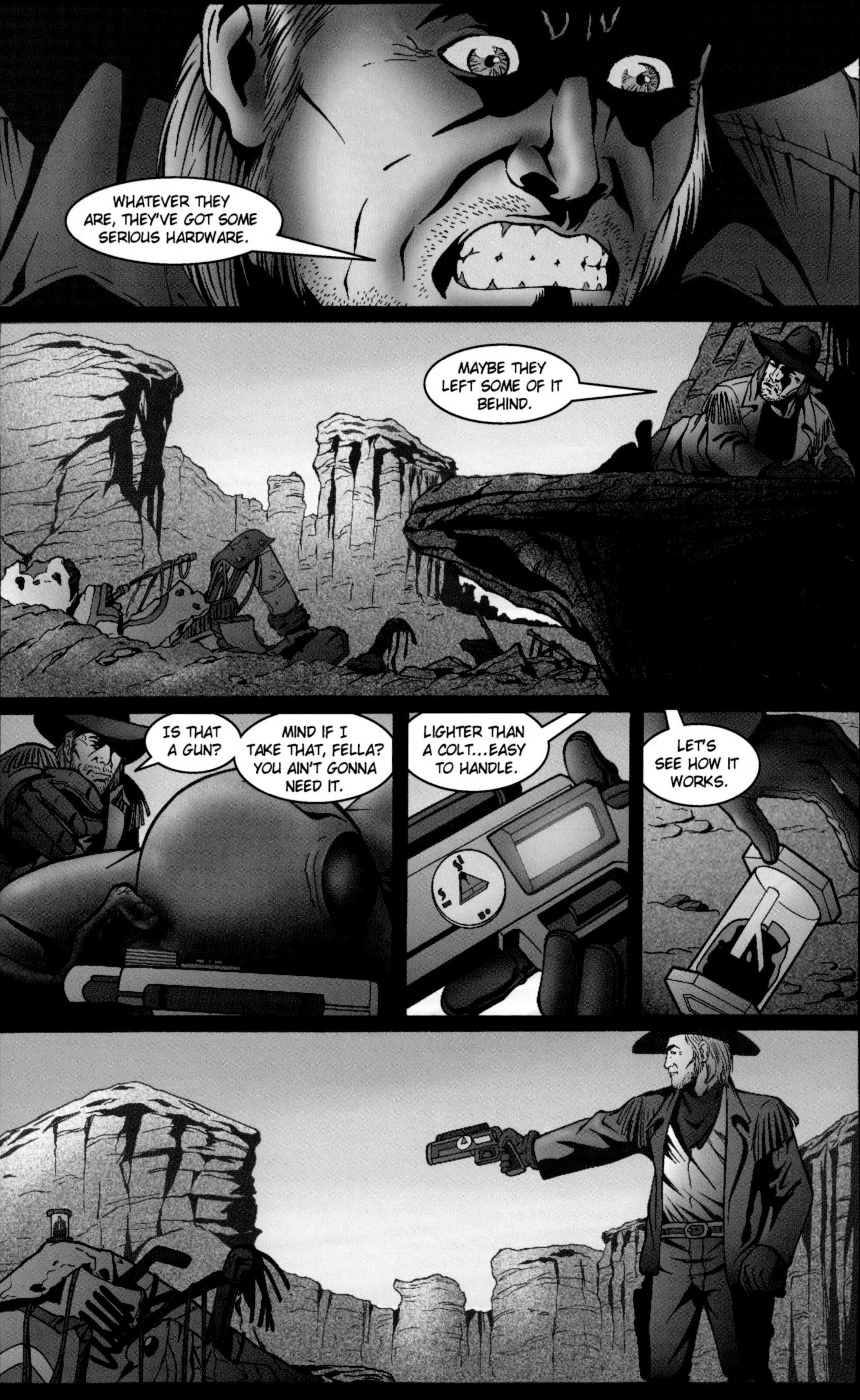
WHATEVER THEY ARE, THEY'VE GOT SOME SERIOUS HARDWARE.
MAYBE THEY LEFT SOME OF IT BEHIND.
IS THAT A GUN?
MIND IF I TAKE THAT, FELLA? YOU AIN'T GONNA NEED IT.
LIGHTER THAN A COLT...EASY TO HANDLE.
LET'S SEE HOW IT WORKS.

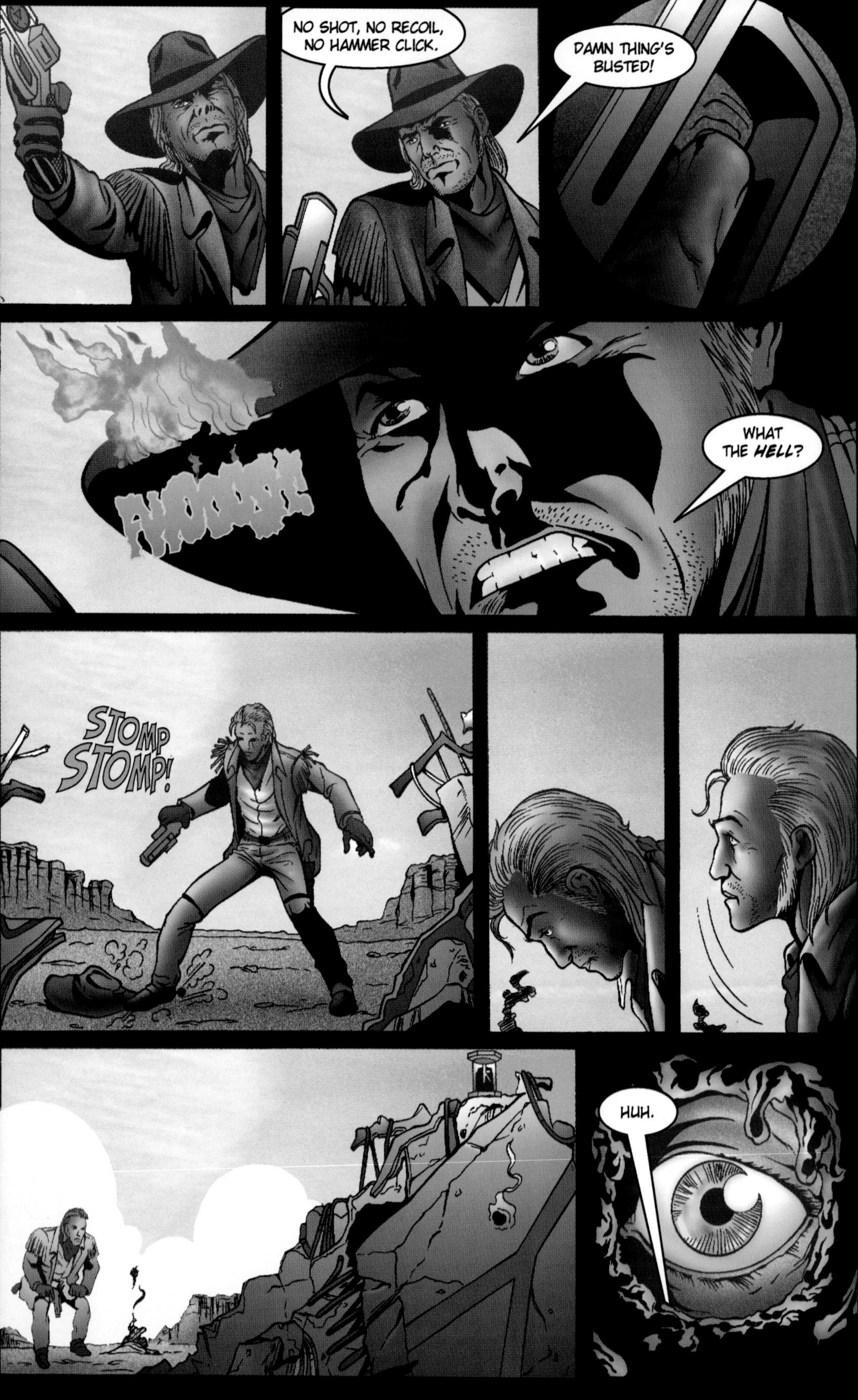
NO SHOT, NO RECOIL, NO HAMMER CLICK.
DAMN THING'S BUSTED!
FWOOSH!
WHAT THE HELL?
STOMP STOMP!
HUH.

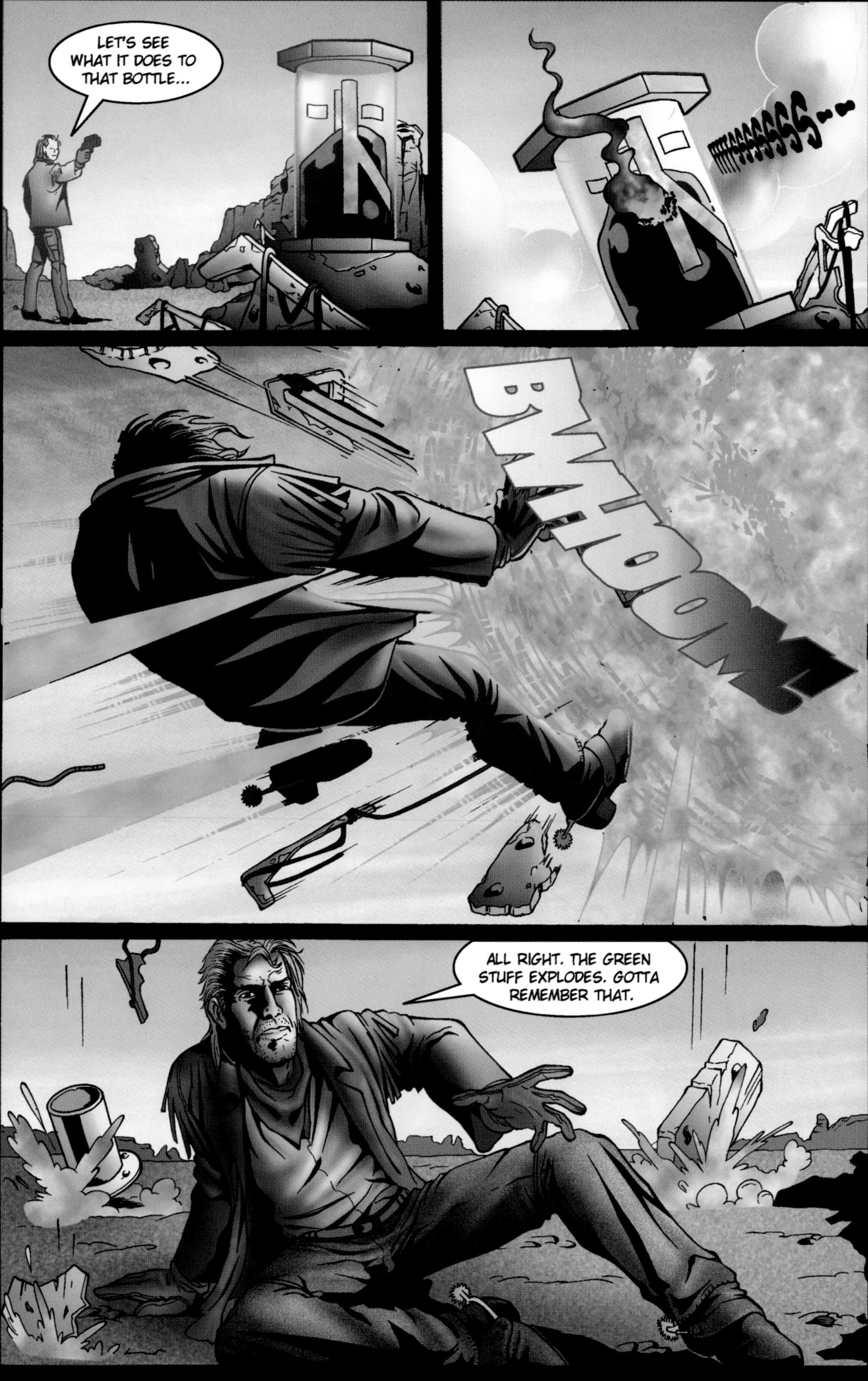
LET'S SEE WHAT IT DOES TO THAT BOTTLE...
BWHOOM!
ALL RIGHT. THE GREEN STUFF EXPLODES. GOTTA REMEMBER THAT.

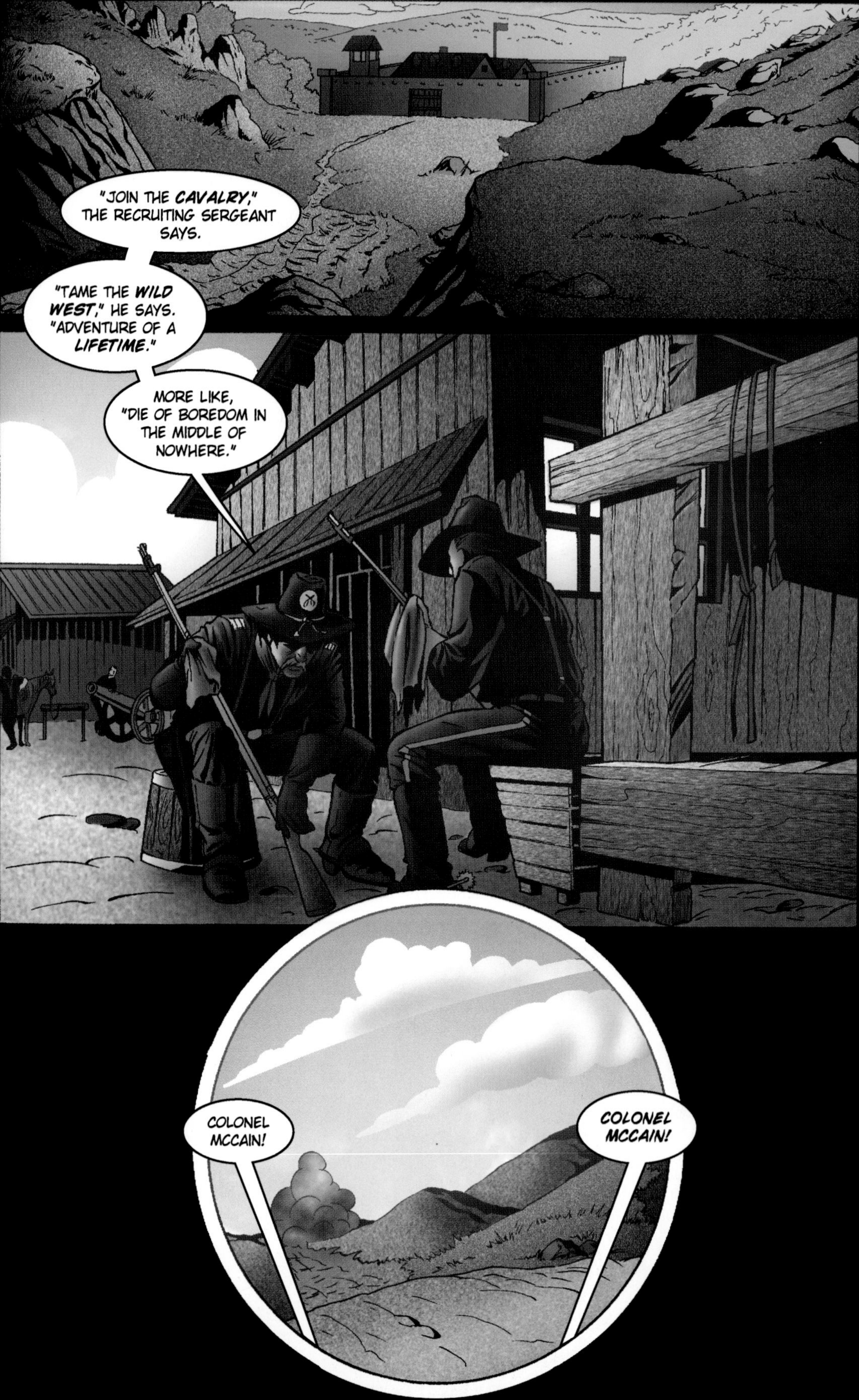
"JOIN THE CAVALRY," THE RECRUITING SERGEANT SAYS.
"TAME THE WILD WEST," HE SAYS. "ADVENTURE OF A LIFETIME."
MORE LIKE, "DIE OF BOREDOM IN THE MIDDLE OF NOWHERE."
COLONEL MCCAIN!
COLONEL MCCAIN!

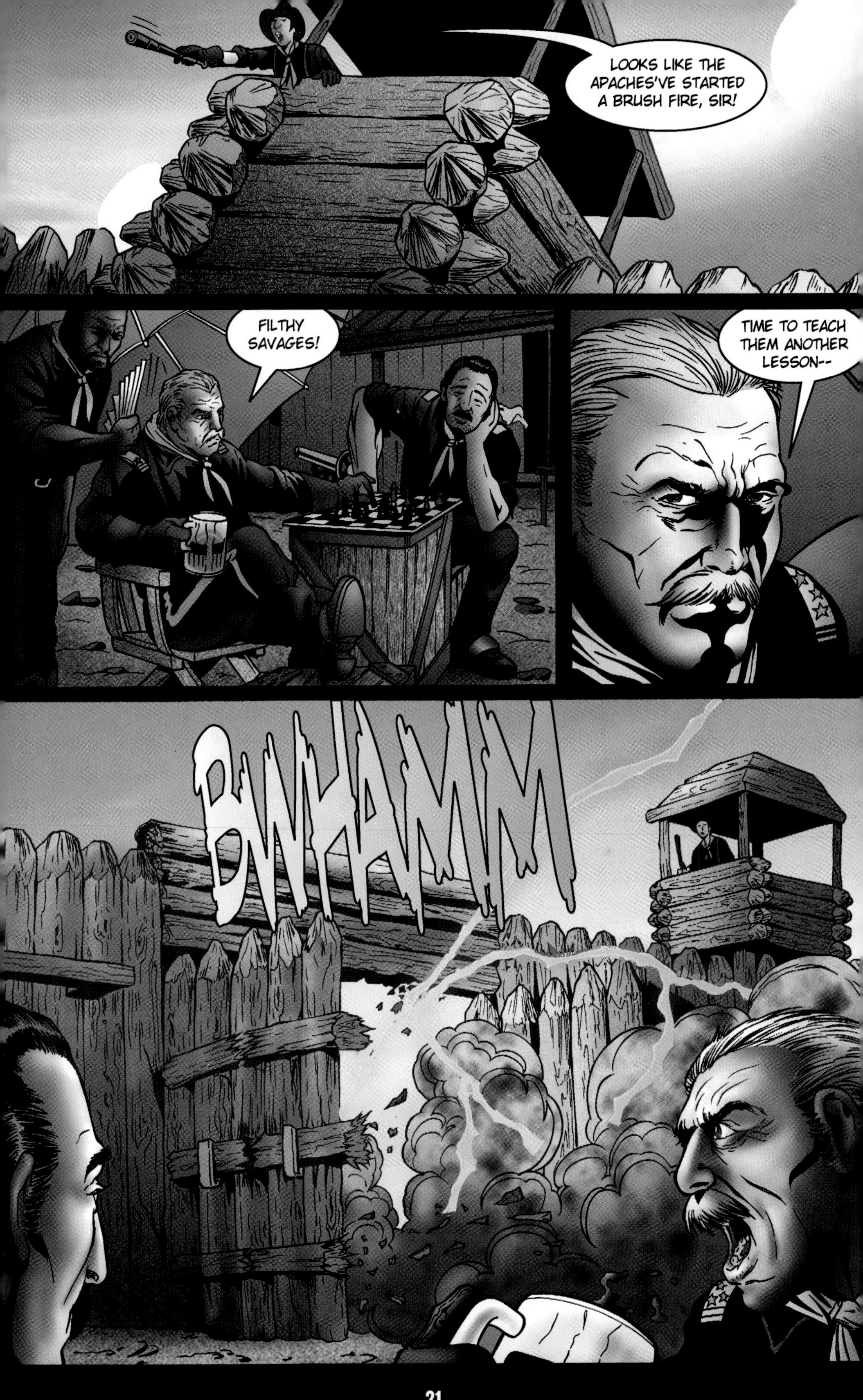
LOOKS LIKE THE APACHES'VE STARTED A BRUSH FIRE, SIR!
FILTHY SAVAGES!
TIME TO TEACH THEM ANOTHER LESSON--
BWHAMM

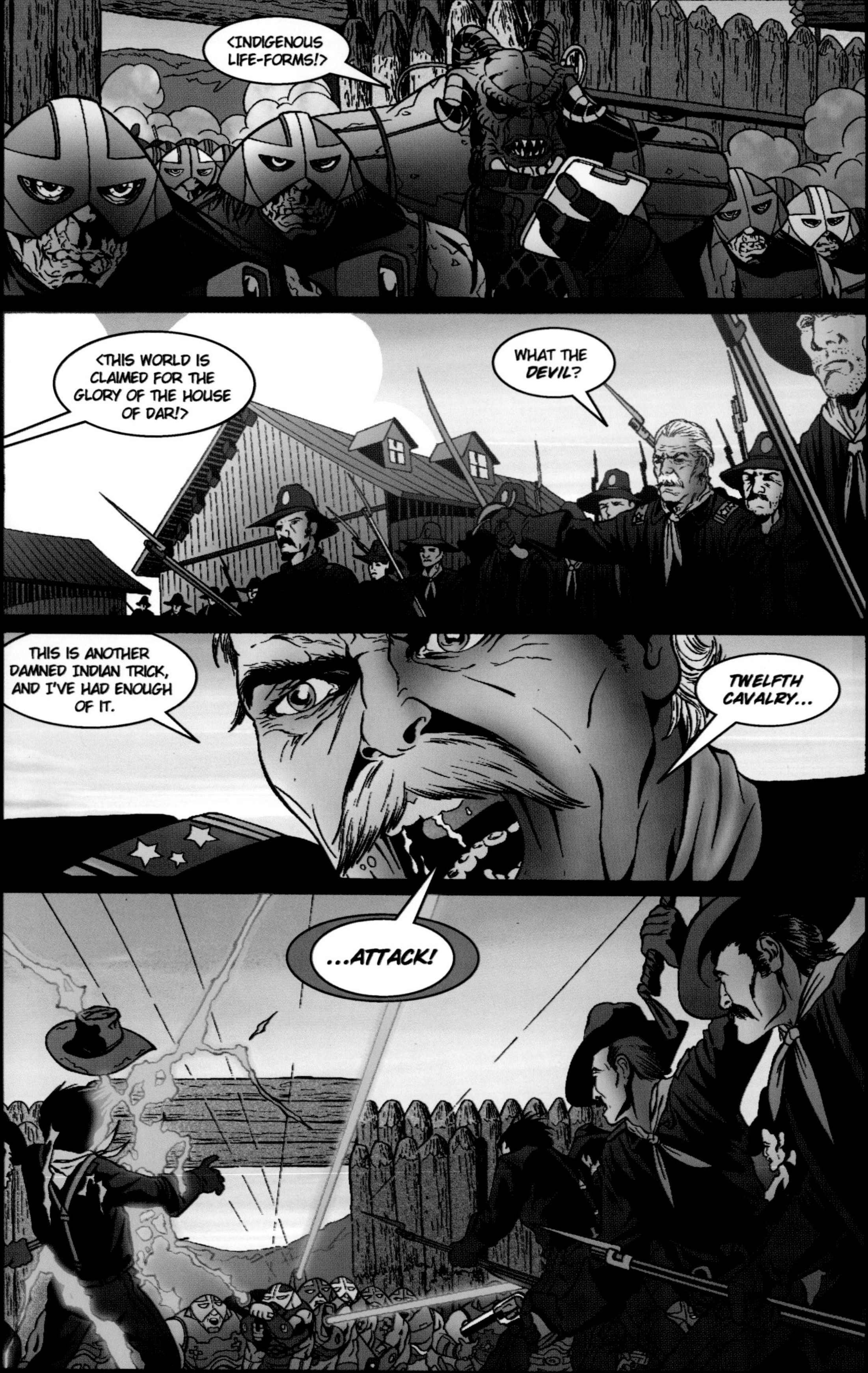
<INDIGENOUS LIFE-FORMS!>
<THIS WORLD IS CLAIMED FOR THE GLORY OF THE HOUSE OF DAR!>
WHAT THE DEVIL?
THIS IS ANOTHER DAMNED INDIAN TRICK, AND I'VE HAD ENOUGH OF IT.
TWELFTH CAVALRY...
...ATTACK!

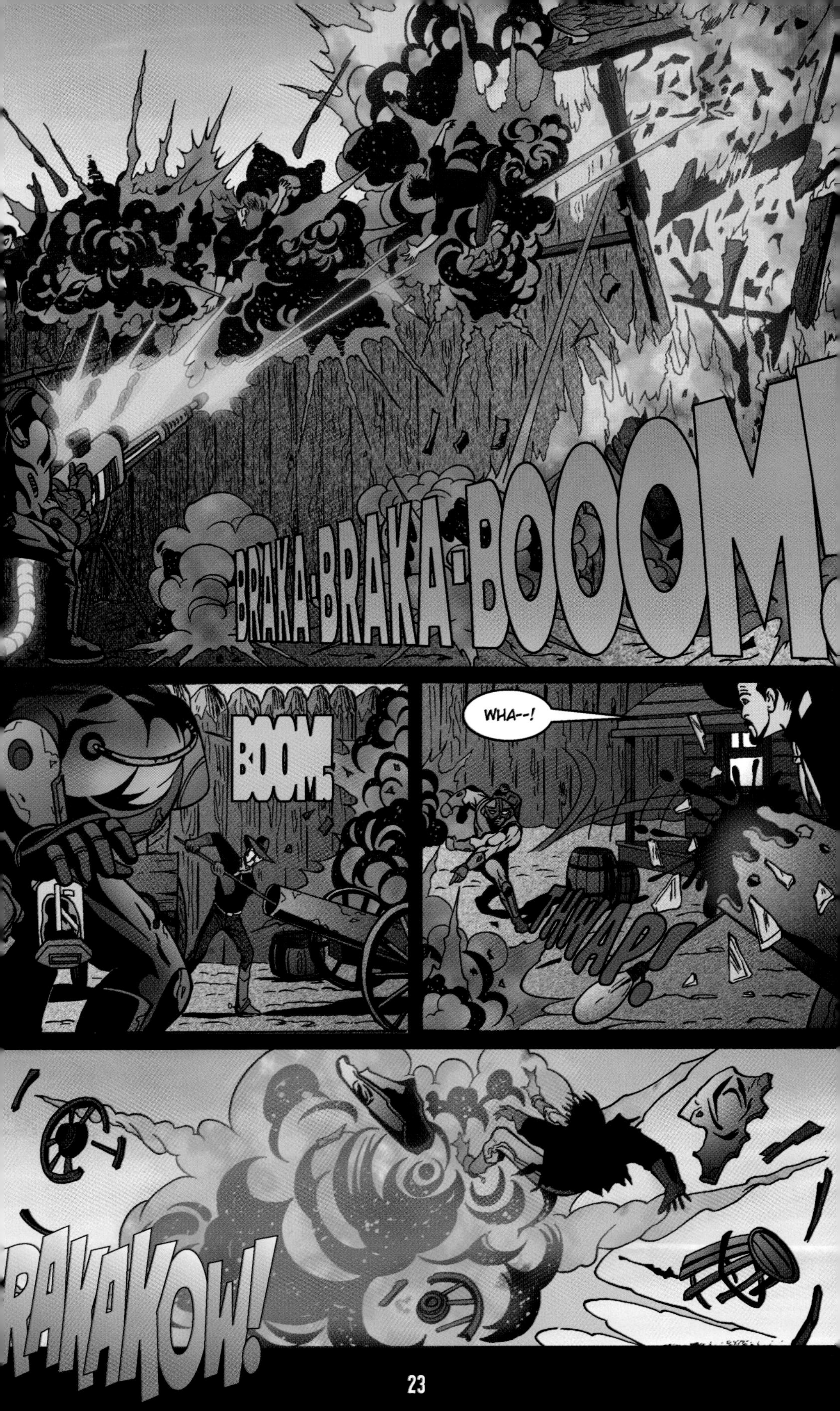
BRAKA-BRAKA-BOOOM!
BOOM!
WHA--!
THWAP!
RAKAKOW!

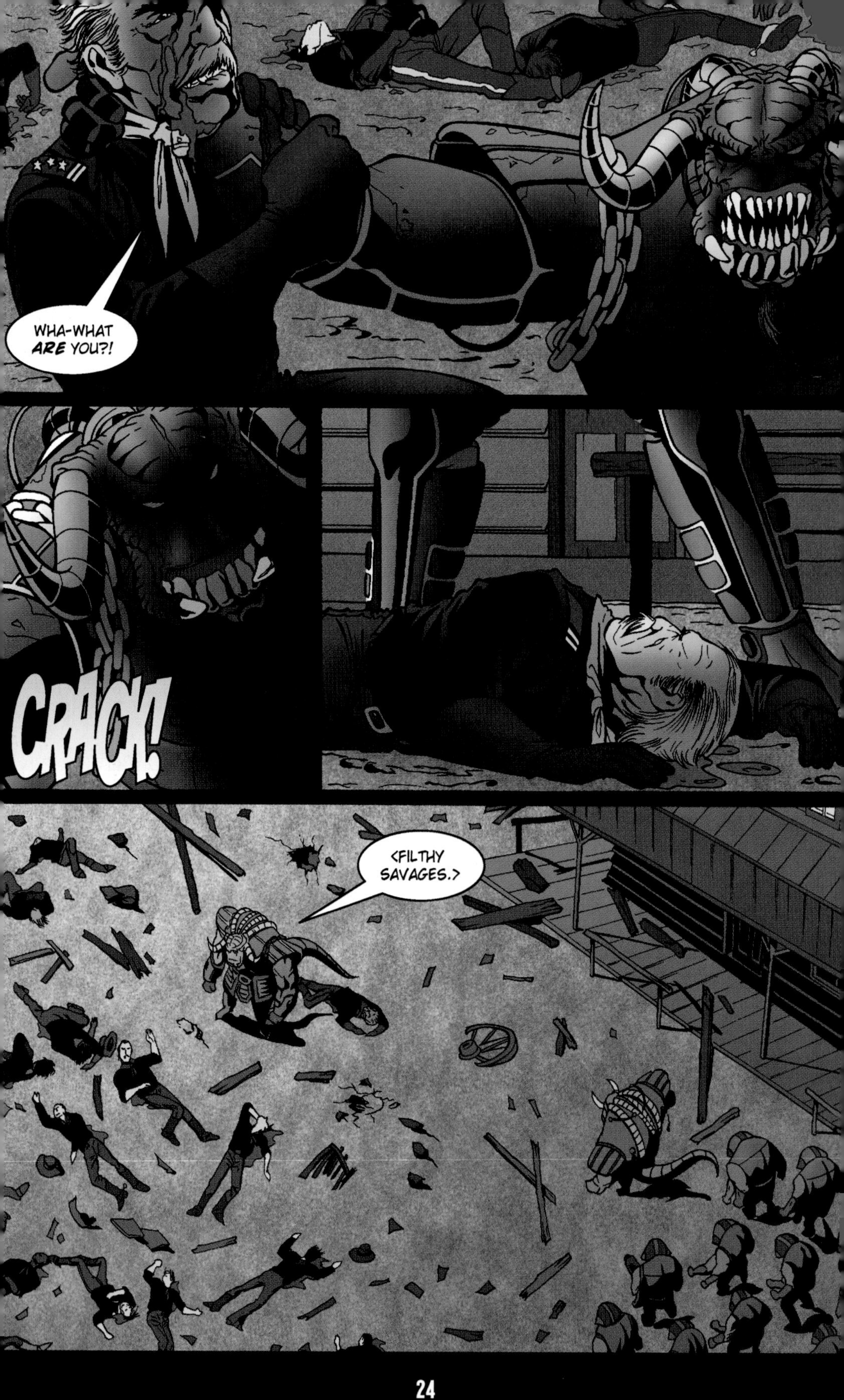
WHA-WHAT ARE YOU?!
CRACK!
<FILTHY SAVAGES.>

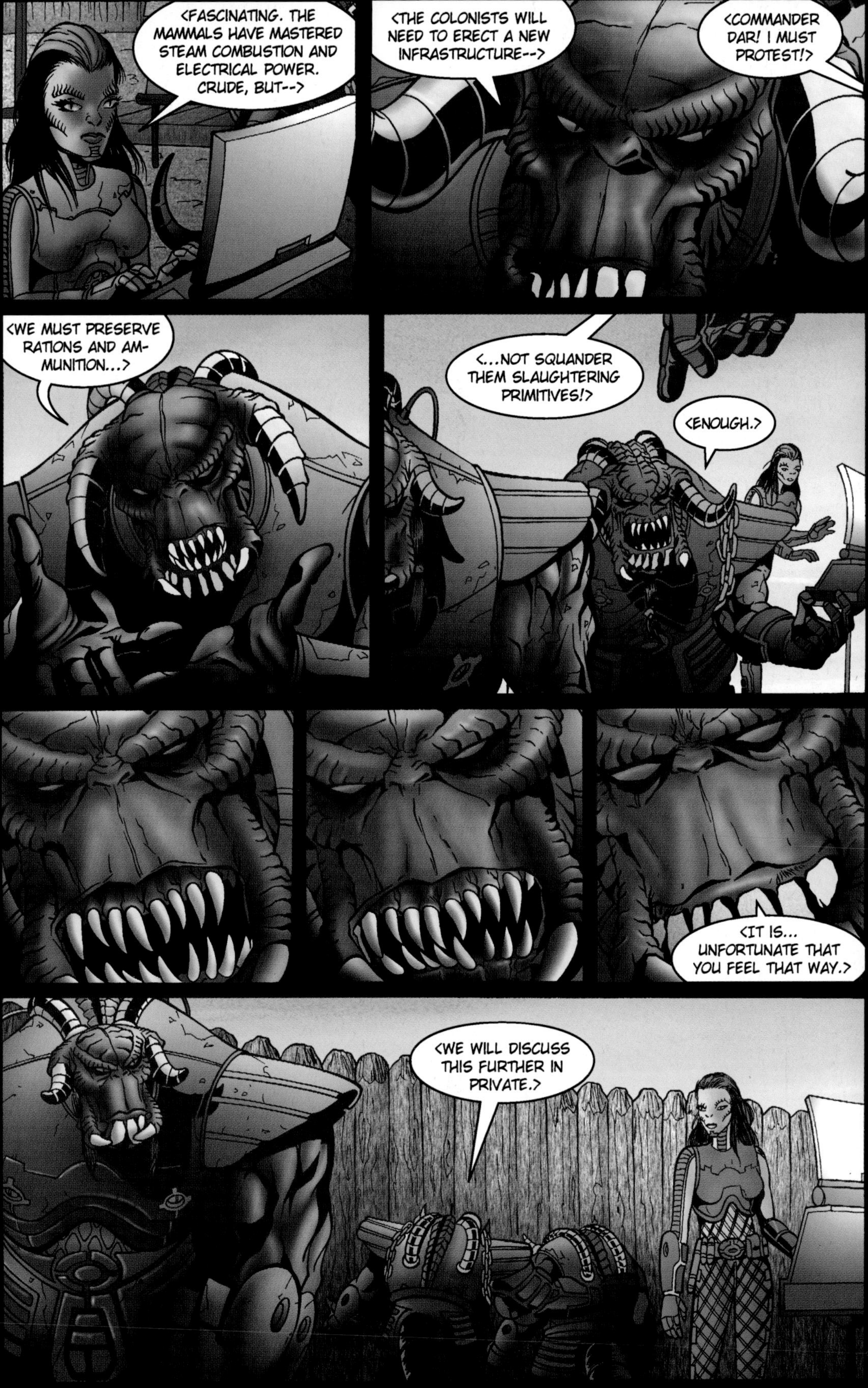
<FASCINATING. THE MAMMALS HAVE MASTERED STEAM COMBUSTION AND ELECTRICAL POWER. CRUDE, BUT-->
<THE COLONISTS WILL NEED TO ERECT A NEW INFRASTRUCTURE-->
<COMMANDER DAR! I MUST PROTEST!>
<WE MUST PRESERVE RATIONS AND AM-MUNITION...>
<...NOT SQUANDER THEM SLAUGHTERING PRIMITIVES!>
<ENOUGH.>
<IT IS... UNFORTUNATE THAT YOU FEEL THAT WAY.>
<WE WILL DISCUSS THIS FURTHER IN PRIVATE.>

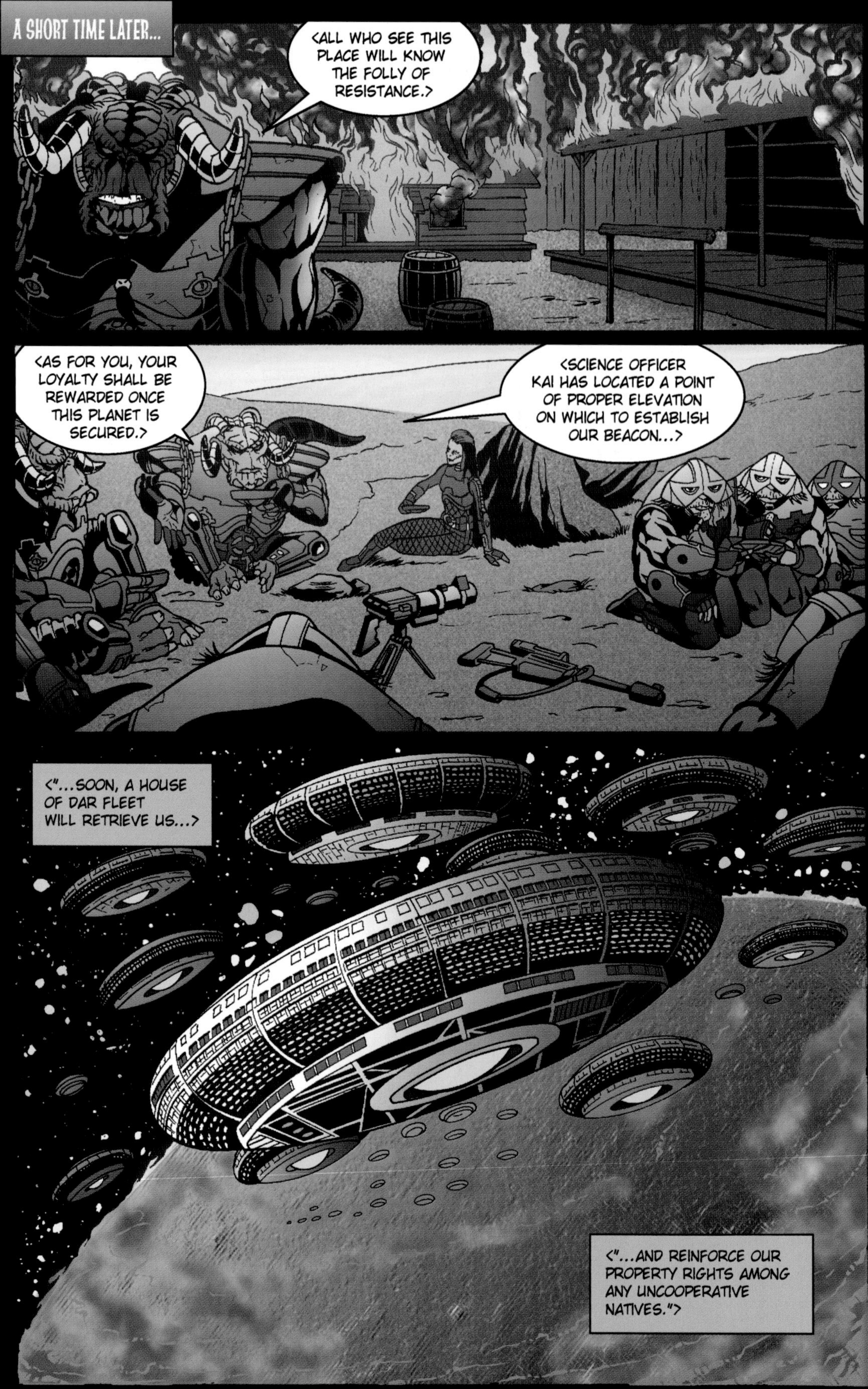
A SHORT TIME LATER...
<ALL WHO SEE THIS PLACE WILL KNOW THE FOLLY OF RESISTANCE.>
<AS FOR YOU, YOUR LOYALTY SHALL BE REWARDED ONCE THIS PLANET IS SECURED.>
<SCIENCE OFFICER KAI HAS LOCATED A POINT OF PROPER ELEVATION ON WHICH TO ESTABLISH OUR BEACON...>
<"...SOON, A HOUSE OF DAR FLEET WILL RETRIEVE US...>
<"...AND REINFORCE OUR PROPERTY RIGHTS AMONG ANY UNCOOPERATIVE NATIVES.">

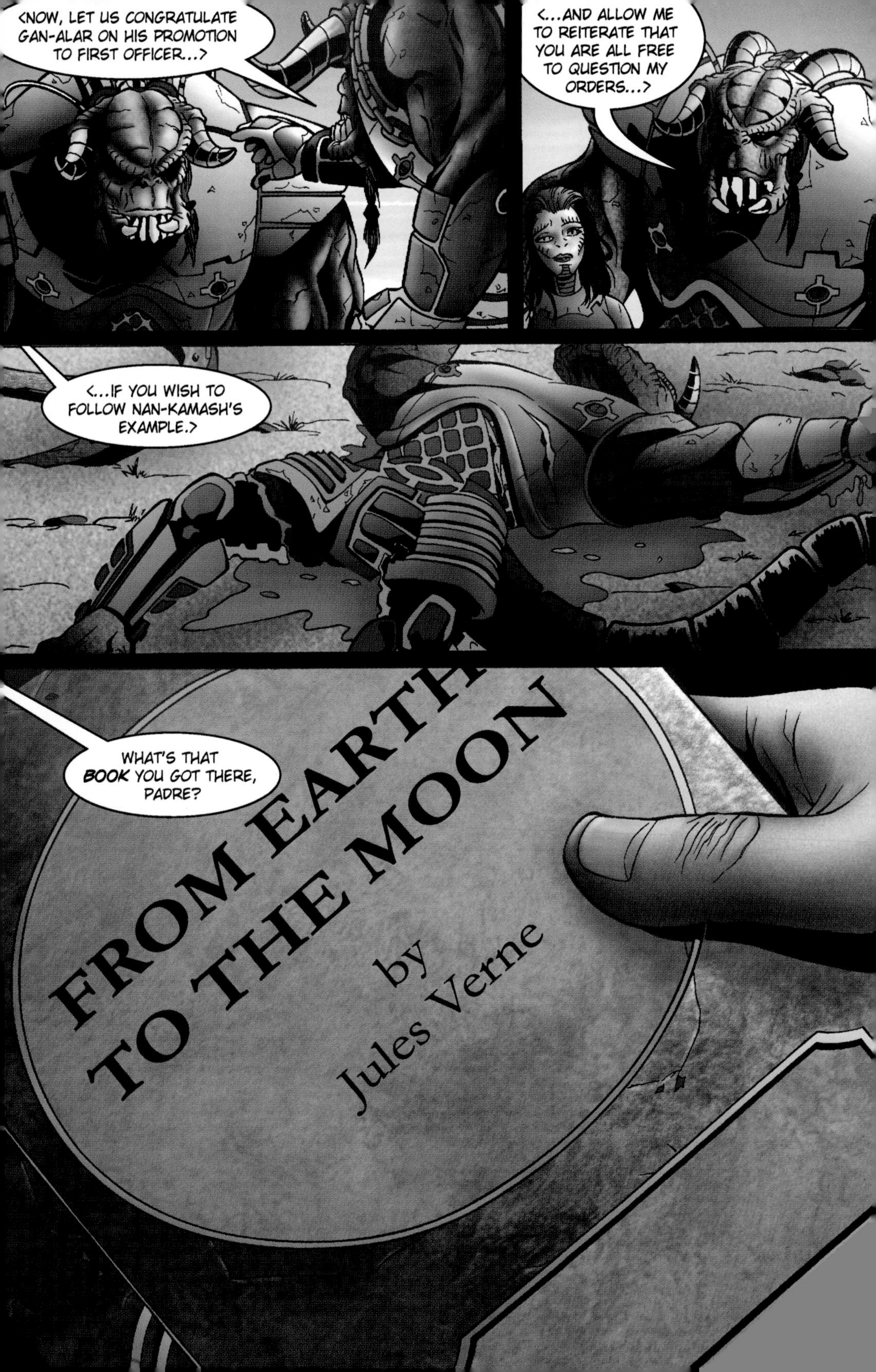
<NOW, LET US CONGRATULATE GAN-ALAR ON HIS PROMOTION TO FIRST OFFICER...>
<...AND ALLOW ME TO REITERATE THAT YOU ARE ALL FREE TO QUESTION MY ORDERS...>
<...IF YOU WISH TO FOLLOW NAN-KAMASH'S EXAMPLE.>
WHAT'S THAT **BOOK** YOU GOT THERE, PADRE?
FROM EARTH TO THE MOON
by
Jules Verne

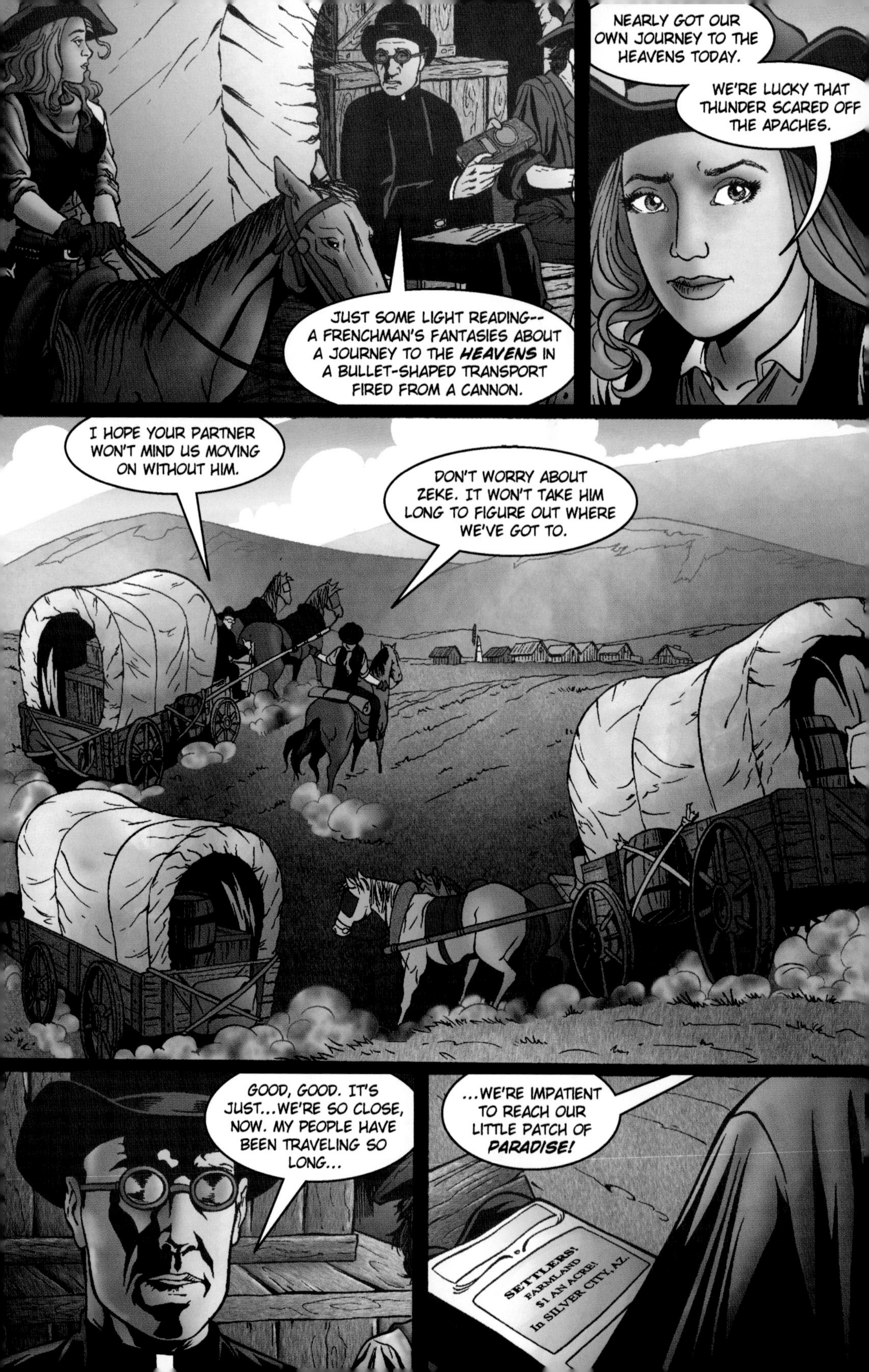
JUST SOME LIGHT READING-- A FRENCHMAN'S FANTASIES ABOUT A JOURNEY TO THE HEAVENS IN A BULLET-SHAPED TRANSPORT FIRED FROM A CANNON.
NEARLY GOT OUR OWN JOURNEY TO THE HEAVENS TODAY.
WE'RE LUCKY THAT THUNDER SCARED OFF THE APACHES.
I HOPE YOUR PARTNER WON'T MIND US MOVING ON WITHOUT HIM.
DON'T WORRY ABOUT ZEKE. IT WON'T TAKE HIM LONG TO FIGURE OUT WHERE WE'VE GOT TO.
GOOD, GOOD. IT'S JUST...WE'RE SO CLOSE, NOW. MY PEOPLE HAVE BEEN TRAVELING SO LONG...
...WE'RE IMPATIENT TO REACH OUR LITTLE PATCH OF PARADISE!
SETTLERS!
FARMLAND
$1 AN ACRE!
In SILVER CITY, AZ.

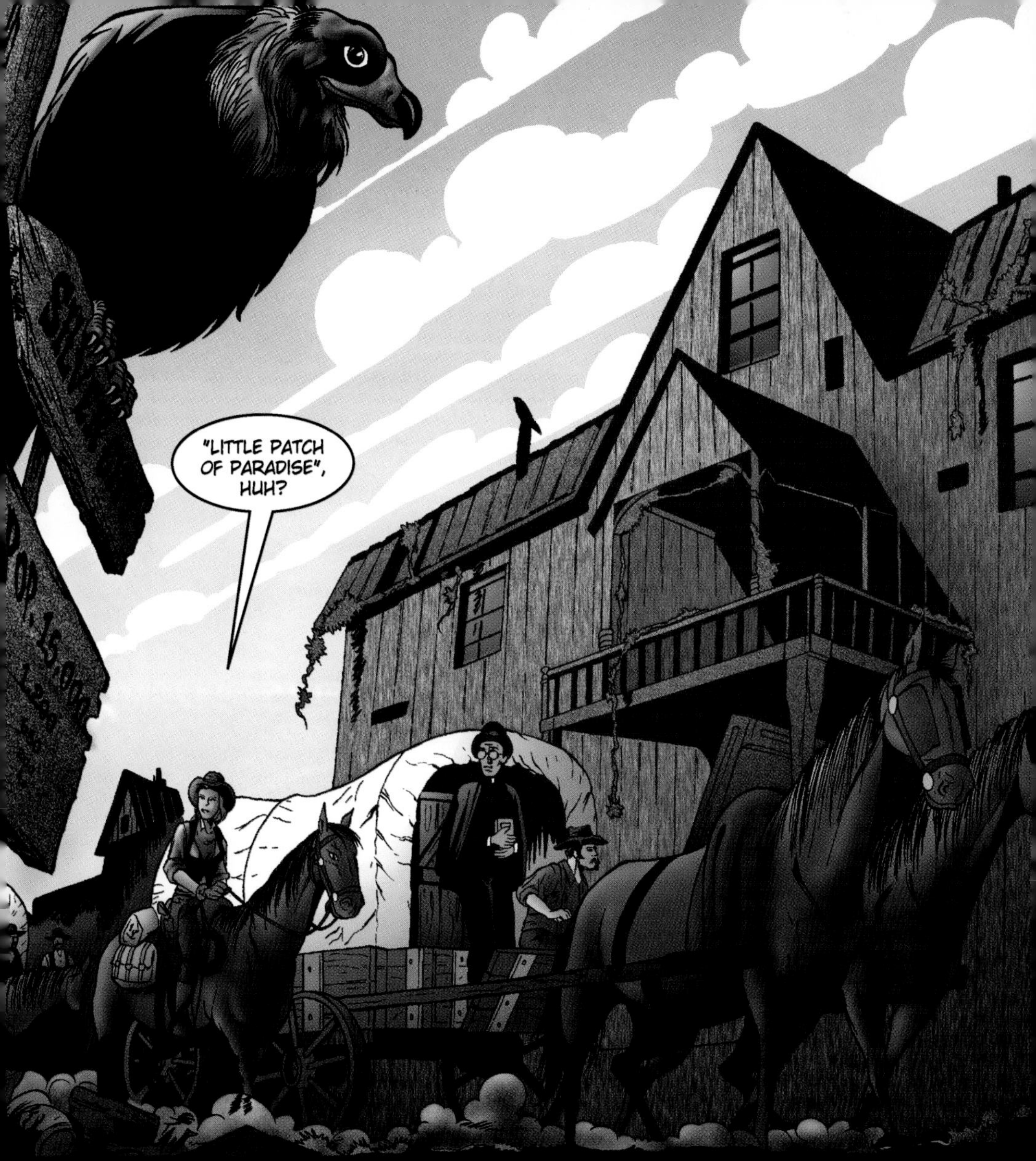
"LITTLE PATCH OF PARADISE", HUH?

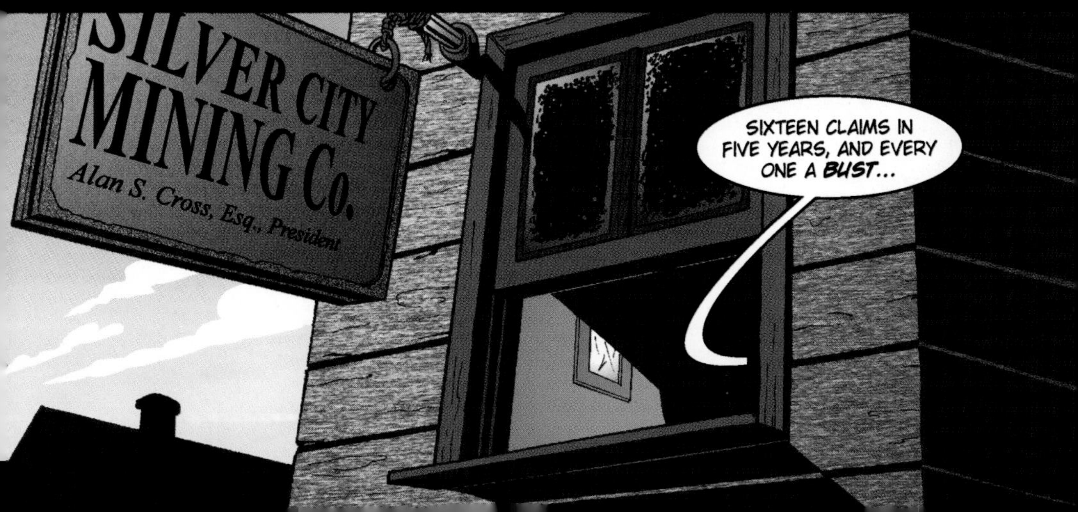
SILVER CITY
MINING Co.
Alan S. Cross, Esq., President
SIXTEEN CLAIMS IN FIVE YEARS, AND EVERY ONE A ***BUST***...

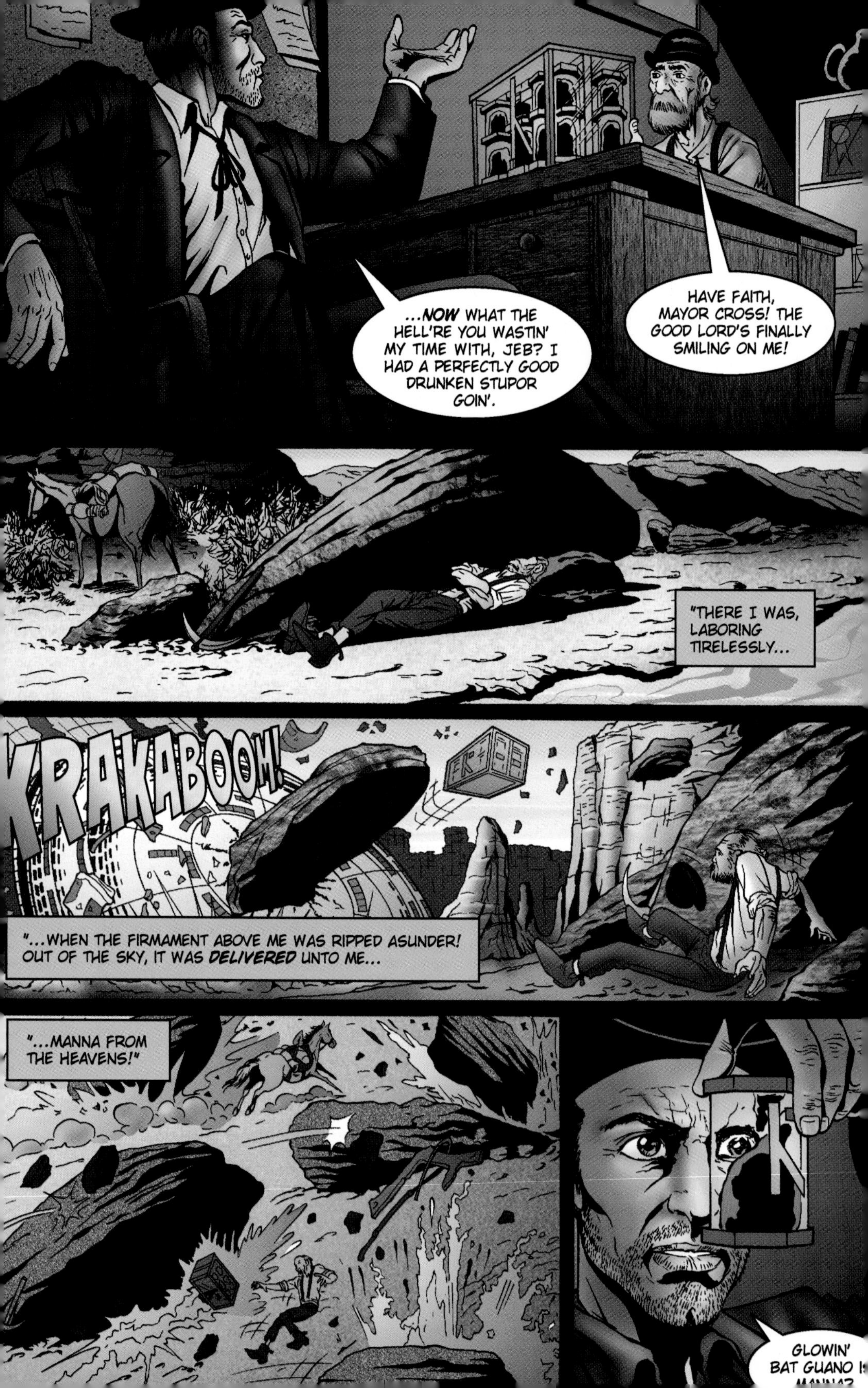
...NOW WHAT THE HELL'RE YOU WASTIN' MY TIME WITH, JEB? I HAD A PERFECTLY GOOD DRUNKEN STUPOR GOIN'.
HAVE FAITH, MAYOR CROSS! THE GOOD LORD'S FINALLY SMILING ON ME!
"THERE I WAS, LABORING TIRELESSLY...
KRAKABOOM!
"...WHEN THE FIRMAMENT ABOVE ME WAS RIPPED ASUNDER! OUT OF THE SKY, IT WAS DELIVERED UNTO ME...
"...MANNA FROM THE HEAVENS!"
GLOWIN' BAT GUANO

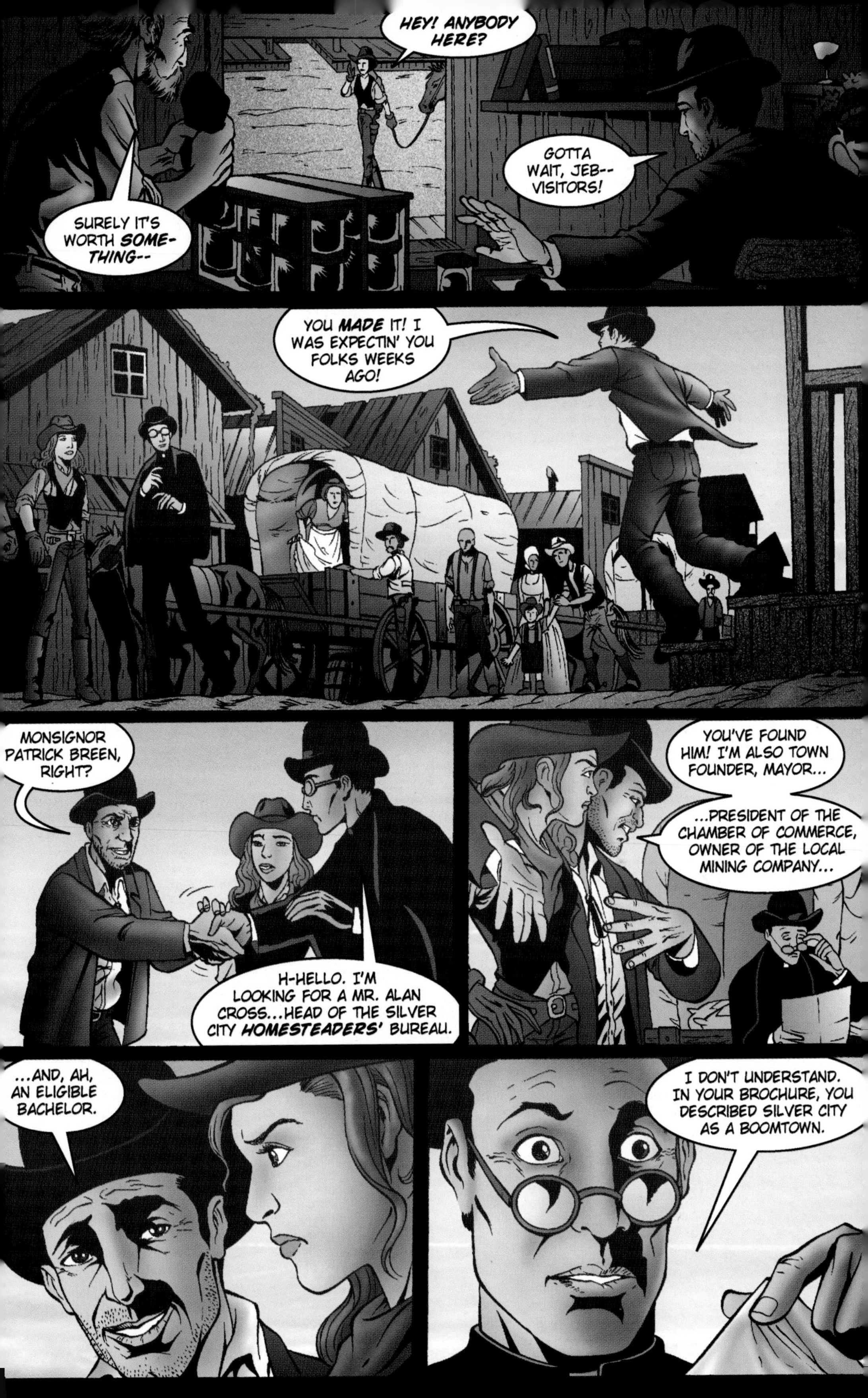
HEY! ANYBODY HERE?
SURELY IT'S WORTH SOME-THING--
GOTTA WAIT, JEB-- VISITORS!
YOU MADE IT! I WAS EXPECTIN' YOU FOLKS WEEKS AGO!
MONSIGNOR PATRICK BREEN, RIGHT?
H-HELLO. I'M LOOKING FOR A MR. ALAN CROSS...HEAD OF THE SILVER CITY HOMESTEADERS' BUREAU.
YOU'VE FOUND HIM! I'M ALSO TOWN FOUNDER, MAYOR...
...PRESIDENT OF THE CHAMBER OF COMMERCE, OWNER OF THE LOCAL MINING COMPANY...
...AND, AH, AN ELIGIBLE BACHELOR.
I DON'T UNDERSTAND. IN YOUR BROCHURE, YOU DESCRIBED SILVER CITY AS A BOOMTOWN.

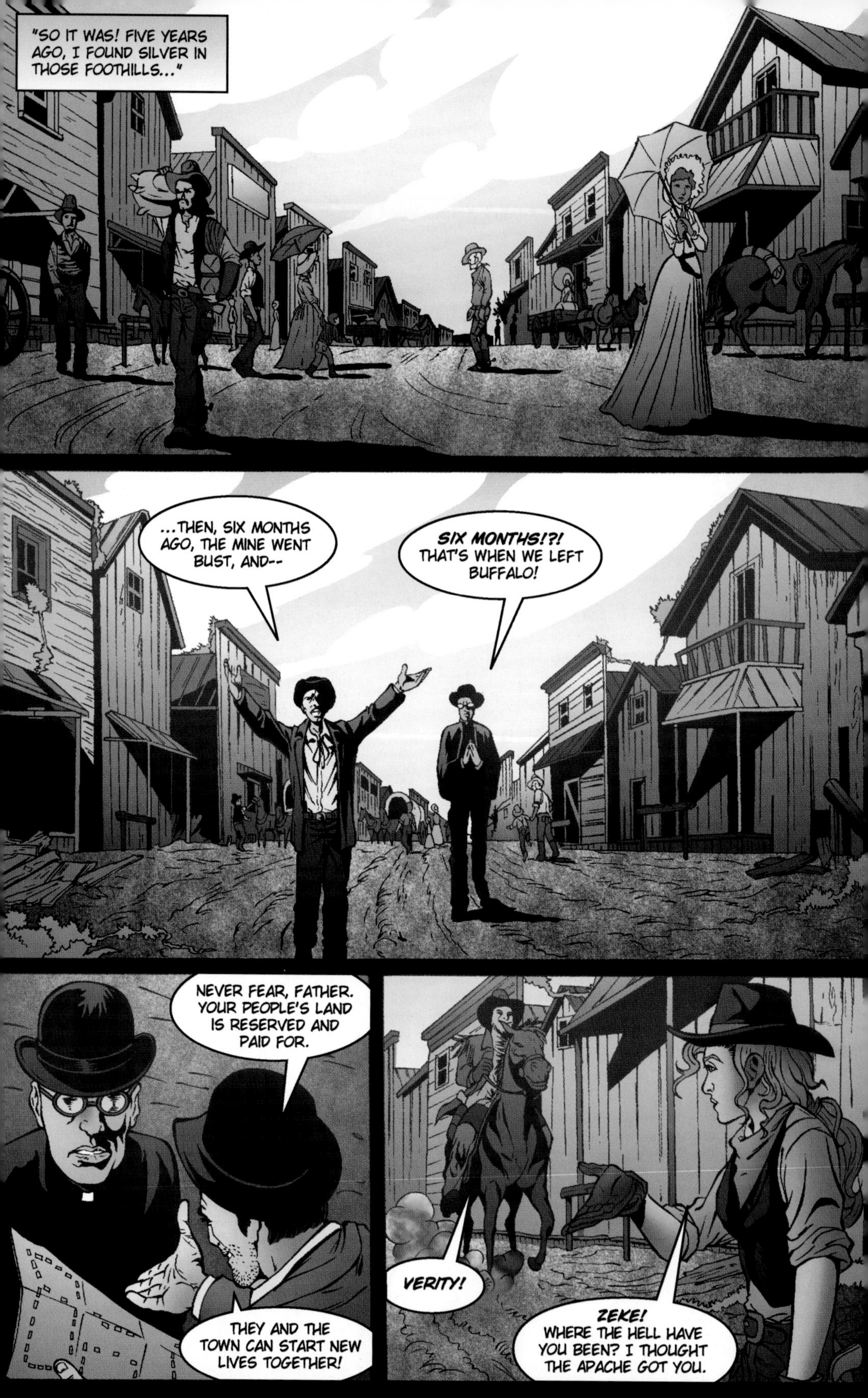
"SO IT WAS! FIVE YEARS AGO, I FOUND SILVER IN THOSE FOOTHILLS..."
...THEN, SIX MONTHS AGO, THE MINE WENT BUST, AND--
SIX MONTHS!?! THAT'S WHEN WE LEFT BUFFALO!
NEVER FEAR, FATHER. YOUR PEOPLE'S LAND IS RESERVED AND PAID FOR.
THEY AND THE TOWN CAN START NEW LIVES TOGETHER!
VERITY!
ZEKE! WHERE THE HELL HAVE YOU BEEN? I THOUGHT THE APACHE GOT YOU.

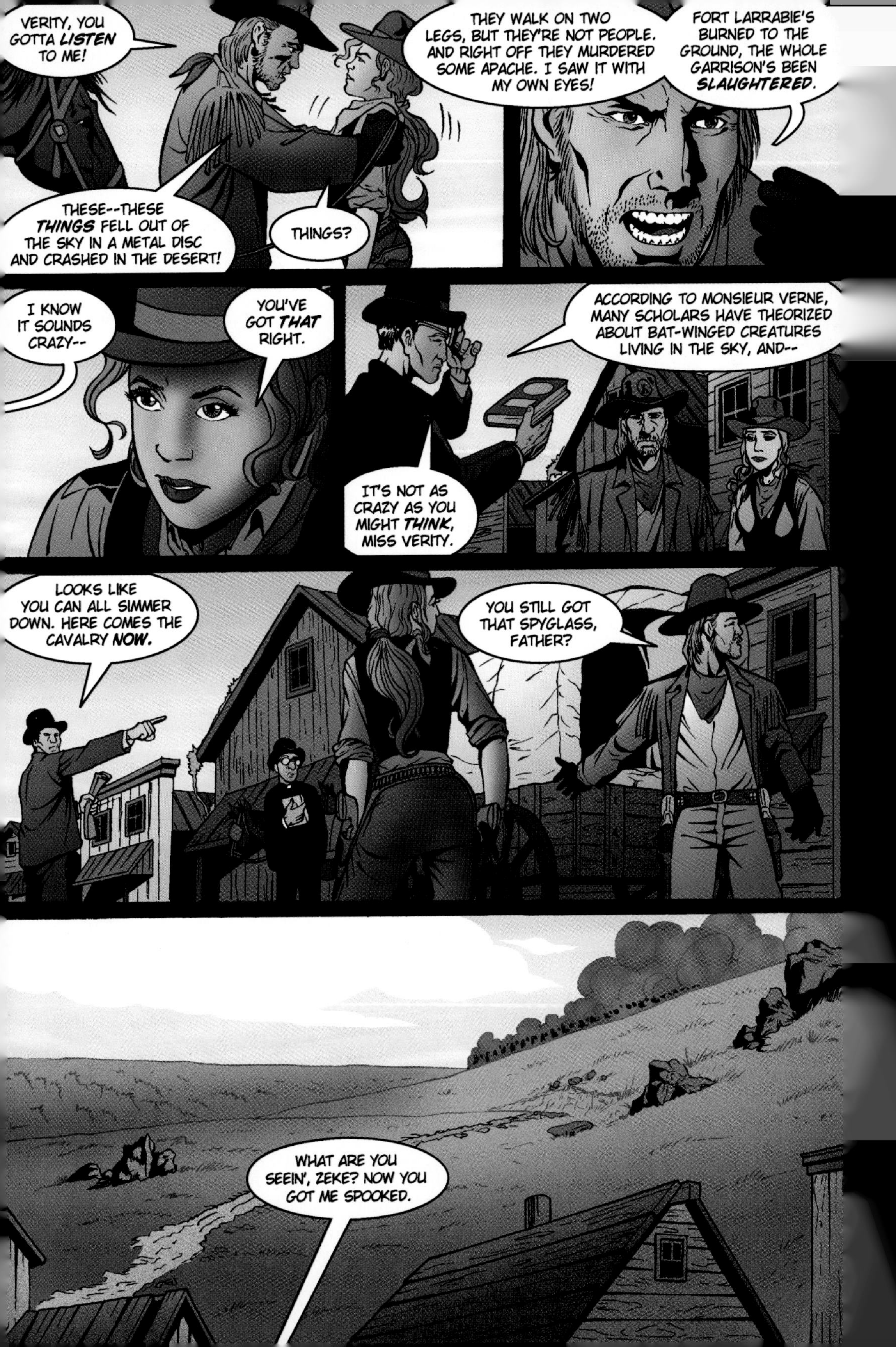
VERITY, YOU GOTTA LISTEN TO ME!
THESE--THESE THINGS FELL OUT OF THE SKY IN A METAL DISC AND CRASHED IN THE DESERT!
THINGS?
THEY WALK ON TWO LEGS, BUT THEY'RE NOT PEOPLE. AND RIGHT OFF THEY MURDERED SOME APACHE. I SAW IT WITH MY OWN EYES!
FORT LARRABIE'S BURNED TO THE GROUND, THE WHOLE GARRISON'S BEEN SLAUGHTERED.
I KNOW IT SOUNDS CRAZY--
YOU'VE GOT THAT RIGHT.
ACCORDING TO MONSIEUR VERNE, MANY SCHOLARS HAVE THEORIZED ABOUT BAT-WINGED CREATURES LIVING IN THE SKY, AND--
IT'S NOT AS CRAZY AS YOU MIGHT THINK, MISS VERITY.
LOOKS LIKE YOU CAN ALL SIMMER DOWN. HERE COMES THE CAVALRY NOW.
YOU STILL GOT THAT SPYGLASS, FATHER?
WHAT ARE YOU SEEIN', ZEKE? NOW YOU GOT ME SPOOKED.

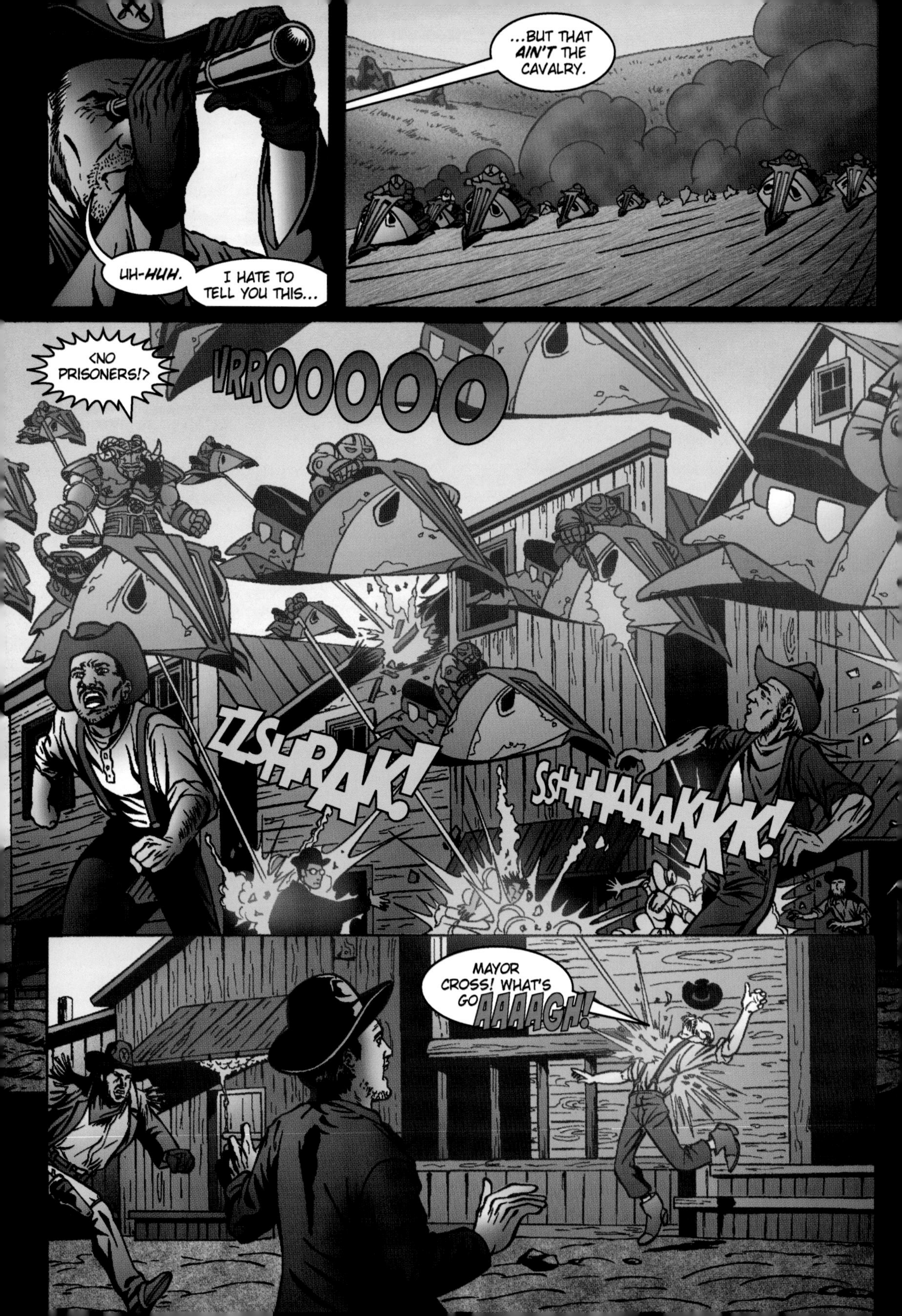
UH-HUH.
I HATE TO TELL YOU THIS...
...BUT THAT AIN'T THE CAVALRY.
<NO PRISONERS!>
VRROOOOOO
ZZSHRAK!
SSHHAAAKKK!
MAYOR CROSS! WHAT'S GOAAAAGH!

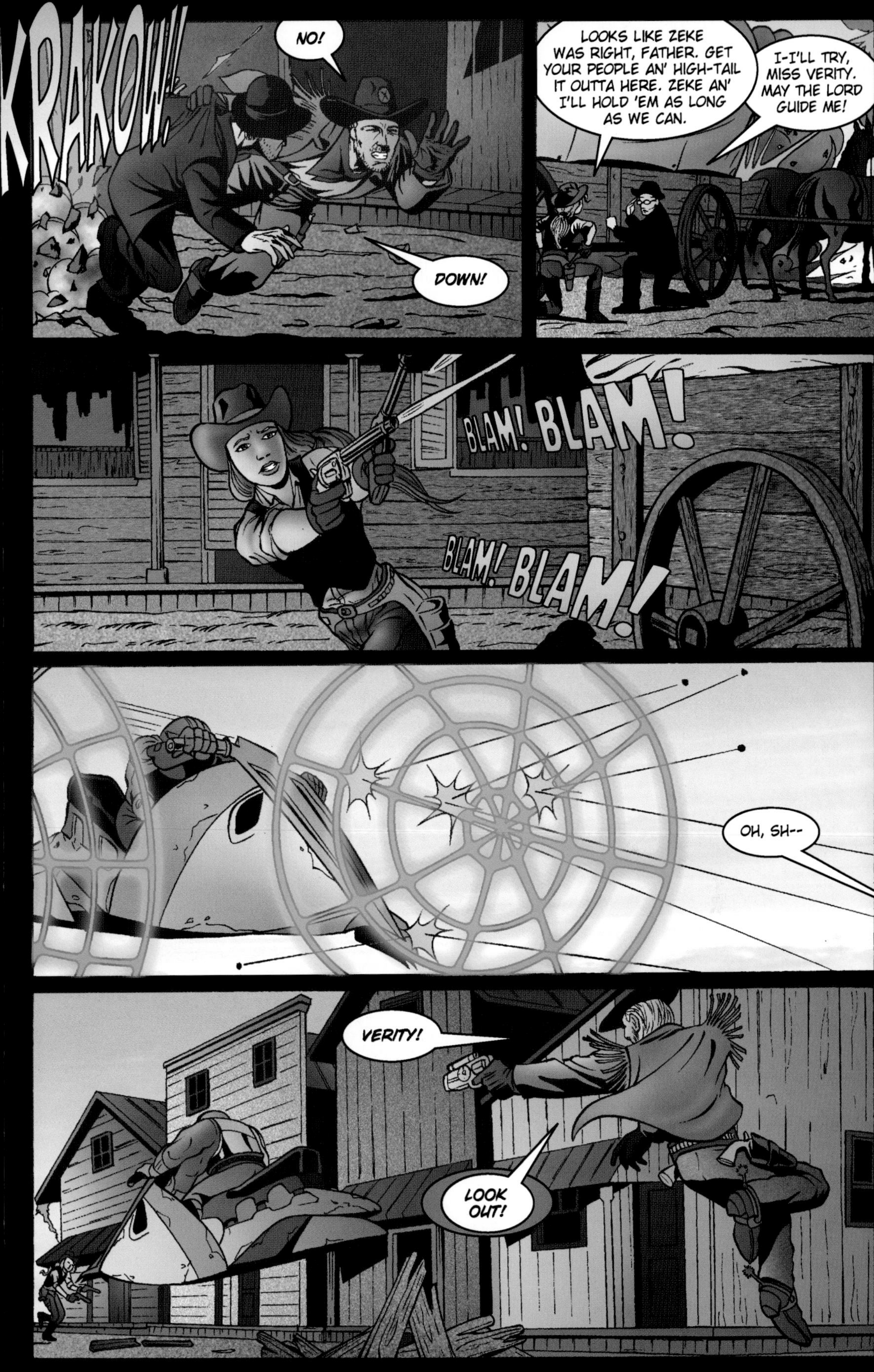
KRAKOW!!
NO!
DOWN!
LOOKS LIKE ZEKE WAS RIGHT, FATHER. GET YOUR PEOPLE AN' HIGH-TAIL IT OUTTA HERE. ZEKE AN' I'LL HOLD 'EM AS LONG AS WE CAN.
I-I'LL TRY, MISS VERITY. MAY THE LORD GUIDE ME!
BLAM! BLAM!
BLAM! BLAM!
OH, SH--
VERITY!
LOOK OUT!

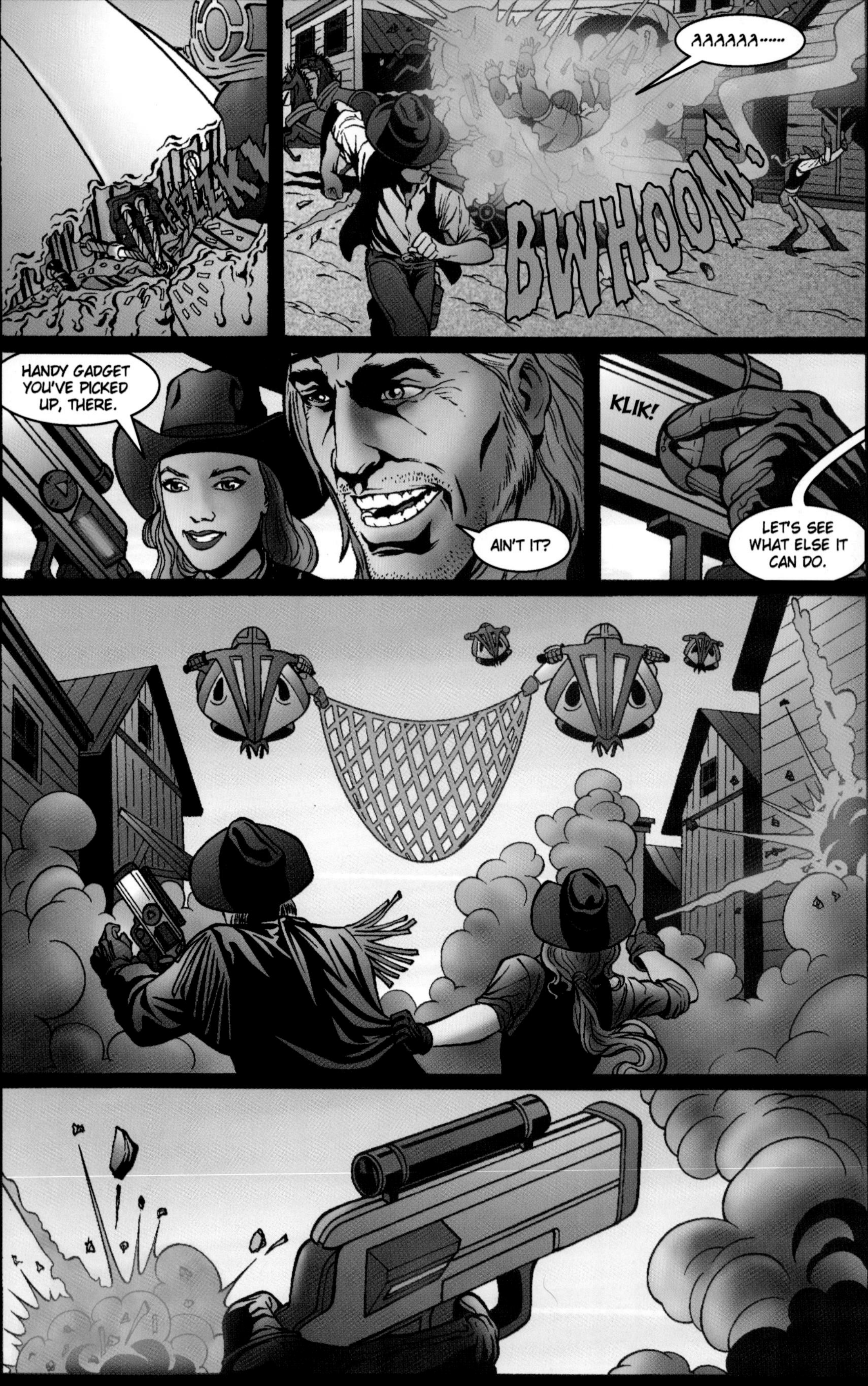
AAAAAA......
BWHOOM!
HANDY GADGET YOU'VE PICKED UP, THERE.
AIN'T IT?
KLIK!
LET'S SEE WHAT ELSE IT CAN DO.

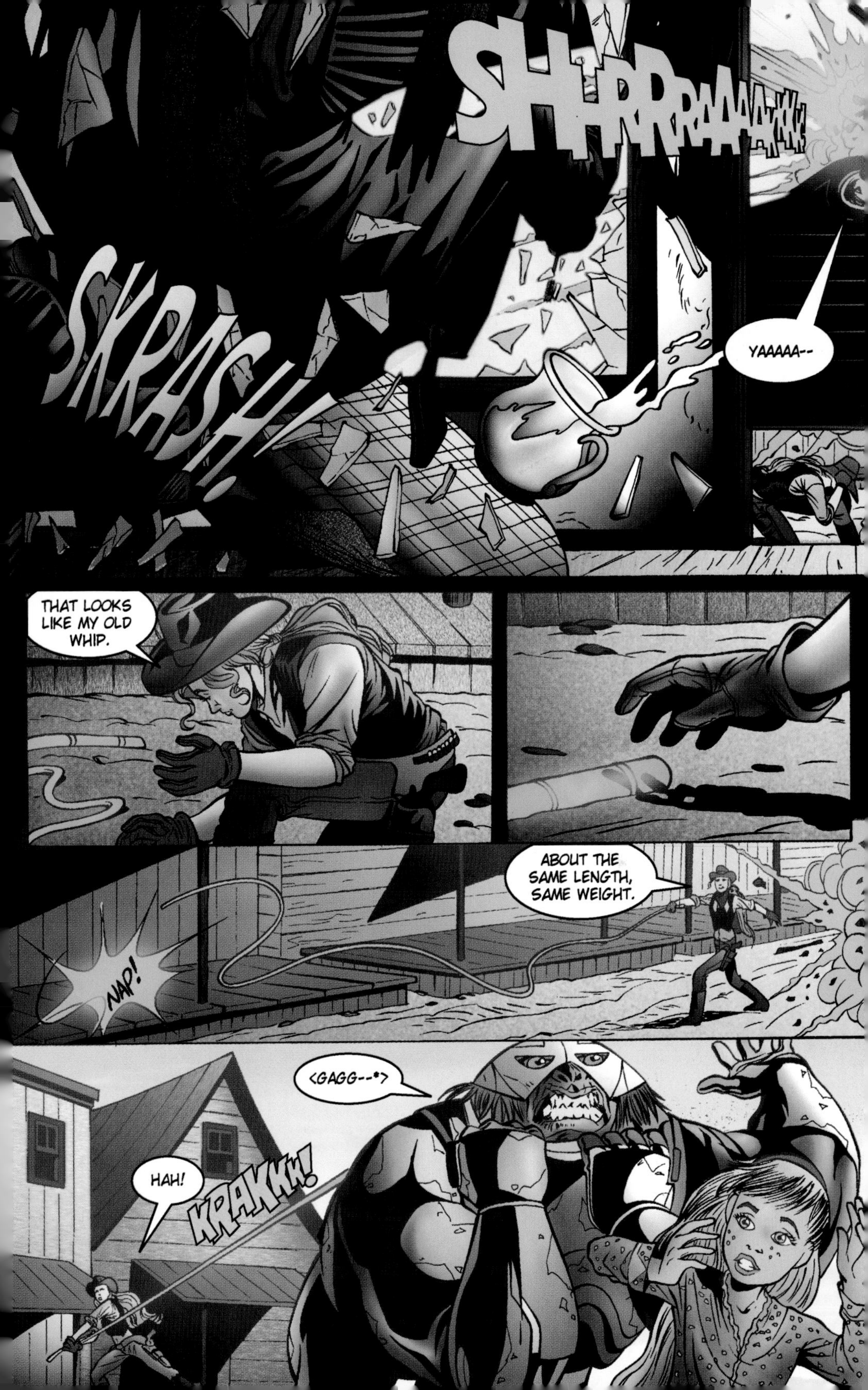
SHRRRAAAAKK!
SKRASH!
YAAAAA--
THAT LOOKS LIKE MY OLD WHIP.
ABOUT THE SAME LENGTH, SAME WEIGHT.
NAP!
<GAGG--*>
HAH!
KRAKKK!

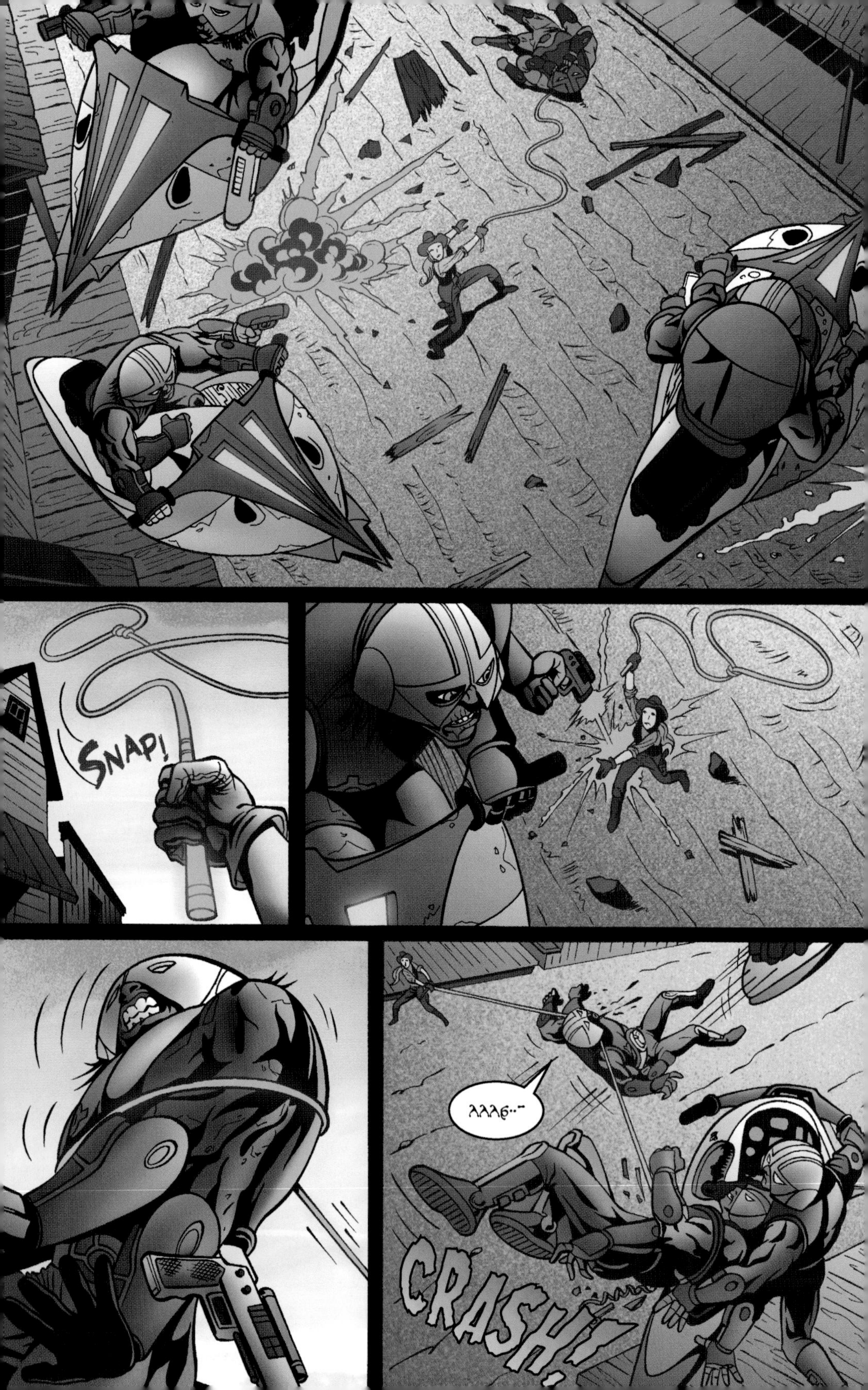
SNAP!
AAAG...
CRASH!

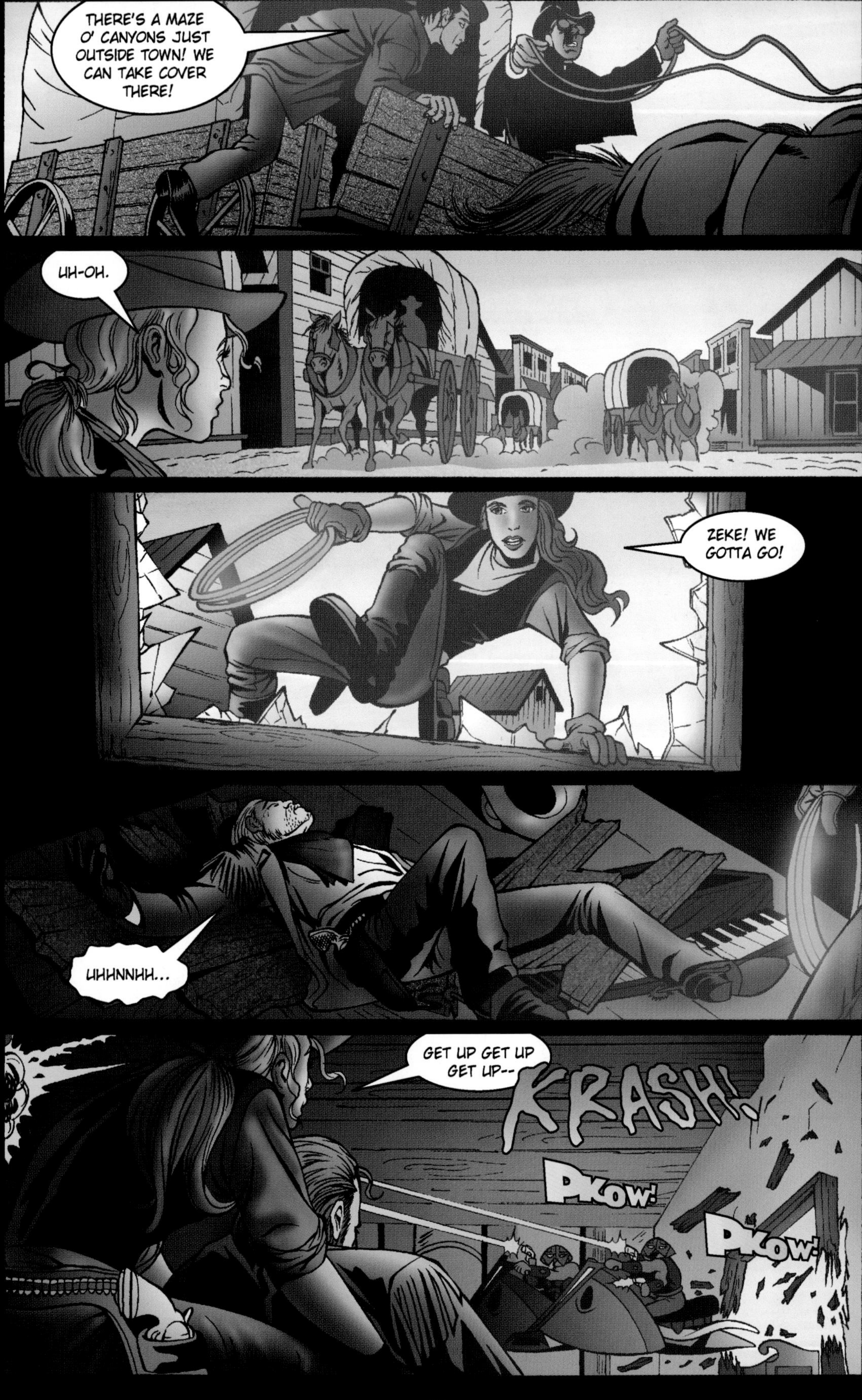
THERE'S A MAZE O' CANYONS JUST OUTSIDE TOWN! WE CAN TAKE COVER THERE!
UH-OH.
ZEKE! WE GOTTA GO!
UHHNNHH...
GET UP GET UP GET UP--
KRASH!
PKOW!
PKOW!

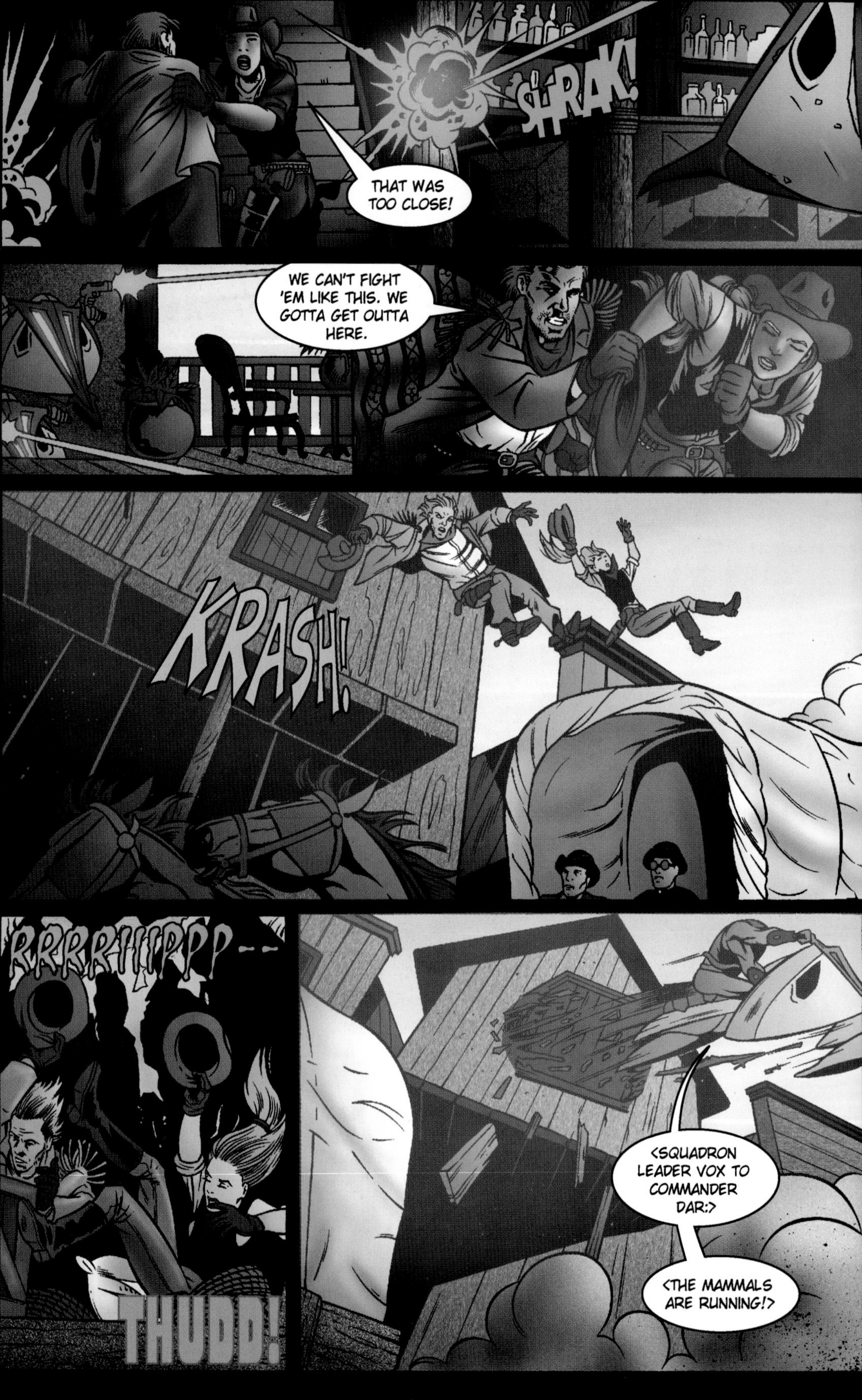
SHRAK!
THAT WAS TOO CLOSE!
WE CAN'T FIGHT 'EM LIKE THIS. WE GOTTA GET OUTTA HERE.
KRASH!
RRRRIIIPPP
THUDD!
<SQUADRON LEADER VOX TO COMMANDER DAR:>
<THE MAMMALS ARE RUNNING!>

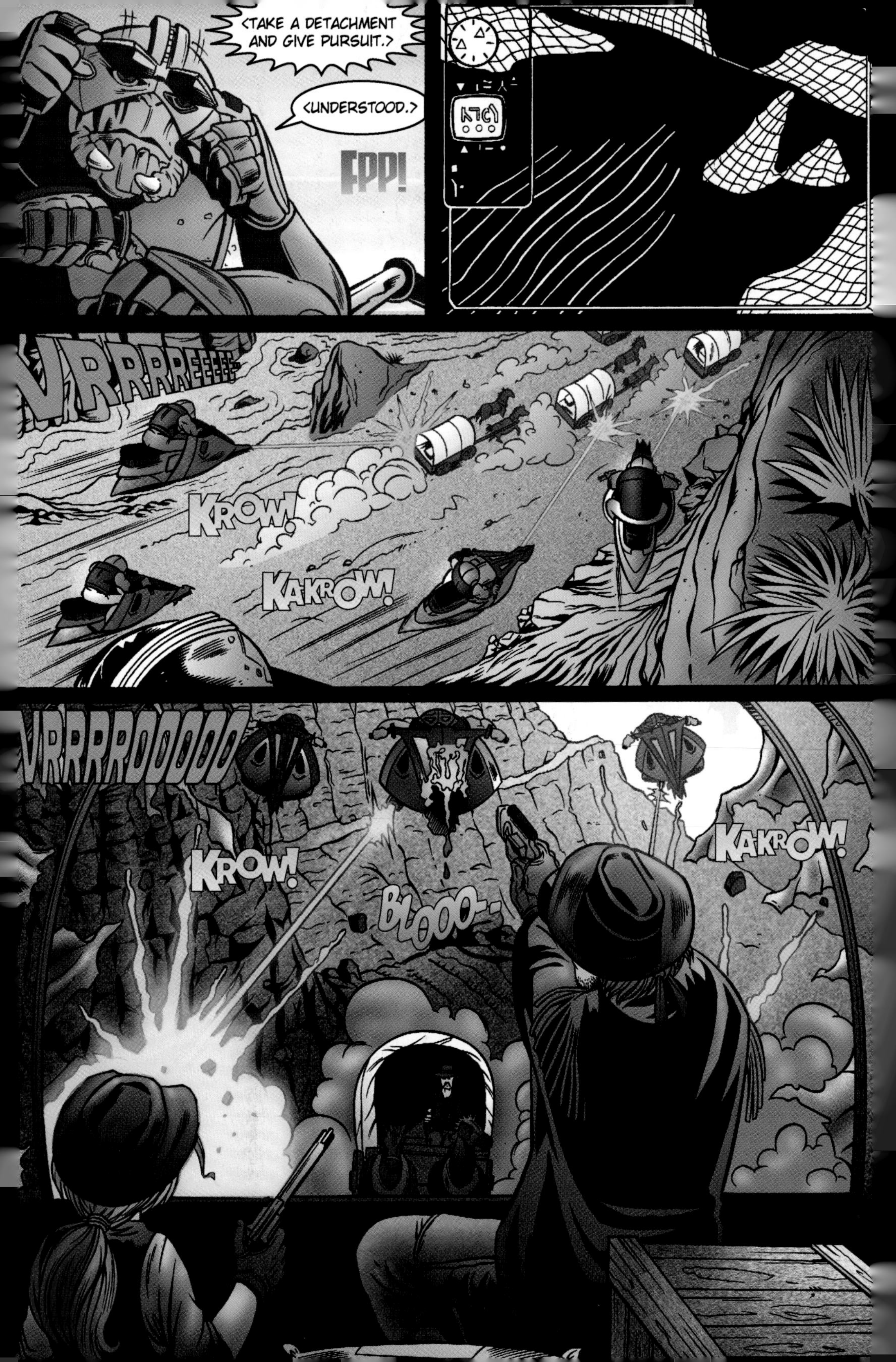
<TAKE A DETACHMENT AND GIVE PURSUIT.>
<UNDERSTOOD.>
FPP!
VRRRREEEE
KROW!
KA-KROW!
VRRRROOOOOO
KROW!
BLOOO-
KA-KROW!

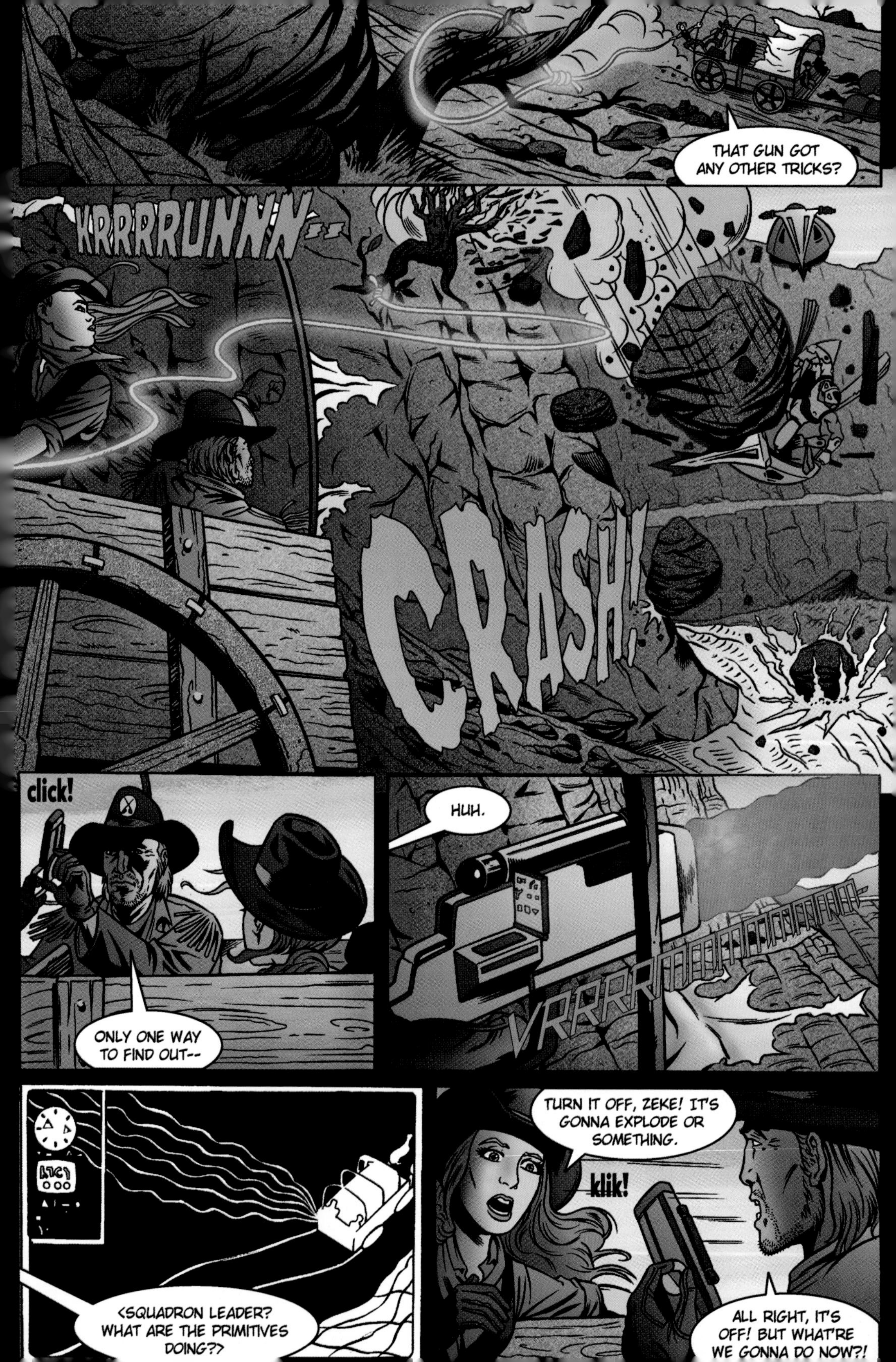
THAT GUN GOT ANY OTHER TRICKS?
KRRRRUNNN--
CRASH!
click!
ONLY ONE WAY TO FIND OUT--
HUH.
VRRRR
<SQUADRON LEADER? WHAT ARE THE PRIMITIVES DOING?>
TURN IT OFF, ZEKE! IT'S GONNA EXPLODE OR SOMETHING.
klik!
ALL RIGHT, IT'S OFF! BUT WHAT'RE WE GONNA DO NOW?!

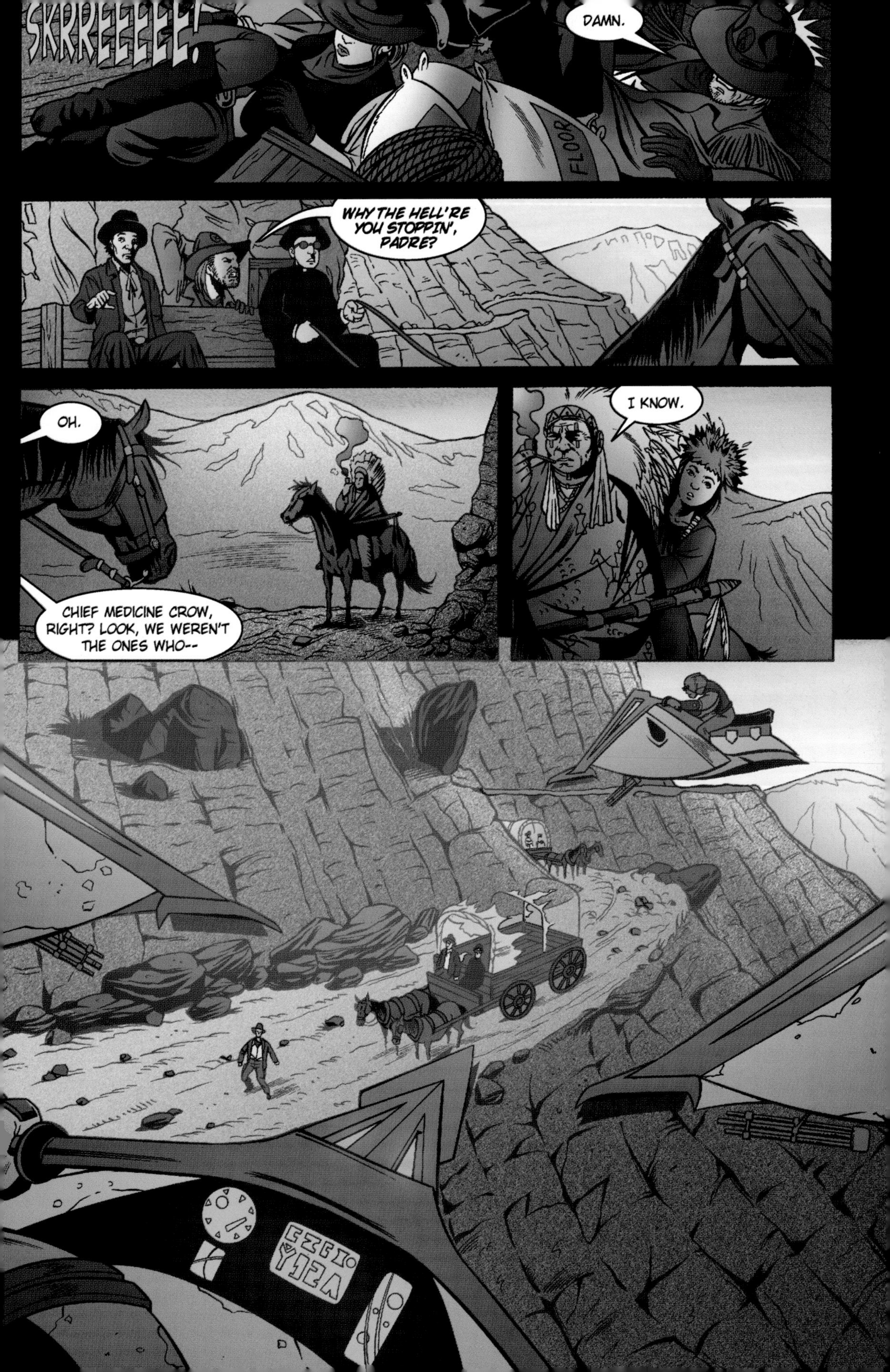
SKRREEEEE!
DAMN.
WHY THE HELL'RE YOU STOPPIN', PADRE?
OH.
CHIEF MEDICINE CROW, RIGHT? LOOK, WE WEREN'T THE ONES WHO--
I KNOW.
FLOOR

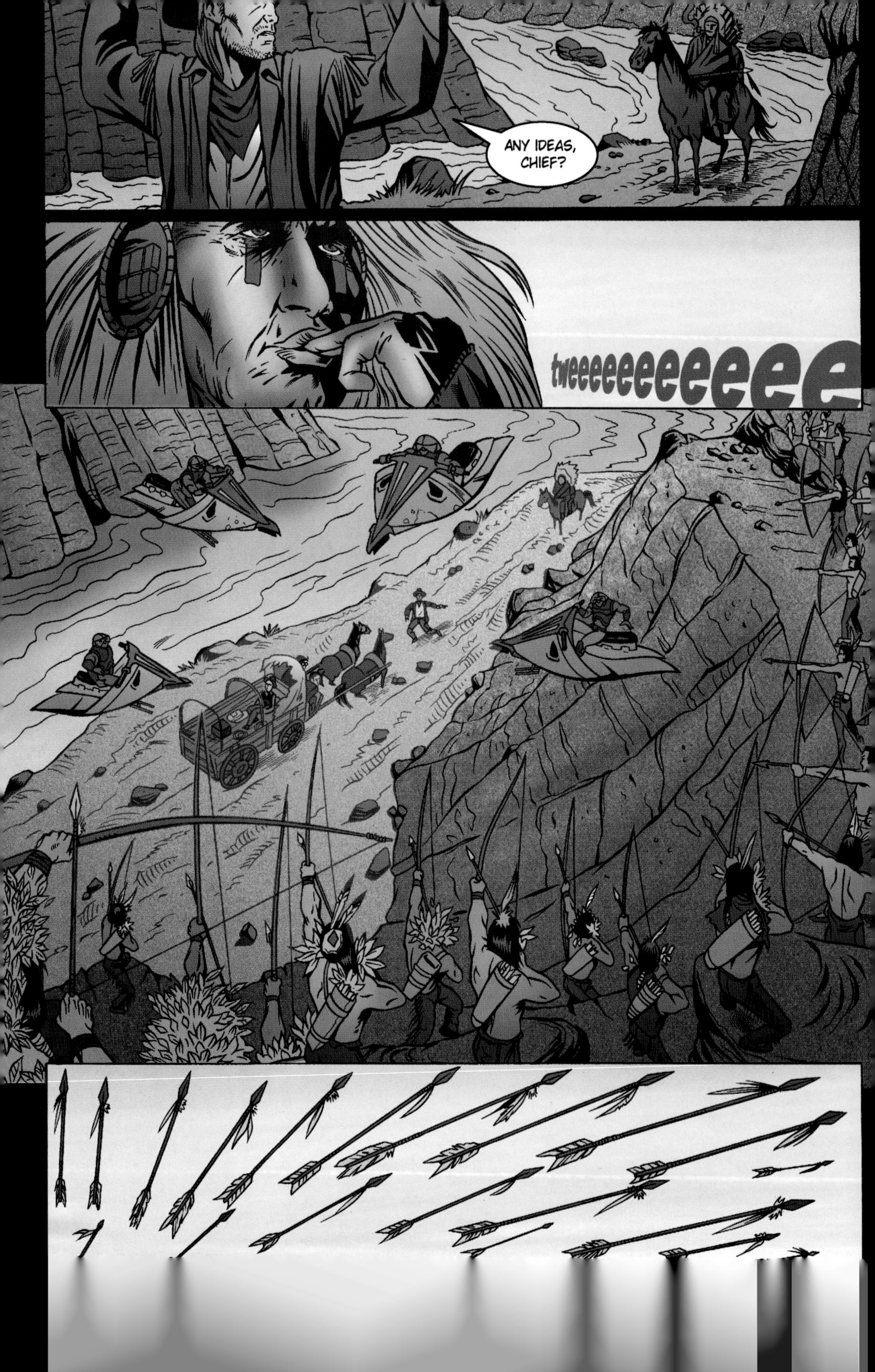
ANY IDEAS, CHIEF?
tweeeeeeeeeee

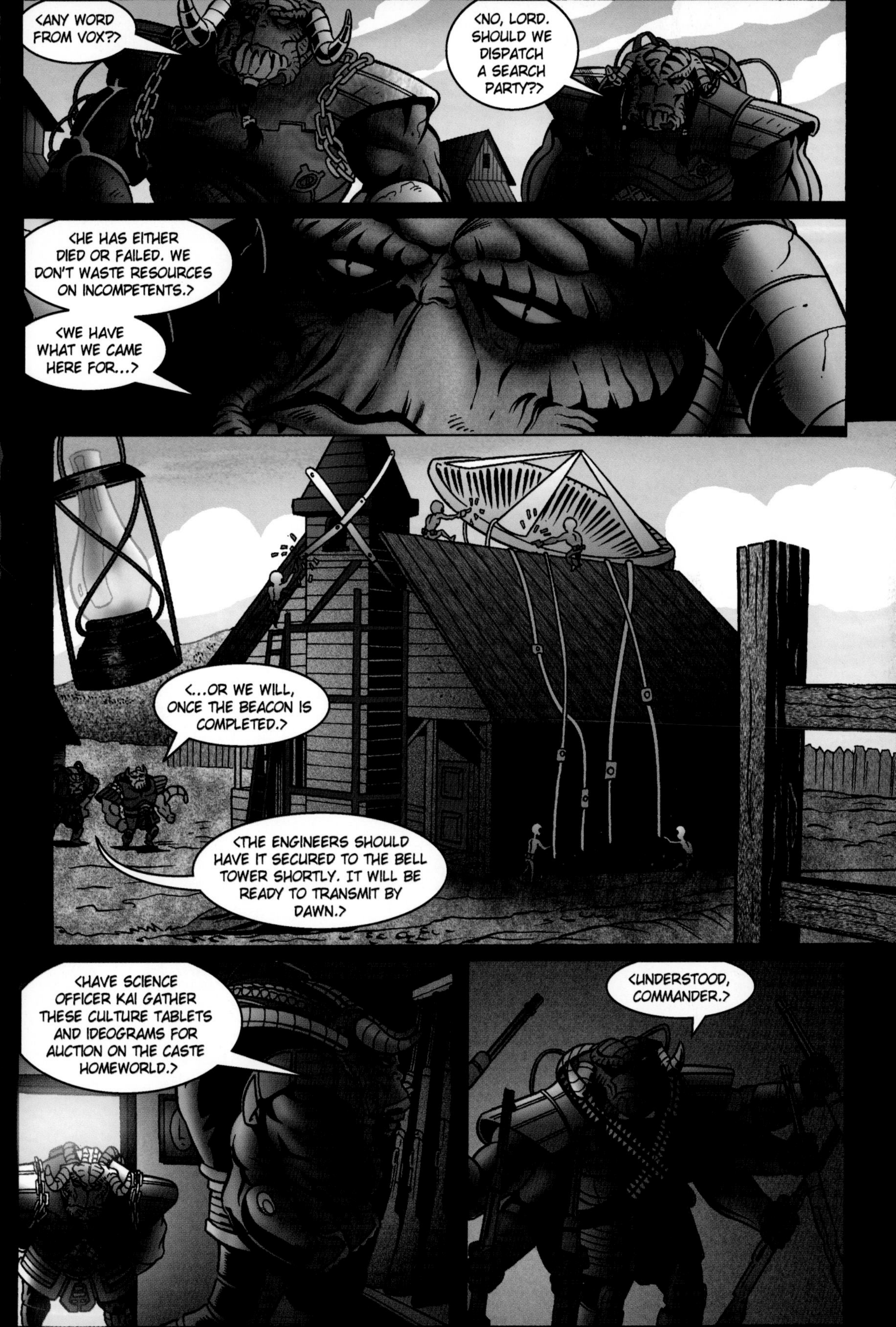
<ANY WORD FROM VOX?>
<NO, LORD. SHOULD WE DISPATCH A SEARCH PARTY?>
<HE HAS EITHER DIED OR FAILED. WE DON'T WASTE RESOURCES ON INCOMPETENTS.>
<WE HAVE WHAT WE CAME HERE FOR...>
<...OR WE WILL, ONCE THE BEACON IS COMPLETED.>
<THE ENGINEERS SHOULD HAVE IT SECURED TO THE BELL TOWER SHORTLY. IT WILL BE READY TO TRANSMIT BY DAWN.>
<HAVE SCIENCE OFFICER KAI GATHER THESE CULTURE TABLETS AND IDEOGRAMS FOR AUCTION ON THE CASTE HOMEWORLD.>
<UNDERSTOOD, COMMANDER.>

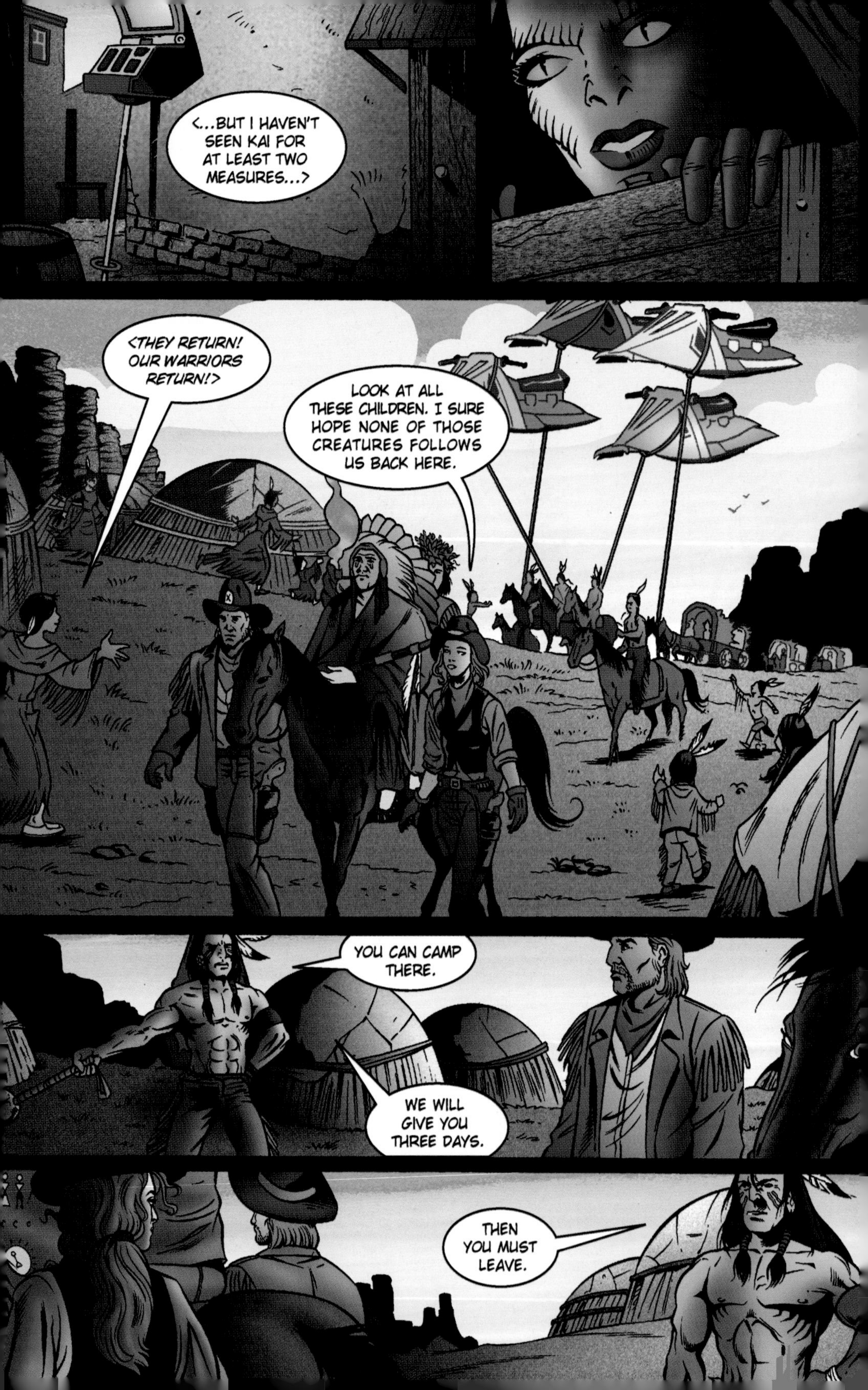

<...BUT I HAVEN'T SEEN KAI FOR AT LEAST TWO MEASURES...>
<THEY RETURN! OUR WARRIORS RETURN!>
LOOK AT ALL THESE CHILDREN. I SURE HOPE NONE OF THOSE CREATURES FOLLOWS US BACK HERE.
YOU CAN CAMP THERE.
WE WILL GIVE YOU THREE DAYS.
THEN YOU MUST LEAVE.

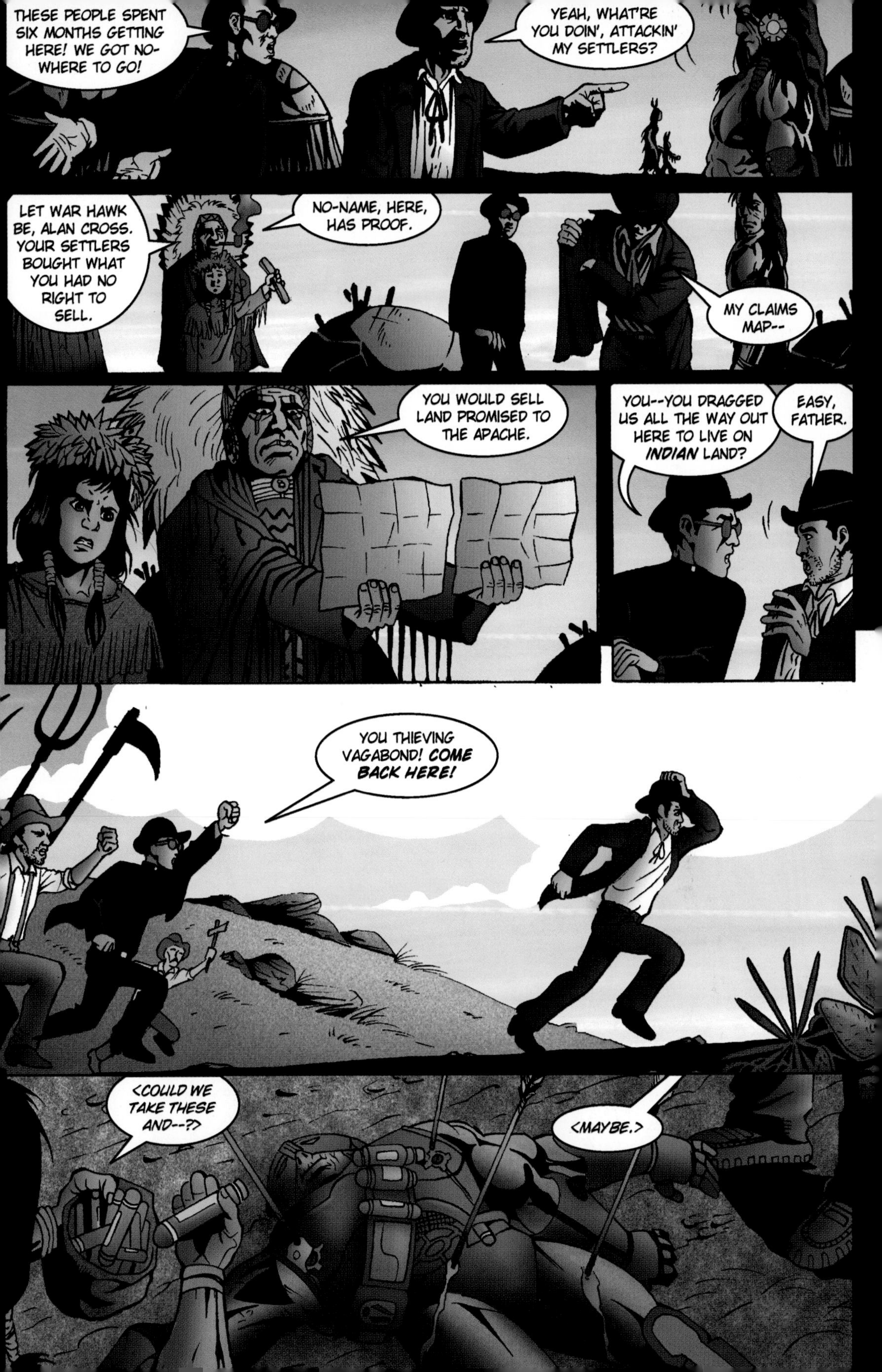
THESE PEOPLE SPENT SIX MONTHS GETTING HERE! WE GOT NO-WHERE TO GO!
YEAH, WHAT'RE YOU DOIN', ATTACKIN' MY SETTLERS?
LET WAR HAWK BE, ALAN CROSS. YOUR SETTLERS BOUGHT WHAT YOU HAD NO RIGHT TO SELL.
NO-NAME, HERE, HAS PROOF.
MY CLAIMS MAP--
YOU WOULD SELL LAND PROMISED TO THE APACHE.
YOU--YOU DRAGGED US ALL THE WAY OUT HERE TO LIVE ON INDIAN LAND?
EASY, FATHER.
YOU THIEVING VAGABOND! COME BACK HERE!
<COULD WE TAKE THESE AND--?>
<MAYBE.>

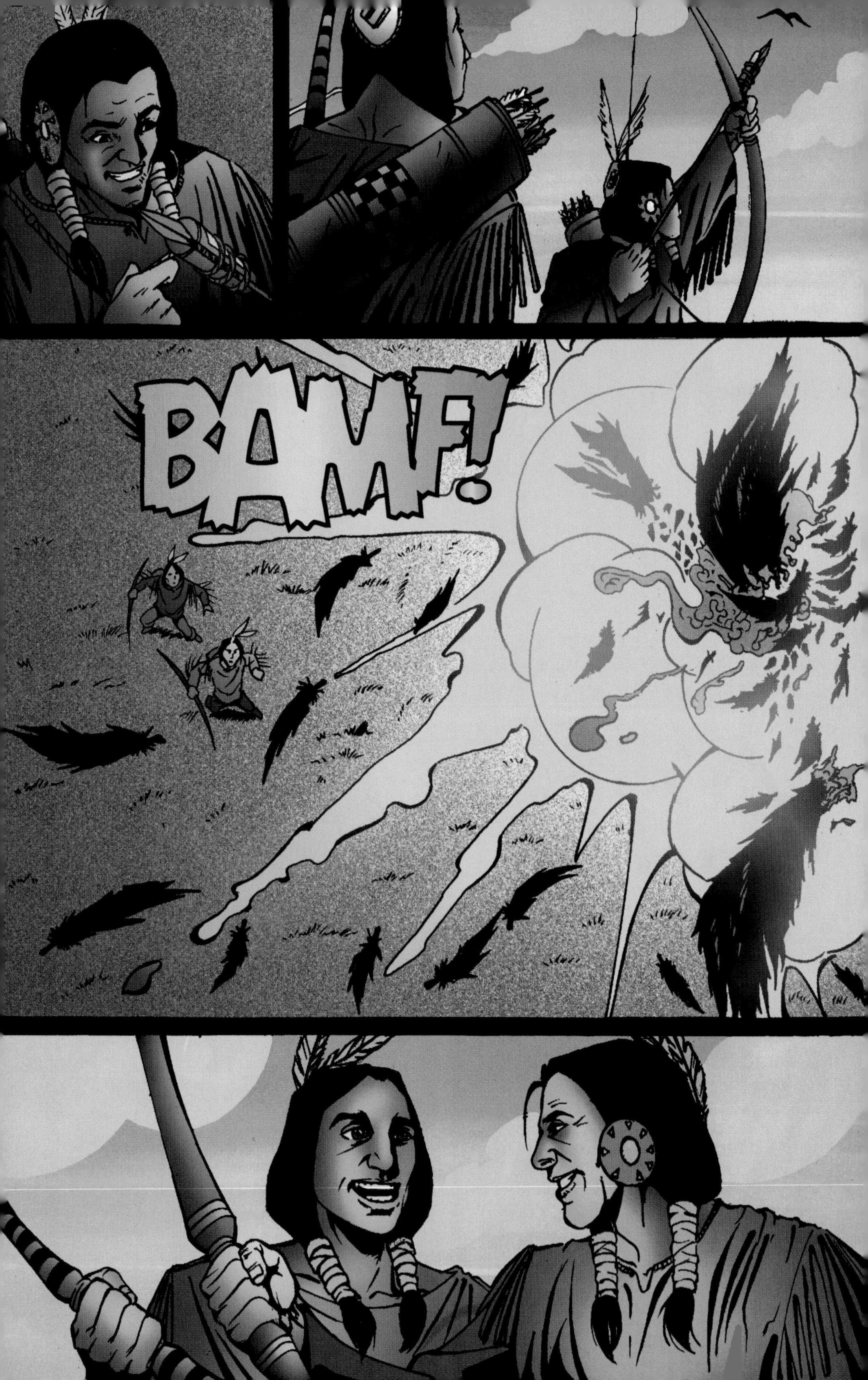
BAMF!

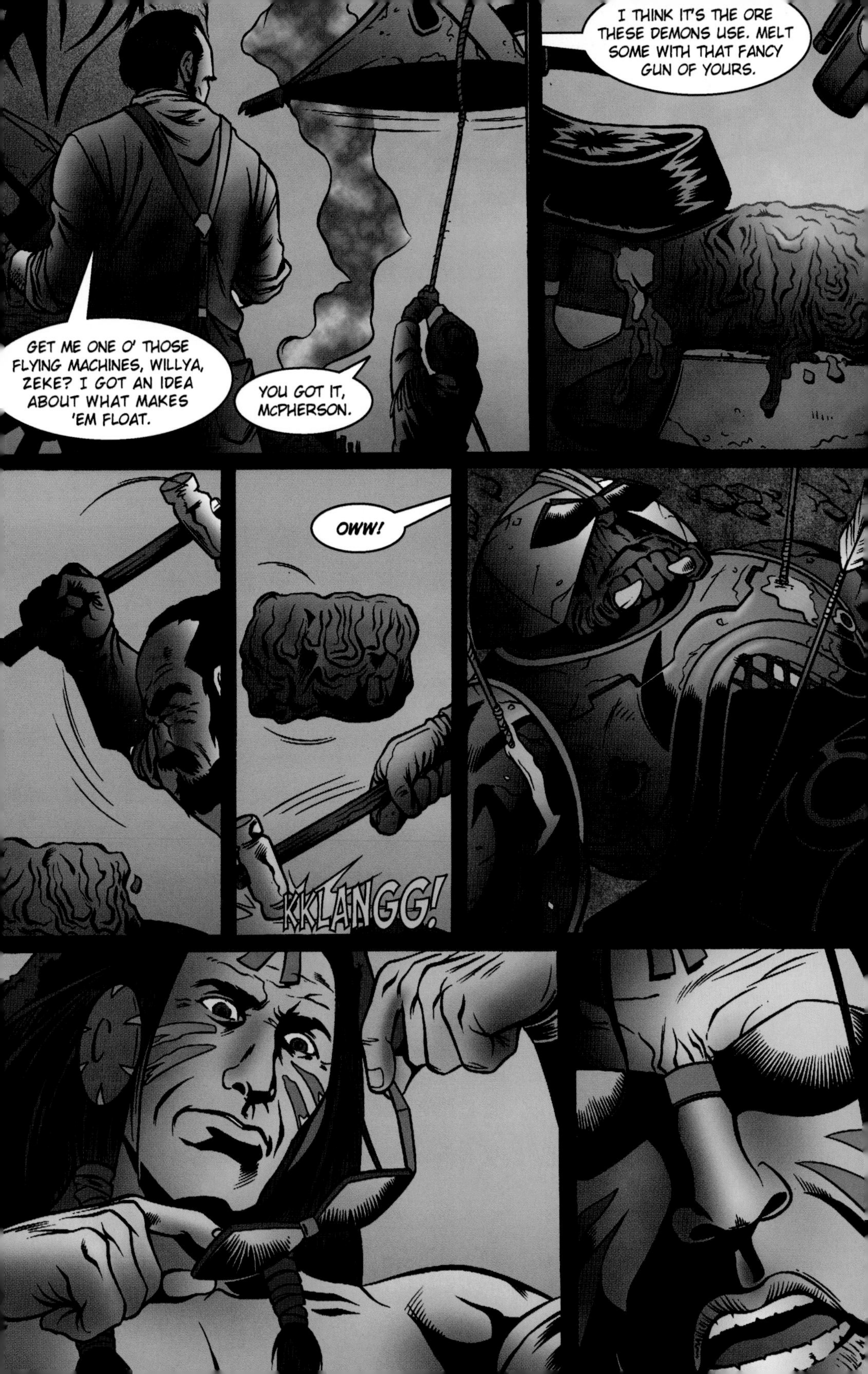
GET ME ONE O' THOSE FLYING MACHINES, WILLYA, ZEKE? I GOT AN IDEA ABOUT WHAT MAKES 'EM FLOAT.
YOU GOT IT, McPHERSON.
I THINK IT'S THE ORE THESE DEMONS USE. MELT SOME WITH THAT FANCY GUN OF YOURS.
OWW!
KKLANGG!

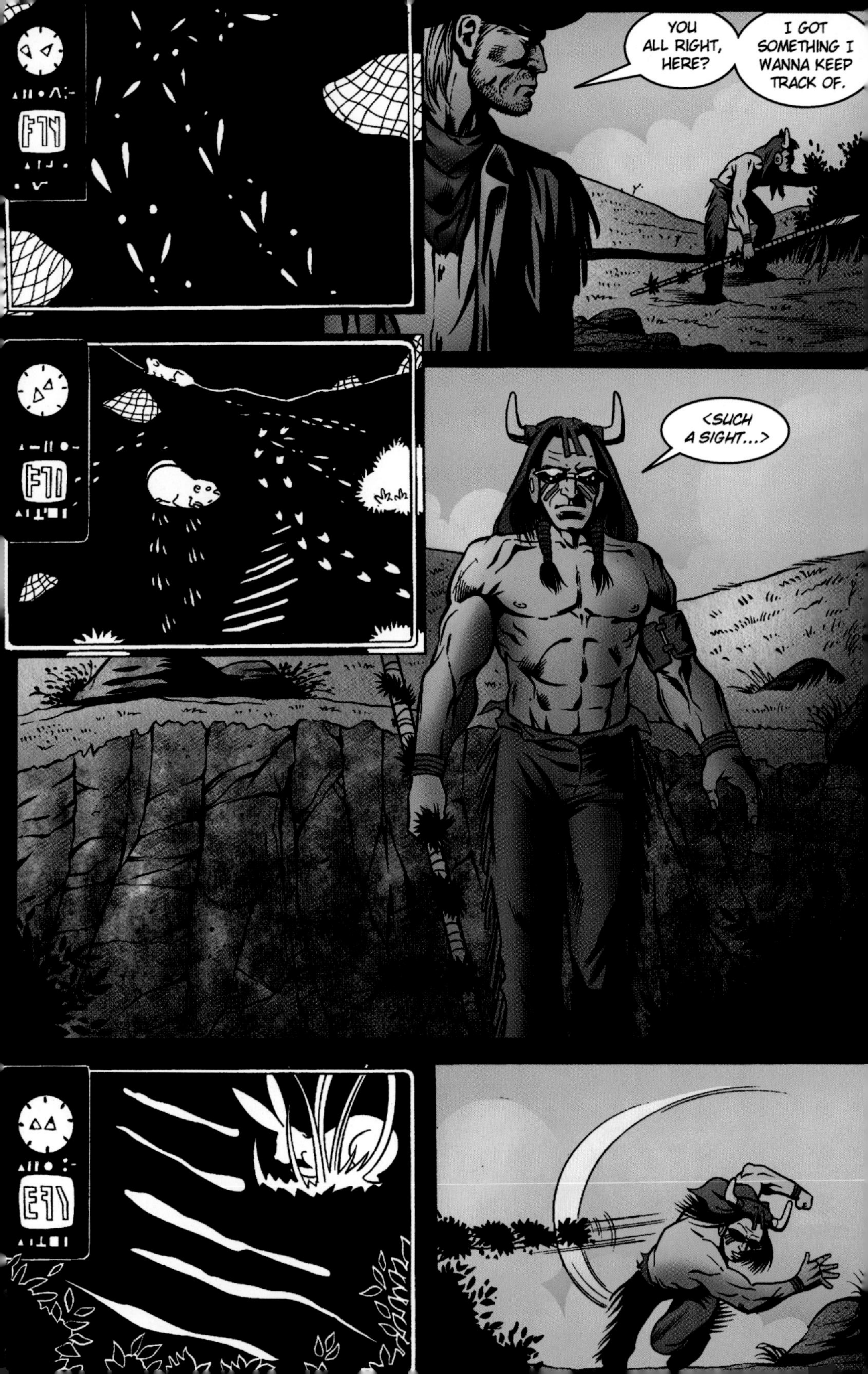
YOU ALL RIGHT, HERE?
I GOT SOMETHING I WANNA KEEP TRACK OF.
<SUCH A SIGHT...>

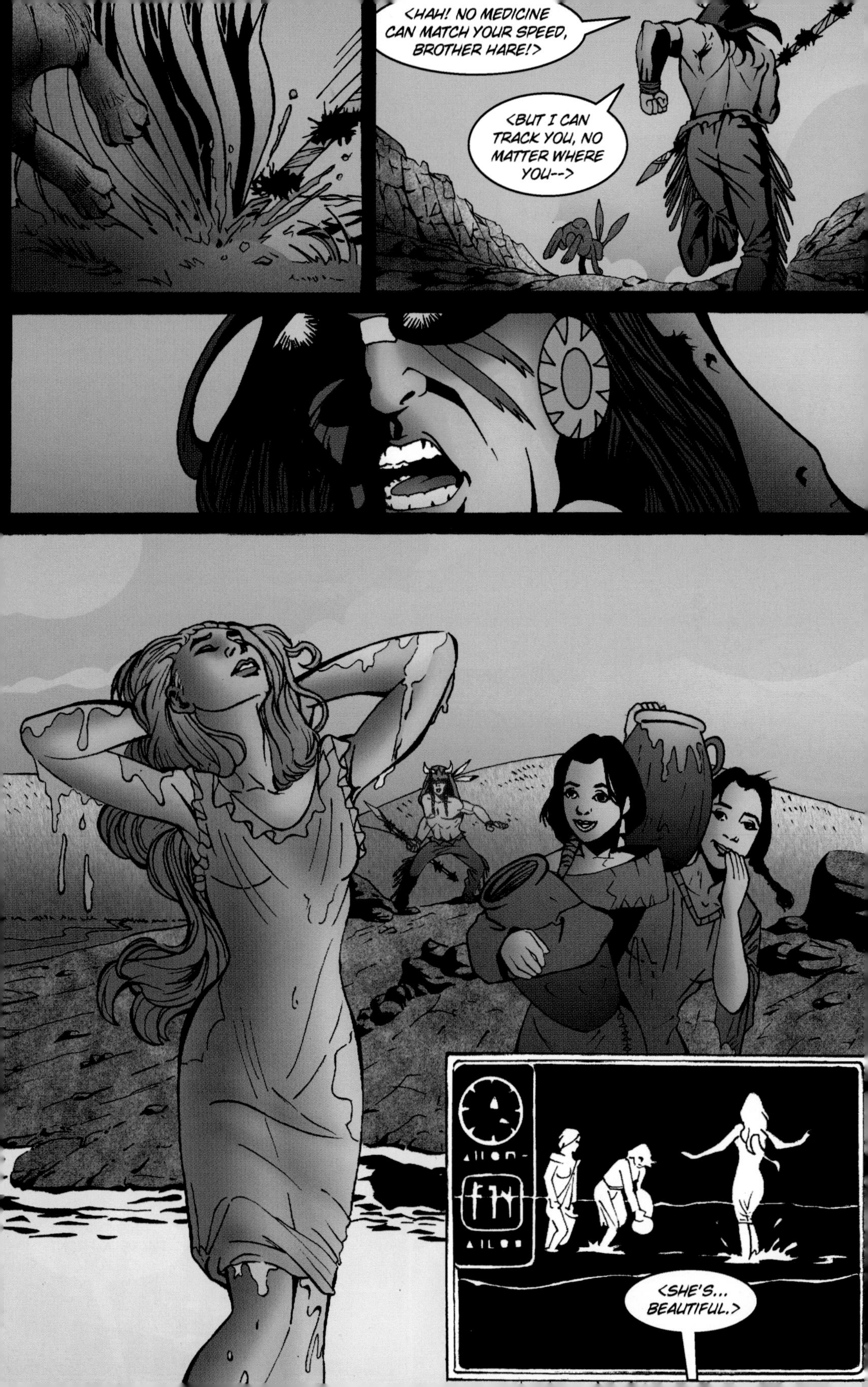
<HAH! NO MEDICINE CAN MATCH YOUR SPEED, BROTHER HARE!>
<BUT I CAN TRACK YOU, NO MATTER WHERE YOU-->
<SHE'S... BEAUTIFUL.>

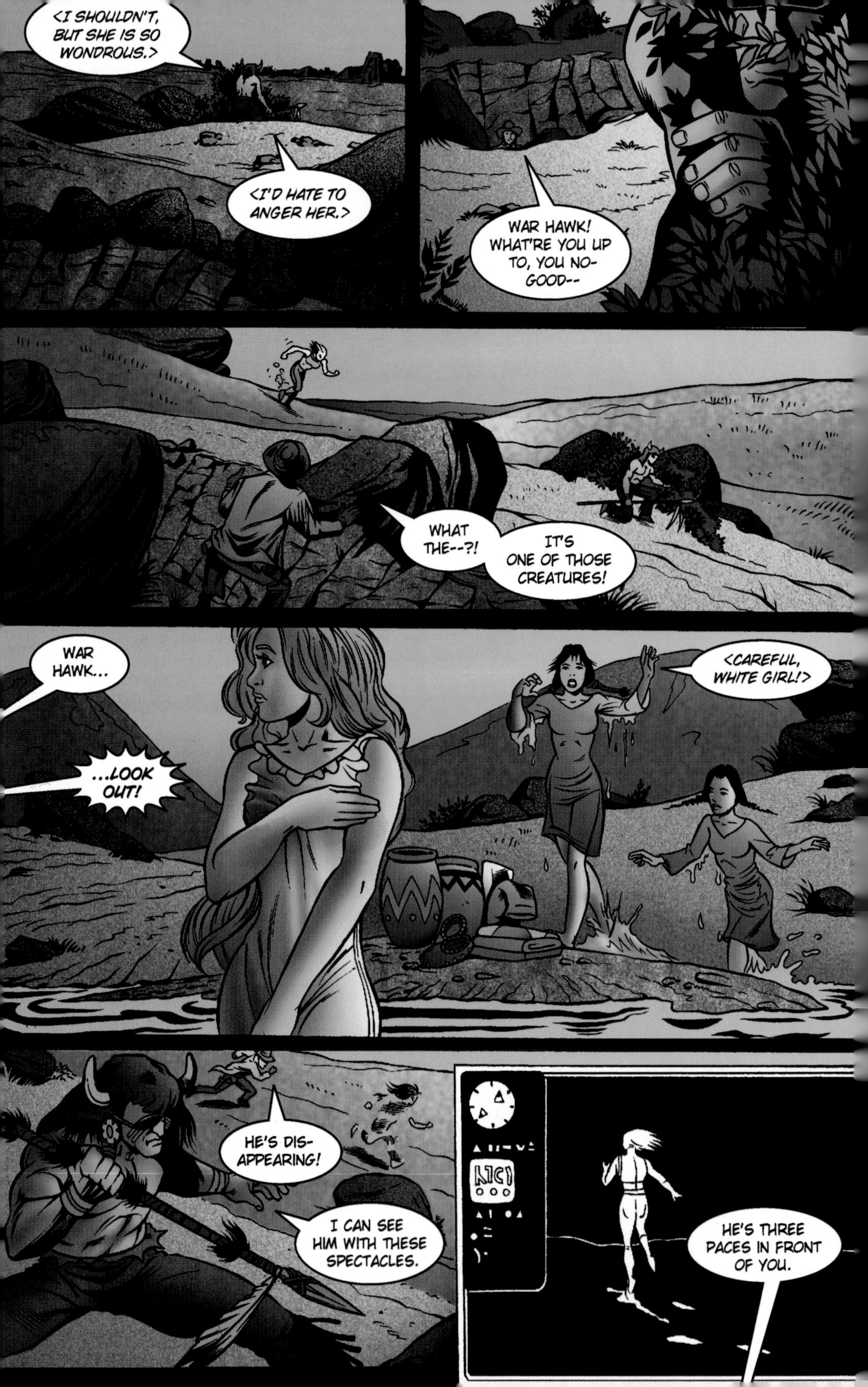
<I SHOULDN'T, BUT SHE IS SO WONDROUS.>
<I'D HATE TO ANGER HER.>
WAR HAWK! WHAT'RE YOU UP TO, YOU NO-GOOD--
WHAT THE--?!
IT'S ONE OF THOSE CREATURES!
WAR HAWK...
...LOOK OUT!
<CAREFUL, WHITE GIRL!>
HE'S DIS-APPEARING!
I CAN SEE HIM WITH THESE SPECTACLES.
HE'S THREE PACES IN FRONT OF YOU.

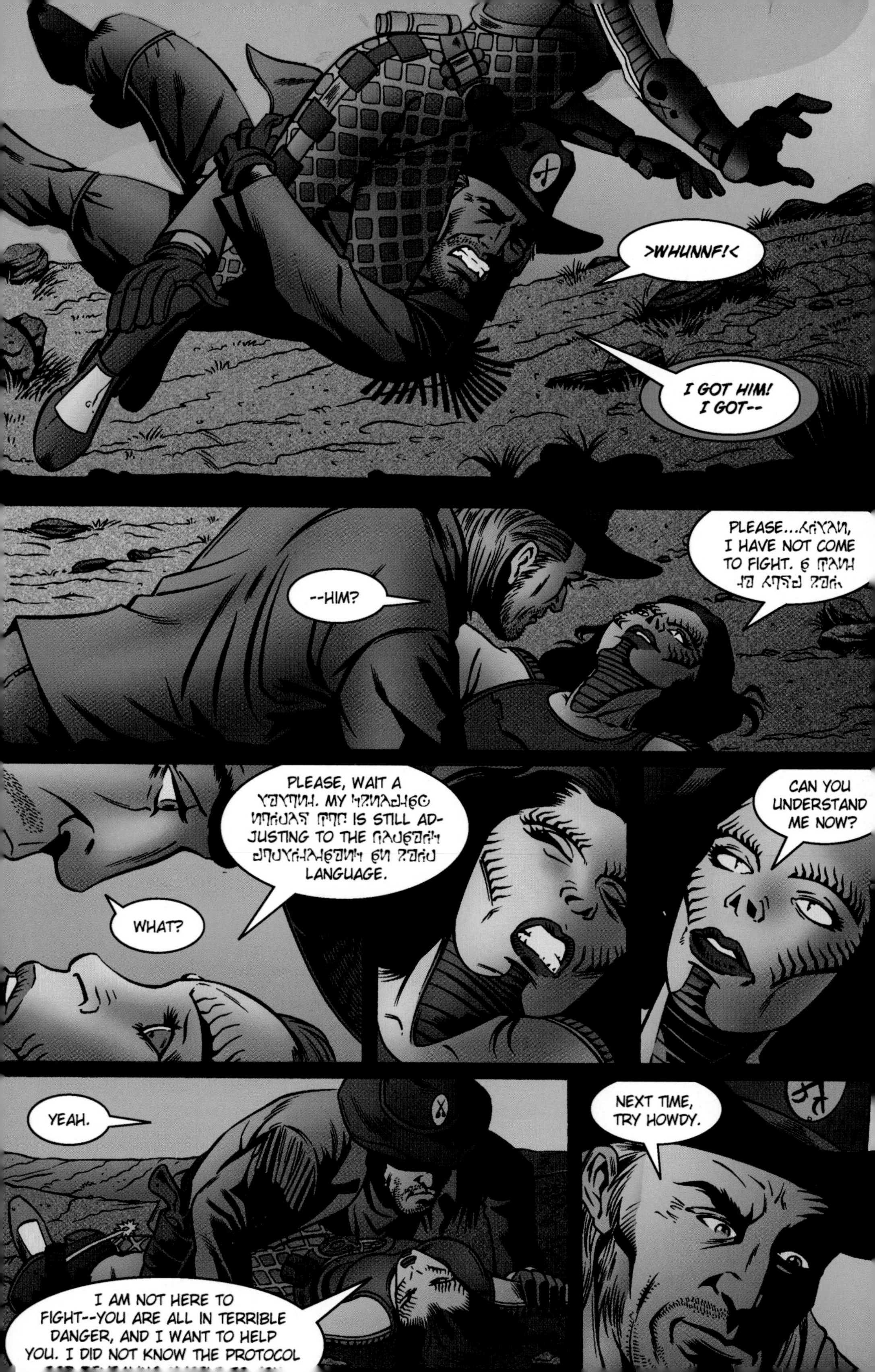

>WHUNNF!<
I GOT HIM! I GOT--
--HIM?
PLEASE... I HAVE NOT COME TO FIGHT.
PLEASE, WAIT A ... MY ... IS STILL ADJUSTING TO THE ... LANGUAGE.
WHAT?
CAN YOU UNDERSTAND ME NOW?
YEAH.
NEXT TIME, TRY HOWDY.
I AM NOT HERE TO FIGHT--YOU ARE ALL IN TERRIBLE DANGER, AND I WANT TO HELP YOU. I DID NOT KNOW THE PROTOCOL

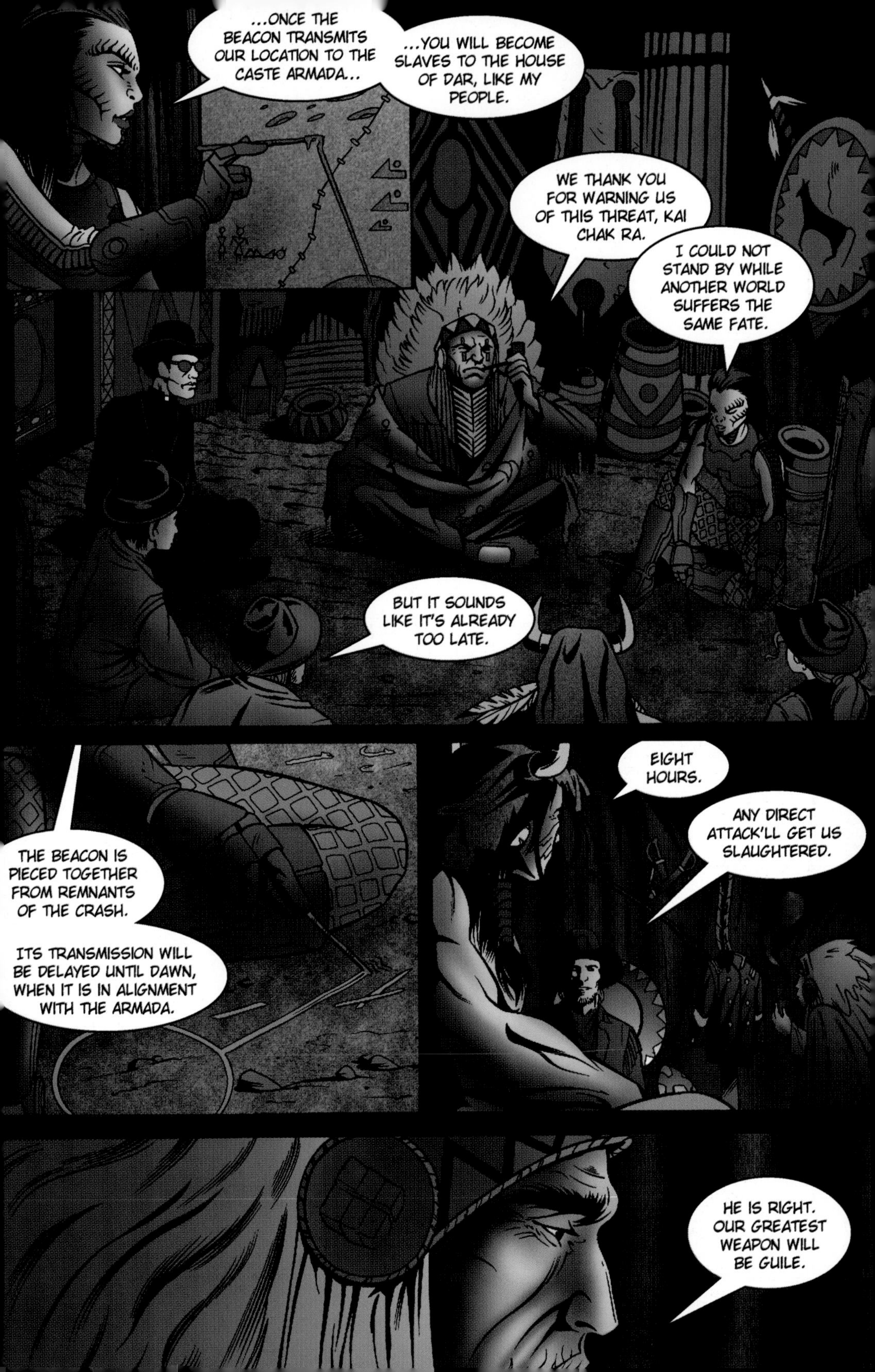
...ONCE THE BEACON TRANSMITS OUR LOCATION TO THE CASTE ARMADA...
...YOU WILL BECOME SLAVES TO THE HOUSE OF DAR, LIKE MY PEOPLE.
WE THANK YOU FOR WARNING US OF THIS THREAT, KAI CHAK RA.
I COULD NOT STAND BY WHILE ANOTHER WORLD SUFFERS THE SAME FATE.
BUT IT SOUNDS LIKE IT'S ALREADY TOO LATE.
THE BEACON IS PIECED TOGETHER FROM REMNANTS OF THE CRASH.
ITS TRANSMISSION WILL BE DELAYED UNTIL DAWN, WHEN IT IS IN ALIGNMENT WITH THE ARMADA.
EIGHT HOURS.
ANY DIRECT ATTACK'LL GET US SLAUGHTERED.
HE IS RIGHT. OUR GREATEST WEAPON WILL BE GUILE.

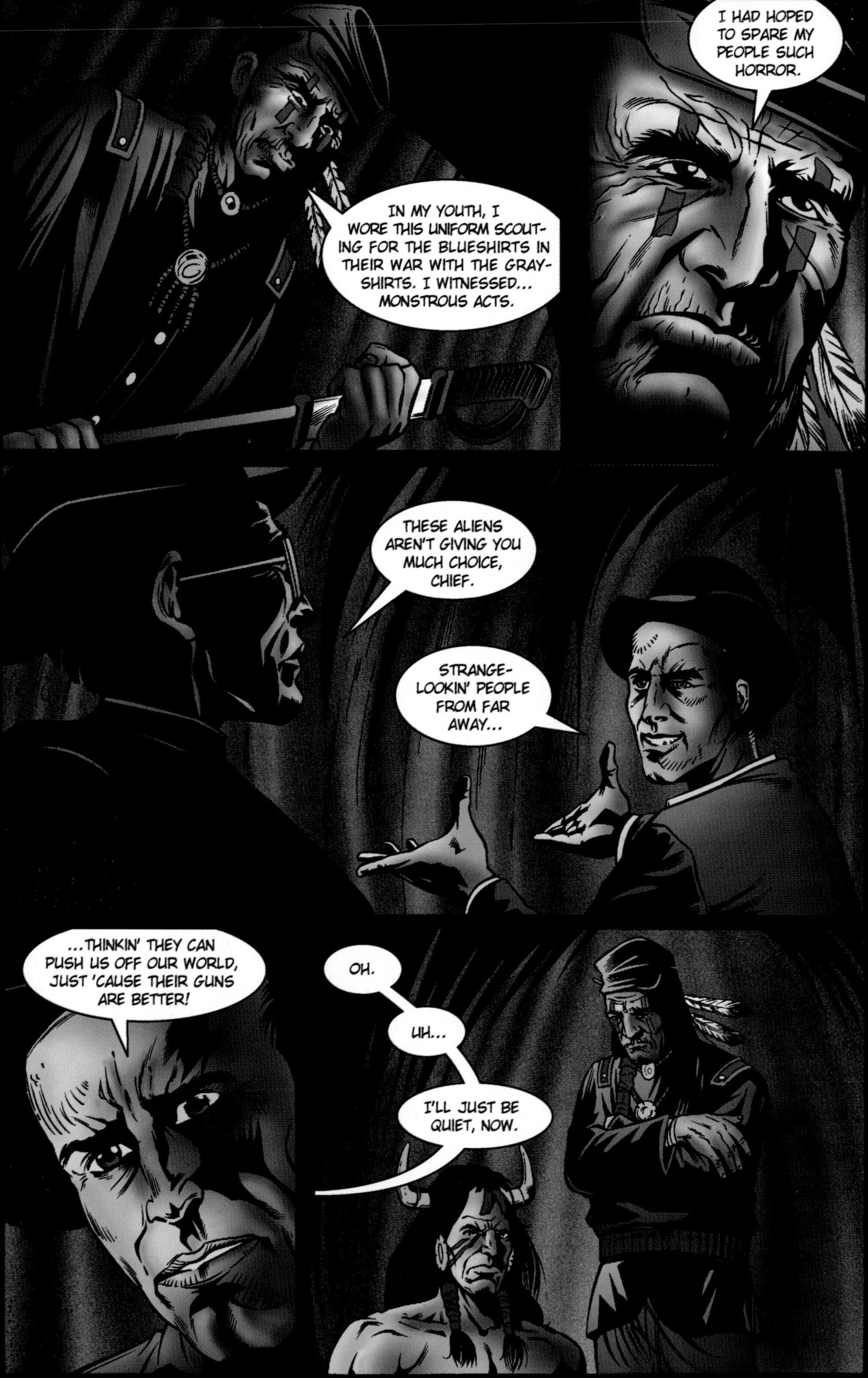
IN MY YOUTH, I WORE THIS UNIFORM SCOUTING FOR THE BLUESHIRTS IN THEIR WAR WITH THE GRAYSHIRTS. I WITNESSED... MONSTROUS ACTS.
I HAD HOPED TO SPARE MY PEOPLE SUCH HORROR.
THESE ALIENS AREN'T GIVING YOU MUCH CHOICE, CHIEF.
STRANGE-LOOKIN' PEOPLE FROM FAR AWAY...
...THINKIN' THEY CAN PUSH US OFF OUR WORLD, JUST 'CAUSE THEIR GUNS ARE BETTER!
OH.
UH...
I'LL JUST BE QUIET, NOW.

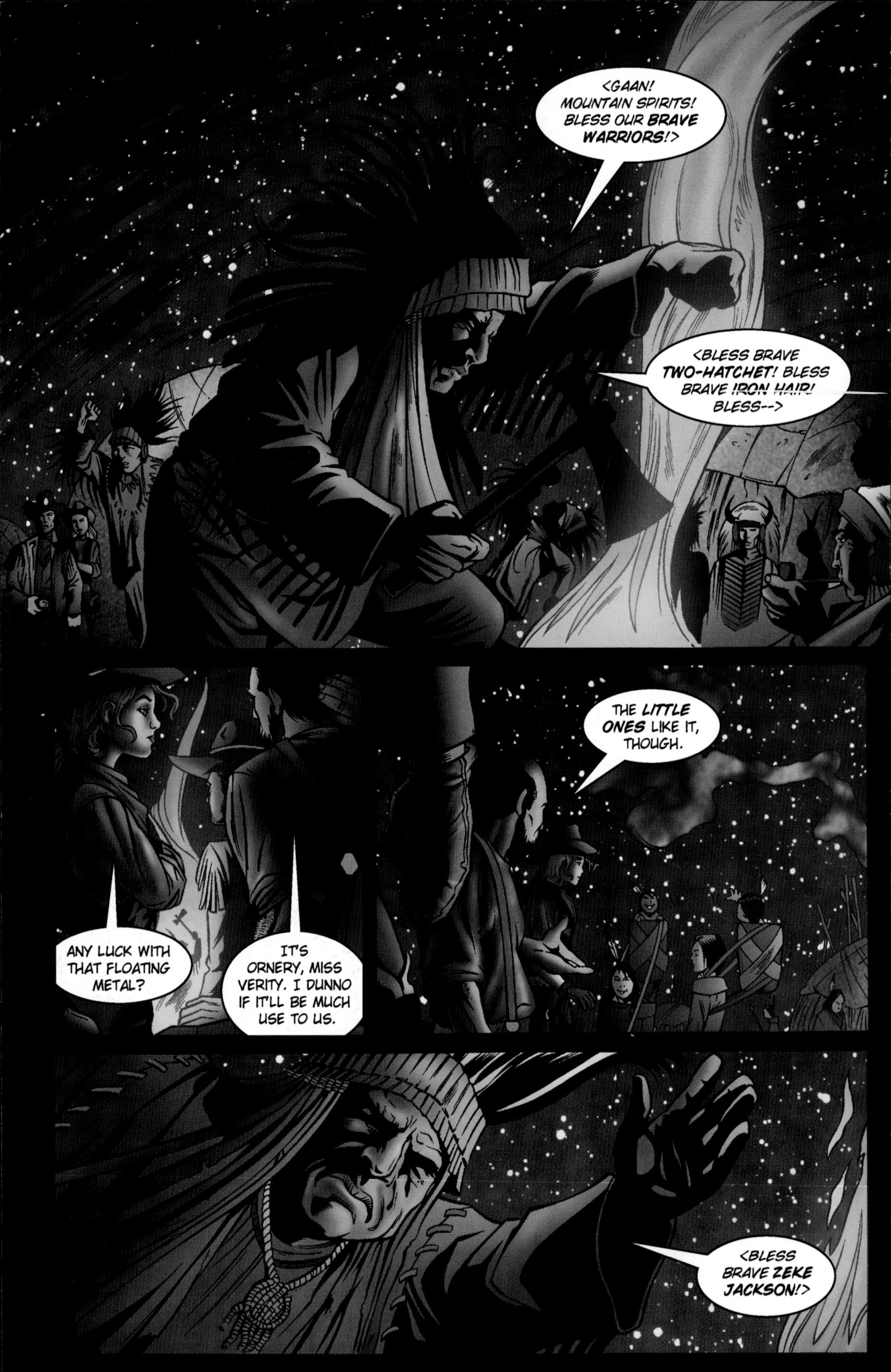
<GAAN! MOUNTAIN SPIRITS! BLESS OUR BRAVE WARRIORS!>
<BLESS BRAVE TWO-HATCHET! BLESS BRAVE IRON HAIR! BLESS-->
ANY LUCK WITH THAT FLOATING METAL?
IT'S ORNERY, MISS VERITY. I DUNNO IF IT'LL BE MUCH USE TO US.
THE LITTLE ONES LIKE IT, THOUGH.
<BLESS BRAVE ZEKE JACKSON!>

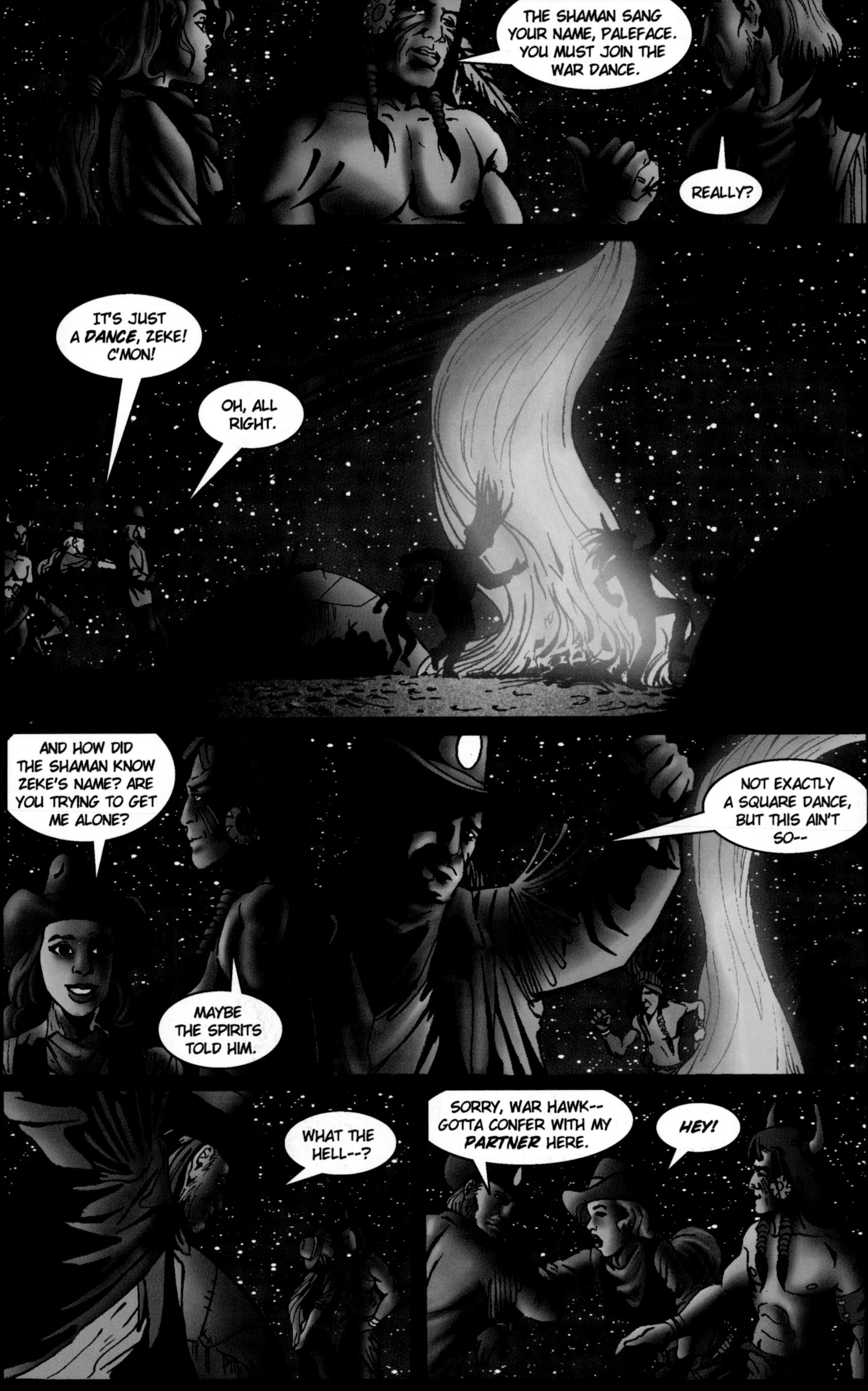
THE SHAMAN SANG YOUR NAME, PALEFACE. YOU MUST JOIN THE WAR DANCE.
REALLY?
IT'S JUST A *DANCE*, ZEKE! C'MON!
OH, ALL RIGHT.
AND HOW DID THE SHAMAN KNOW ZEKE'S NAME? ARE YOU TRYING TO GET ME ALONE?
NOT EXACTLY A SQUARE DANCE, BUT THIS AIN'T SO--
MAYBE THE SPIRITS TOLD HIM.
WHAT THE HELL--?
SORRY, WAR HAWK-- GOTTA CONFER WITH MY *PARTNER* HERE.
HEY!

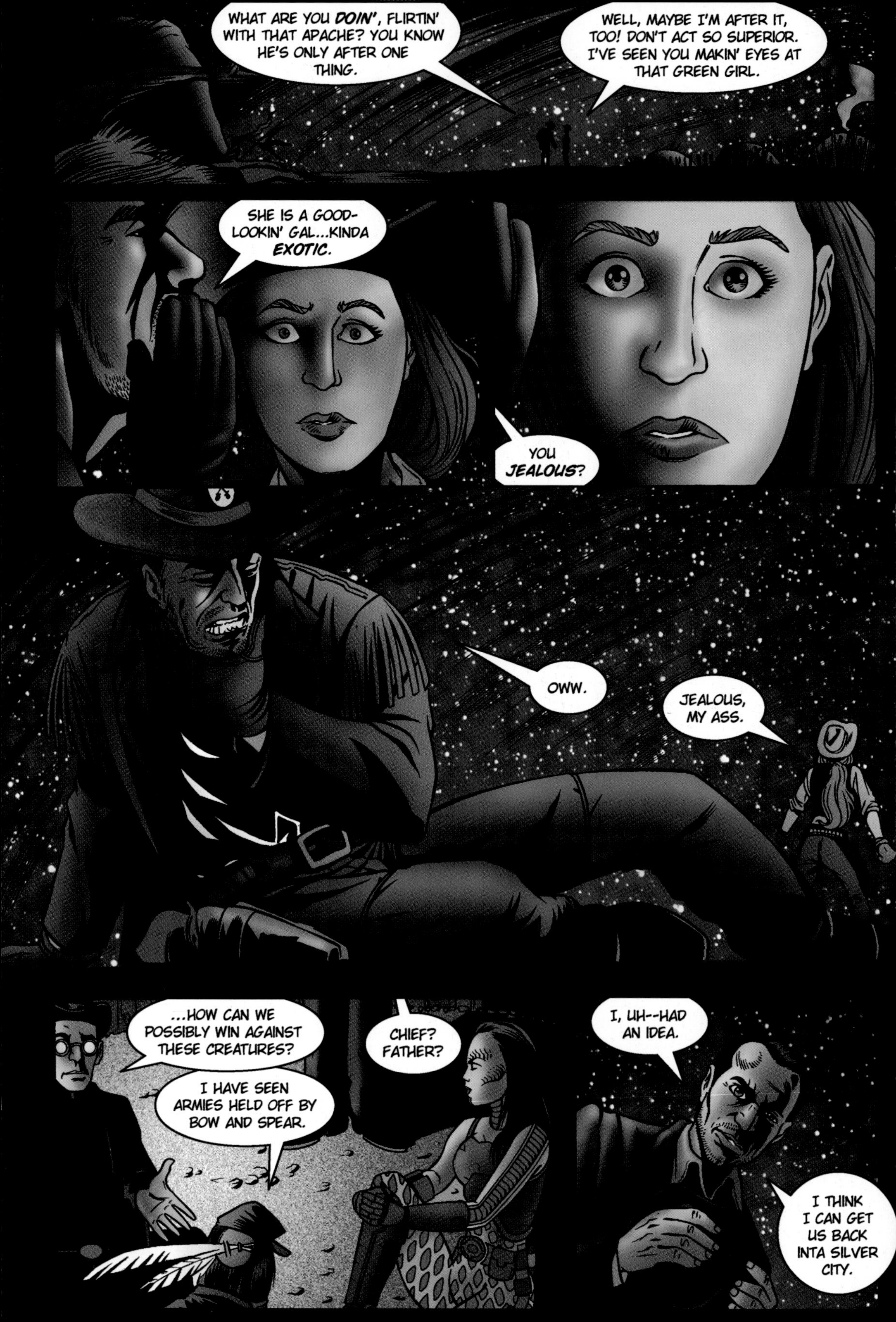
WHAT ARE YOU DOIN', FLIRTIN' WITH THAT APACHE? YOU KNOW HE'S ONLY AFTER ONE THING.
WELL, MAYBE I'M AFTER IT, TOO! DON'T ACT SO SUPERIOR. I'VE SEEN YOU MAKIN' EYES AT THAT GREEN GIRL.
SHE IS A GOOD-LOOKIN' GAL...KINDA EXOTIC.
YOU JEALOUS?
OWW.
JEALOUS, MY ASS.
...HOW CAN WE POSSIBLY WIN AGAINST THESE CREATURES?
I HAVE SEEN ARMIES HELD OFF BY BOW AND SPEAR.
CHIEF? FATHER?
I, UH--HAD AN IDEA.
I THINK I CAN GET US BACK INTA SILVER CITY.

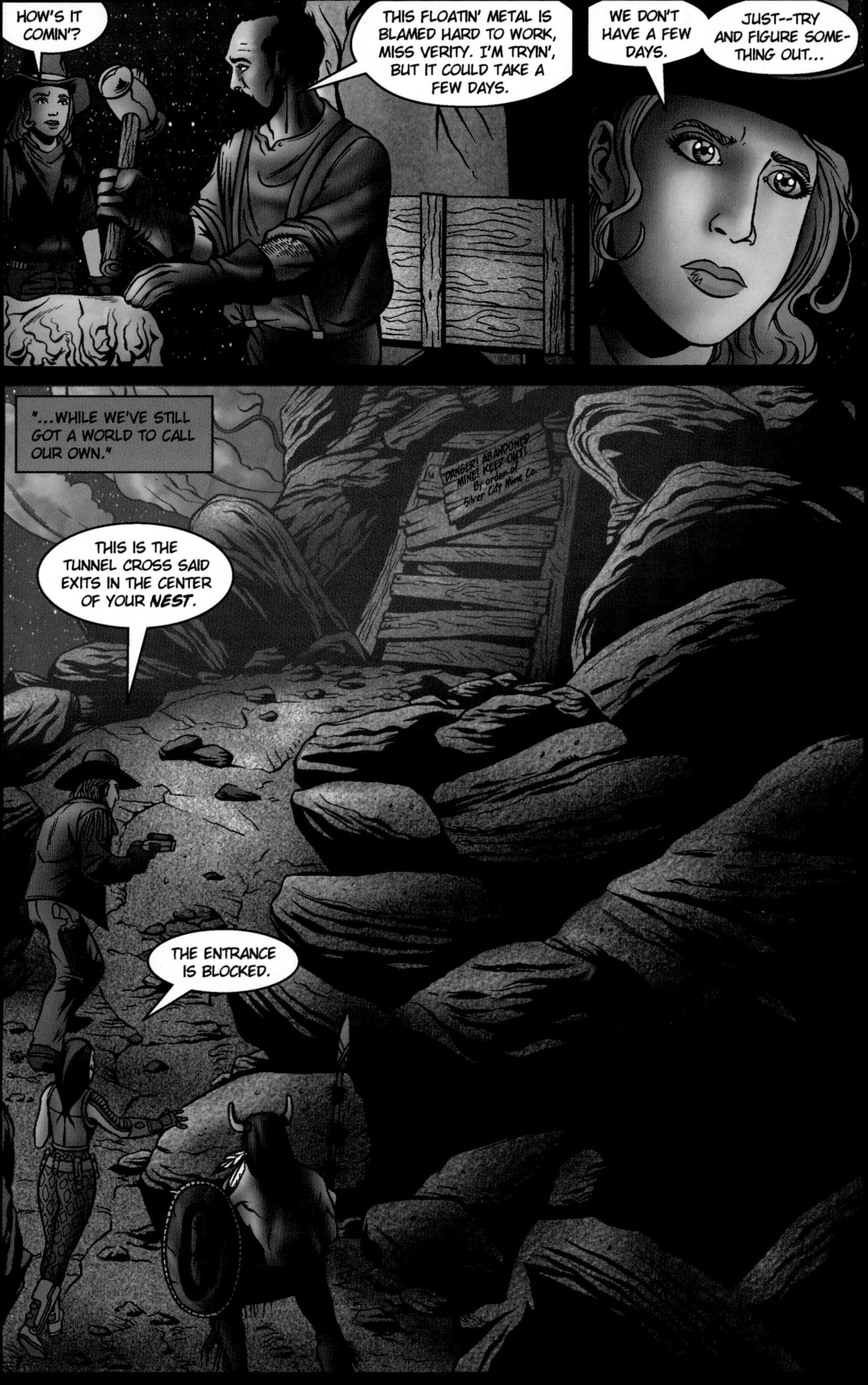
HOW'S IT COMIN'?
THIS FLOATIN' METAL IS BLAMED HARD TO WORK, MISS VERITY. I'M TRYIN', BUT IT COULD TAKE A FEW DAYS.
WE DON'T HAVE A FEW DAYS.
JUST--TRY AND FIGURE SOMETHING OUT...
"...WHILE WE'VE STILL GOT A WORLD TO CALL OUR OWN."
DANGER! ABANDONED MINE! KEEP OUT! By order of Silver City Mine Co.
THIS IS THE TUNNEL CROSS SAID EXITS IN THE CENTER OF YOUR NEST.
THE ENTRANCE IS BLOCKED.

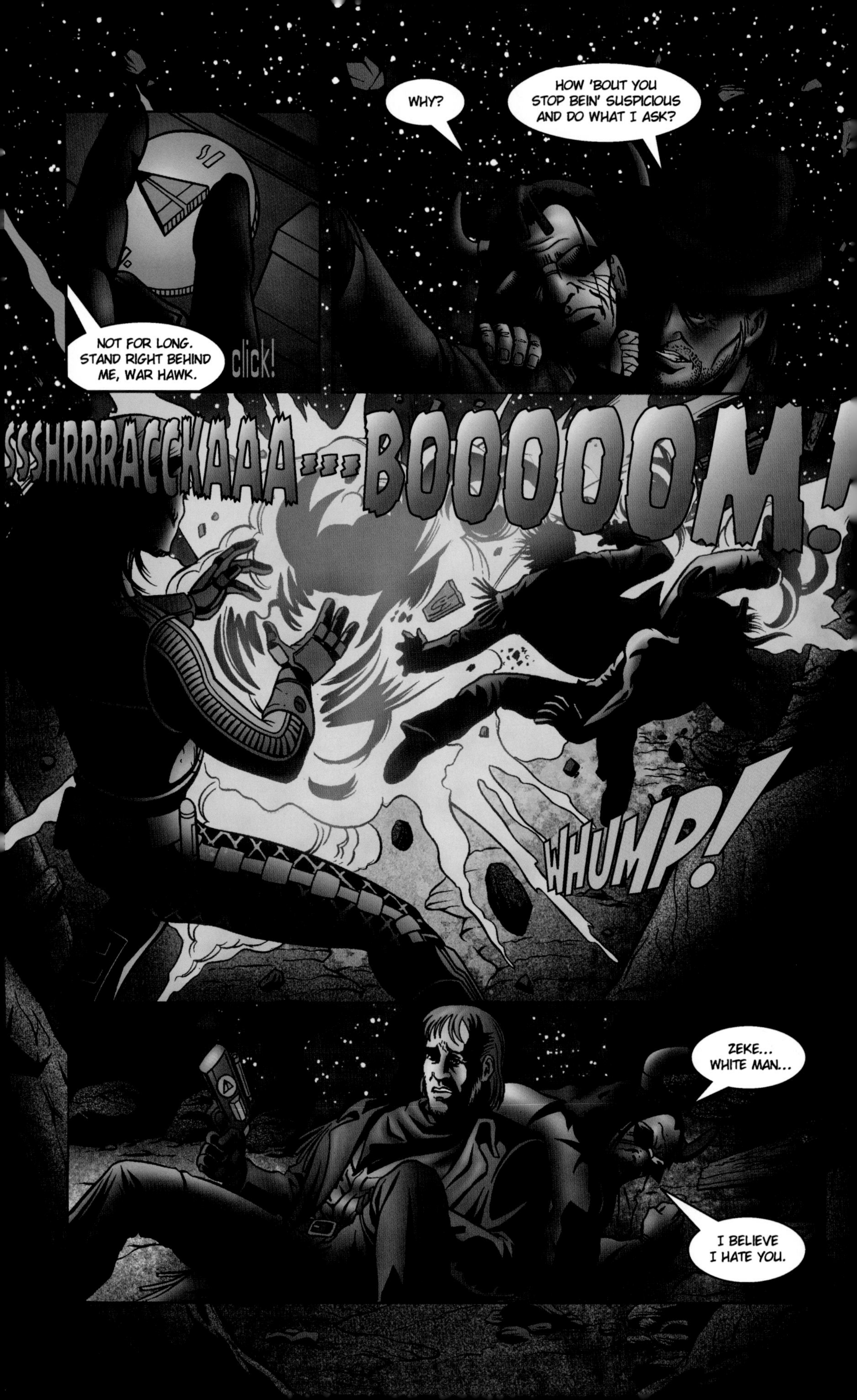
WHY?
HOW 'BOUT YOU STOP BEIN' SUSPICIOUS AND DO WHAT I ASK?
NOT FOR LONG. STAND RIGHT BEHIND ME, WAR HAWK.
click!
SSSHRRRACCKAAA---BOOOOOOM!
WHUMP!
ZEKE... WHITE MAN...
I BELIEVE I HATE YOU.

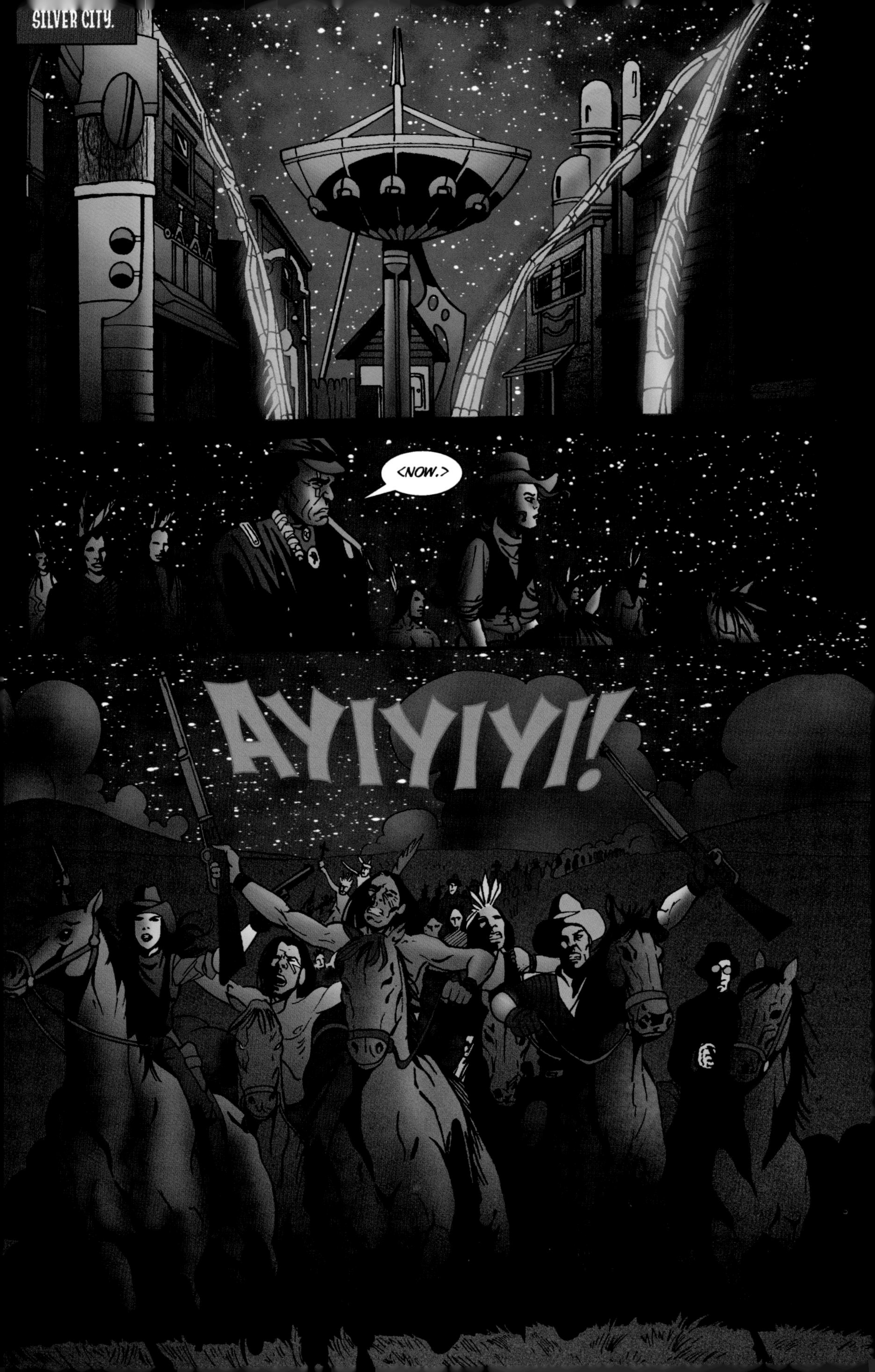
SILVER CITY.
<NOW.>
AYIYIYI!

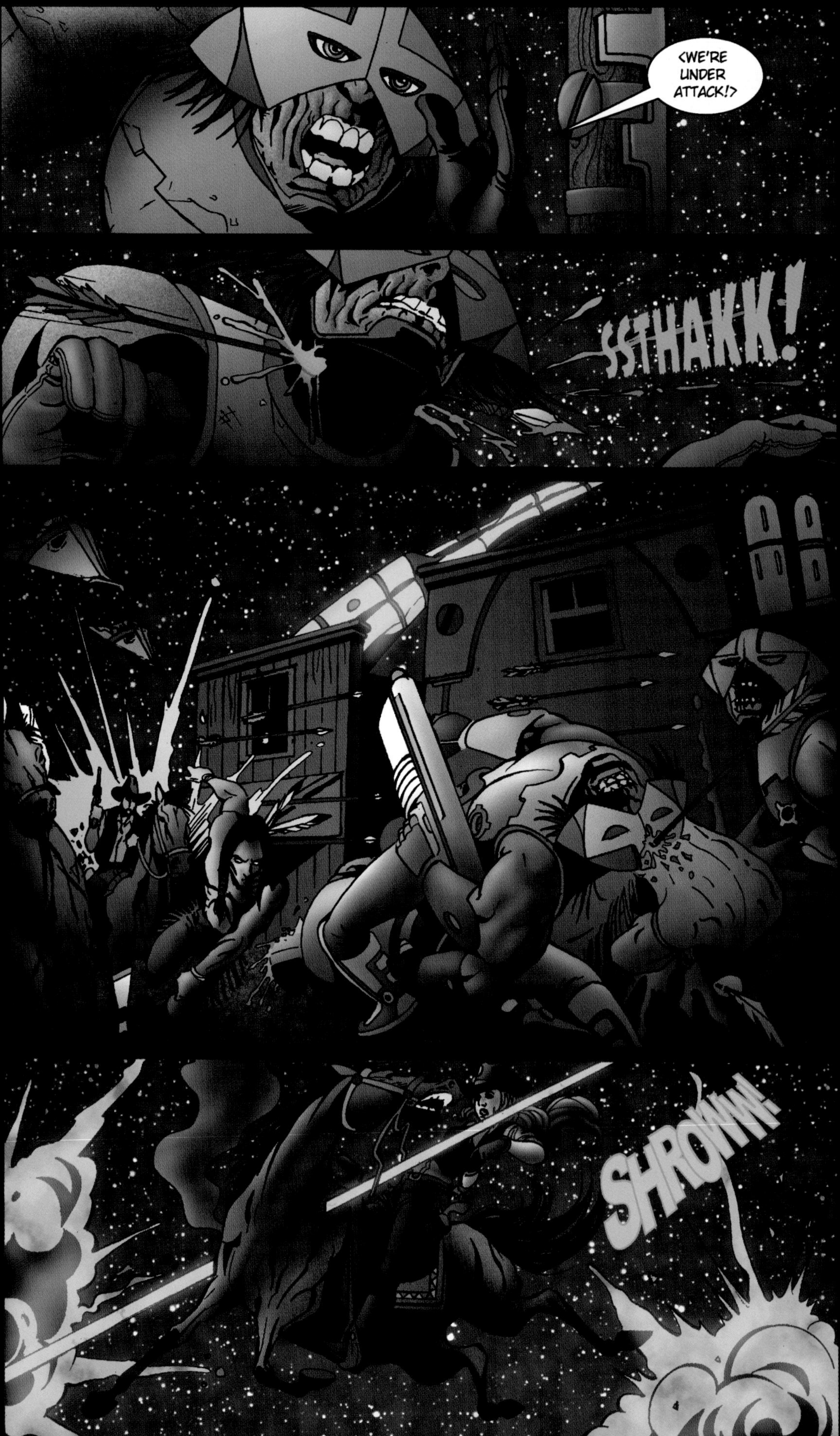
<WE'RE UNDER ATTACK!>
SSTHAKK!
SHROWW!

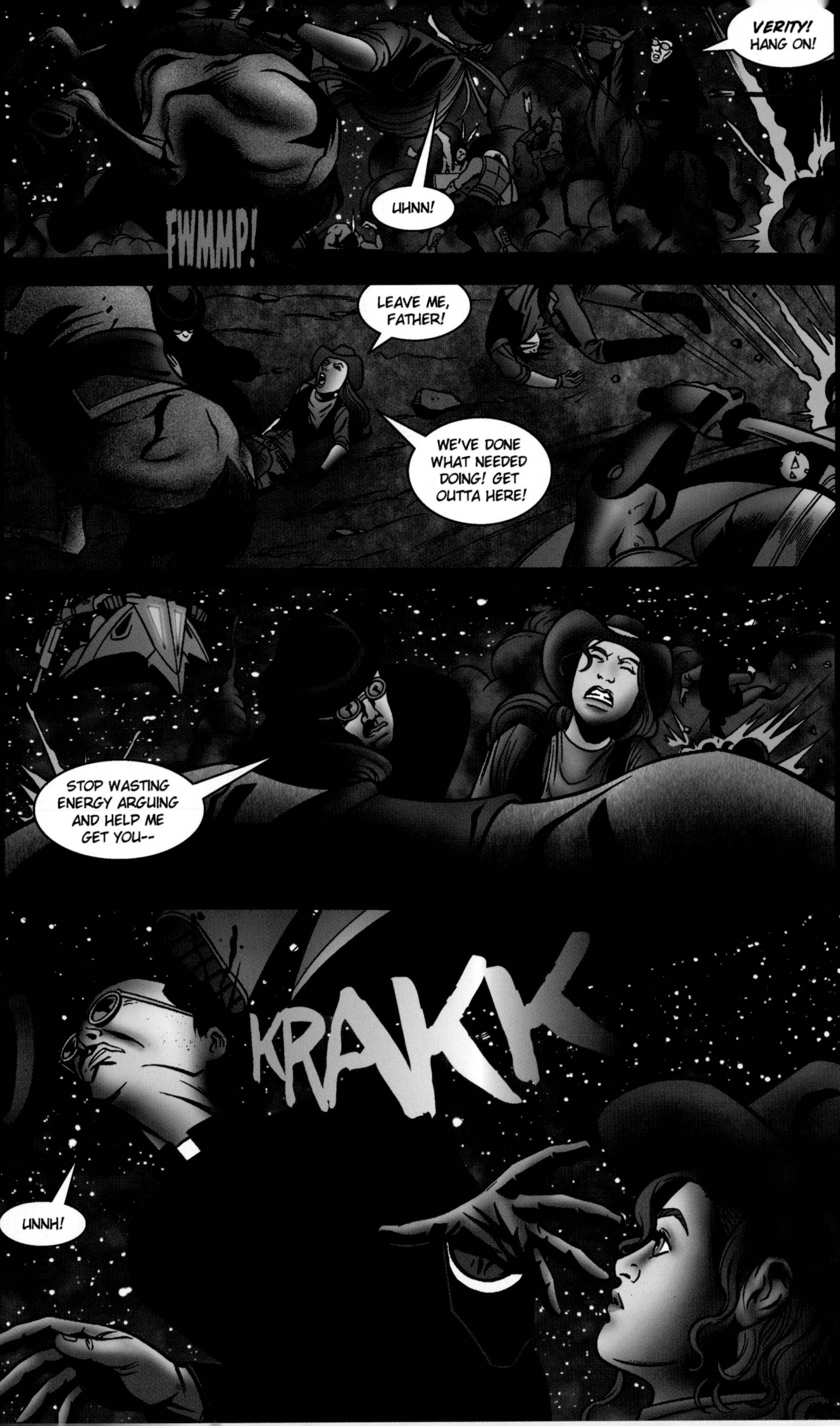
VERITY! HANG ON!
UHNN!
FWMMP!
LEAVE ME, FATHER!
WE'VE DONE WHAT NEEDED DOING! GET OUTTA HERE!
STOP WASTING ENERGY ARGUING AND HELP ME GET YOU--
KRAKK
UNNH!

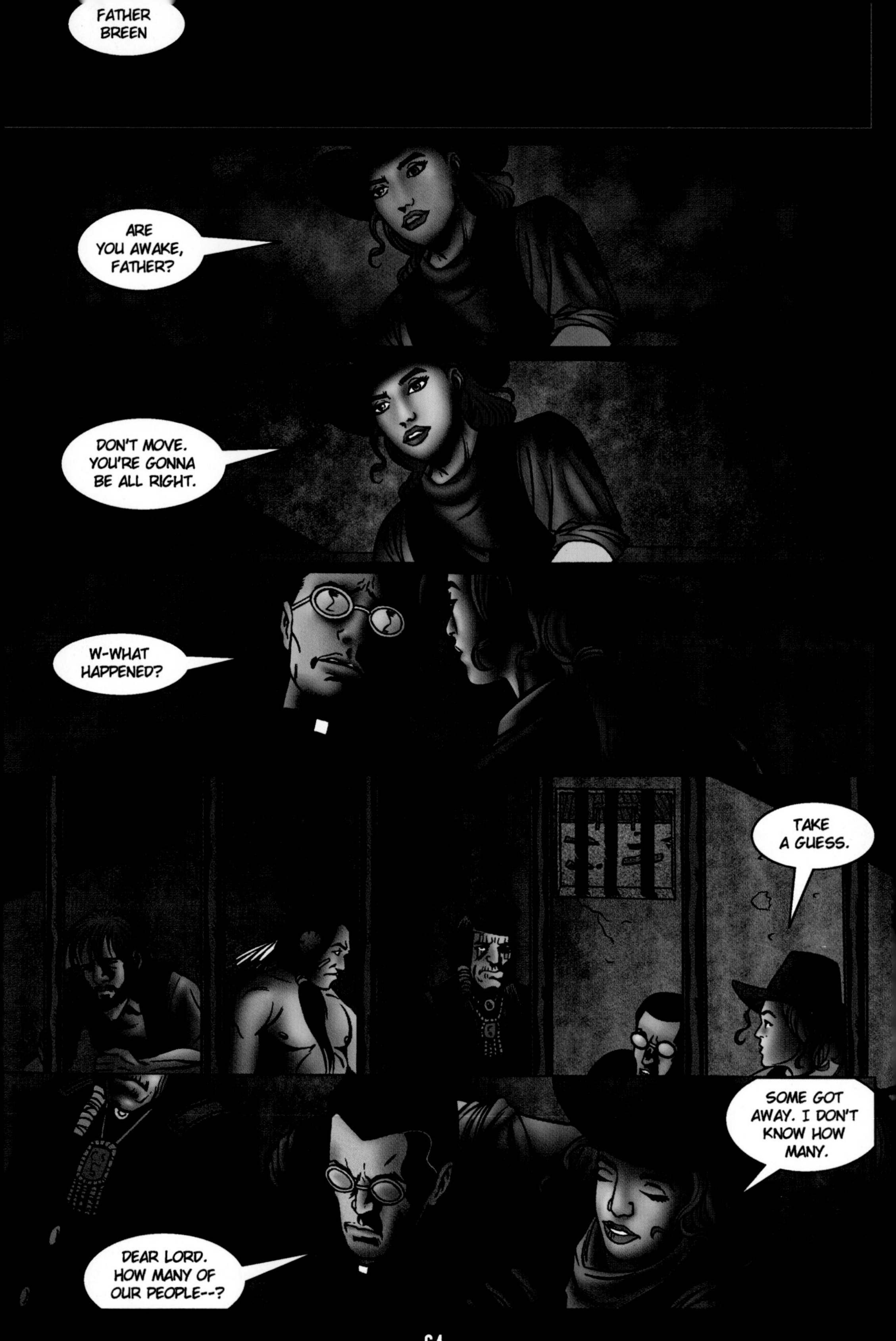
FATHER BREEN
ARE YOU AWAKE, FATHER?
DON'T MOVE. YOU'RE GONNA BE ALL RIGHT.
W-WHAT HAPPENED?
TAKE A GUESS.
SOME GOT AWAY. I DON'T KNOW HOW MANY.
DEAR LORD. HOW MANY OF OUR PEOPLE--?

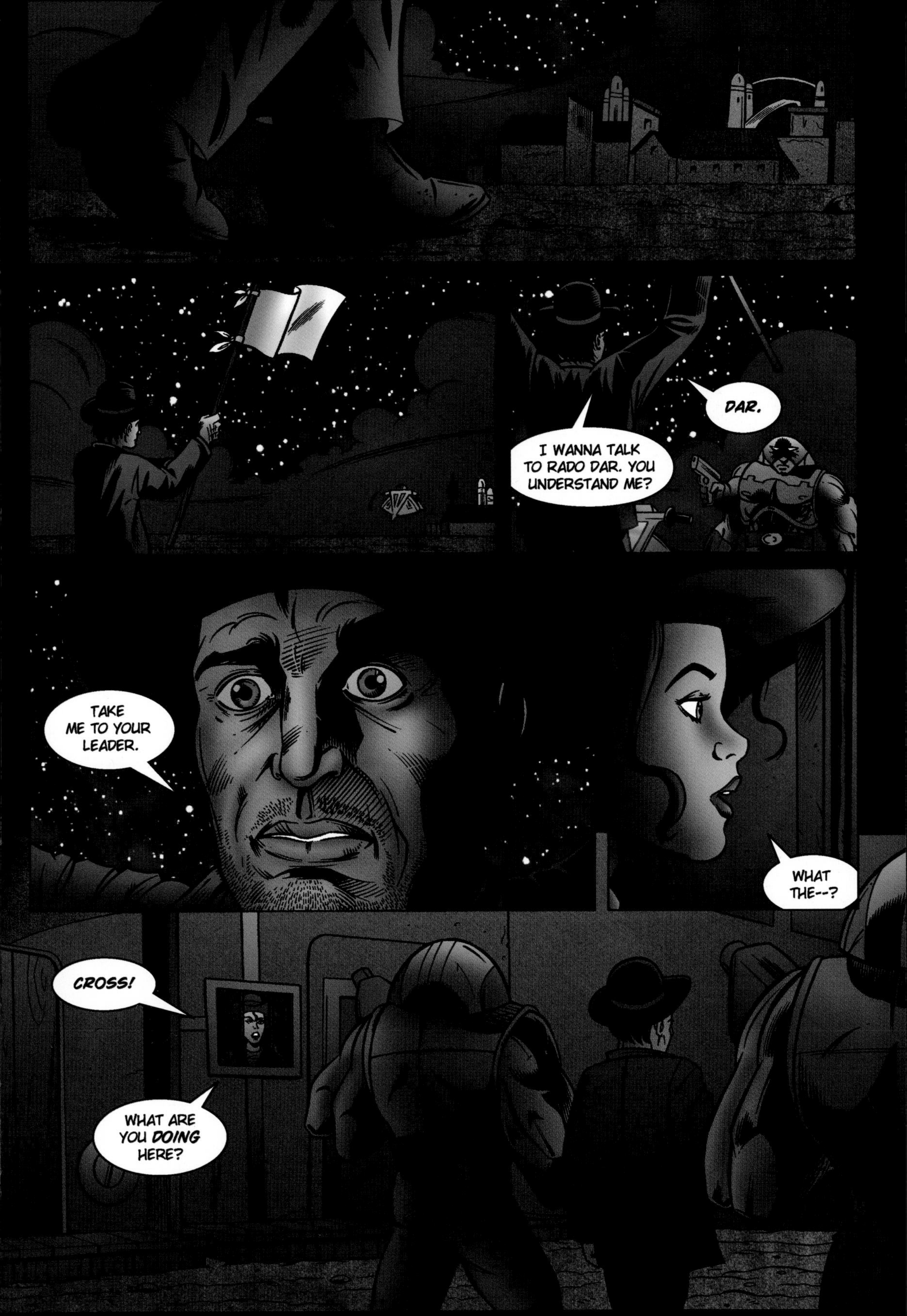
DAR.
I WANNA TALK TO RADO DAR. YOU UNDERSTAND ME?
TAKE ME TO YOUR LEADER.
WHAT THE--?
CROSS!
WHAT ARE YOU *DOING* HERE?

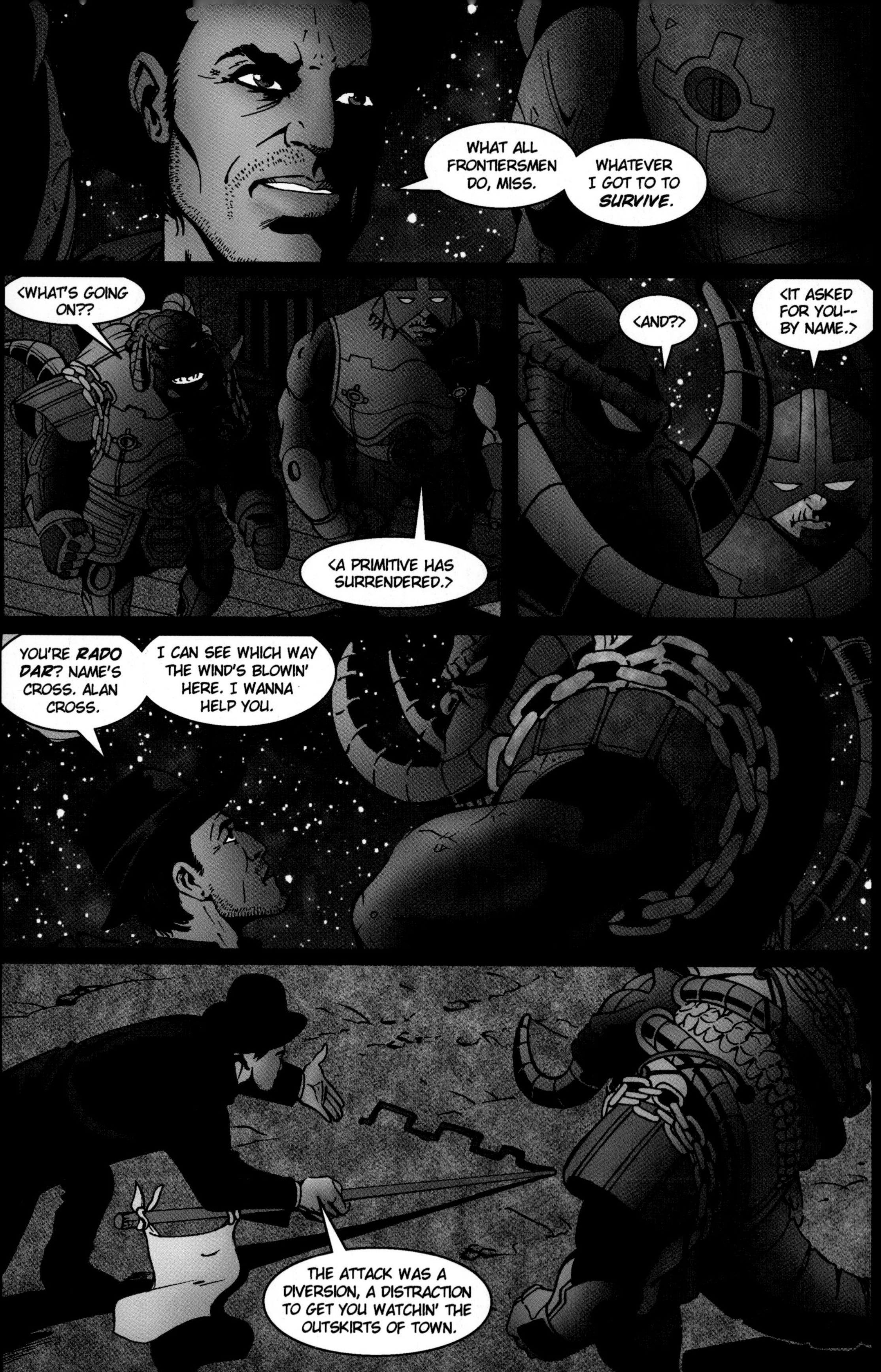
WHAT ALL FRONTIERSMEN DO, MISS.
WHATEVER I GOT TO TO *SURVIVE*.
<WHAT'S GOING ON??
<A PRIMITIVE HAS SURRENDERED.>
<AND?>
<IT ASKED FOR YOU-- BY NAME.>
YOU'RE *RADO DAR*? NAME'S CROSS. ALAN CROSS.
I CAN SEE WHICH WAY THE WIND'S BLOWIN' HERE. I WANNA HELP YOU.
THE ATTACK WAS A DIVERSION, A DISTRACTION TO GET YOU WATCHIN' THE OUTSKIRTS OF TOWN.

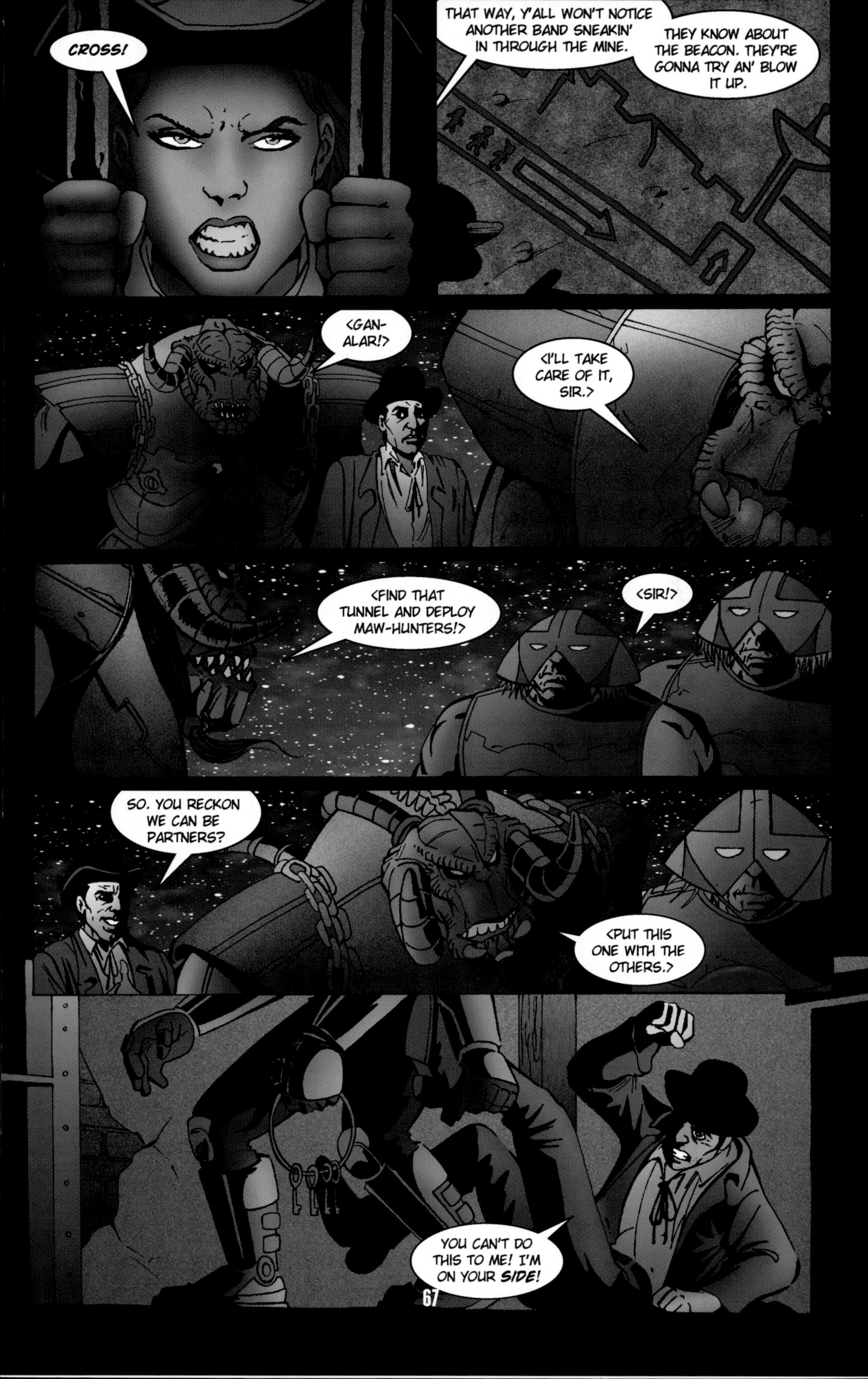
CROSS!
THAT WAY, Y'ALL WON'T NOTICE ANOTHER BAND SNEAKIN' IN THROUGH THE MINE.
THEY KNOW ABOUT THE BEACON. THEY'RE GONNA TRY AN' BLOW IT UP.
<GAN-ALAR!>
<I'LL TAKE CARE OF IT, SIR.>
<FIND THAT TUNNEL AND DEPLOY MAW-HUNTERS!>
<SIR!>
SO. YOU RECKON WE CAN BE PARTNERS?
<PUT THIS ONE WITH THE OTHERS.>
YOU CAN'T DO THIS TO ME! I'M ON YOUR *SIDE!*

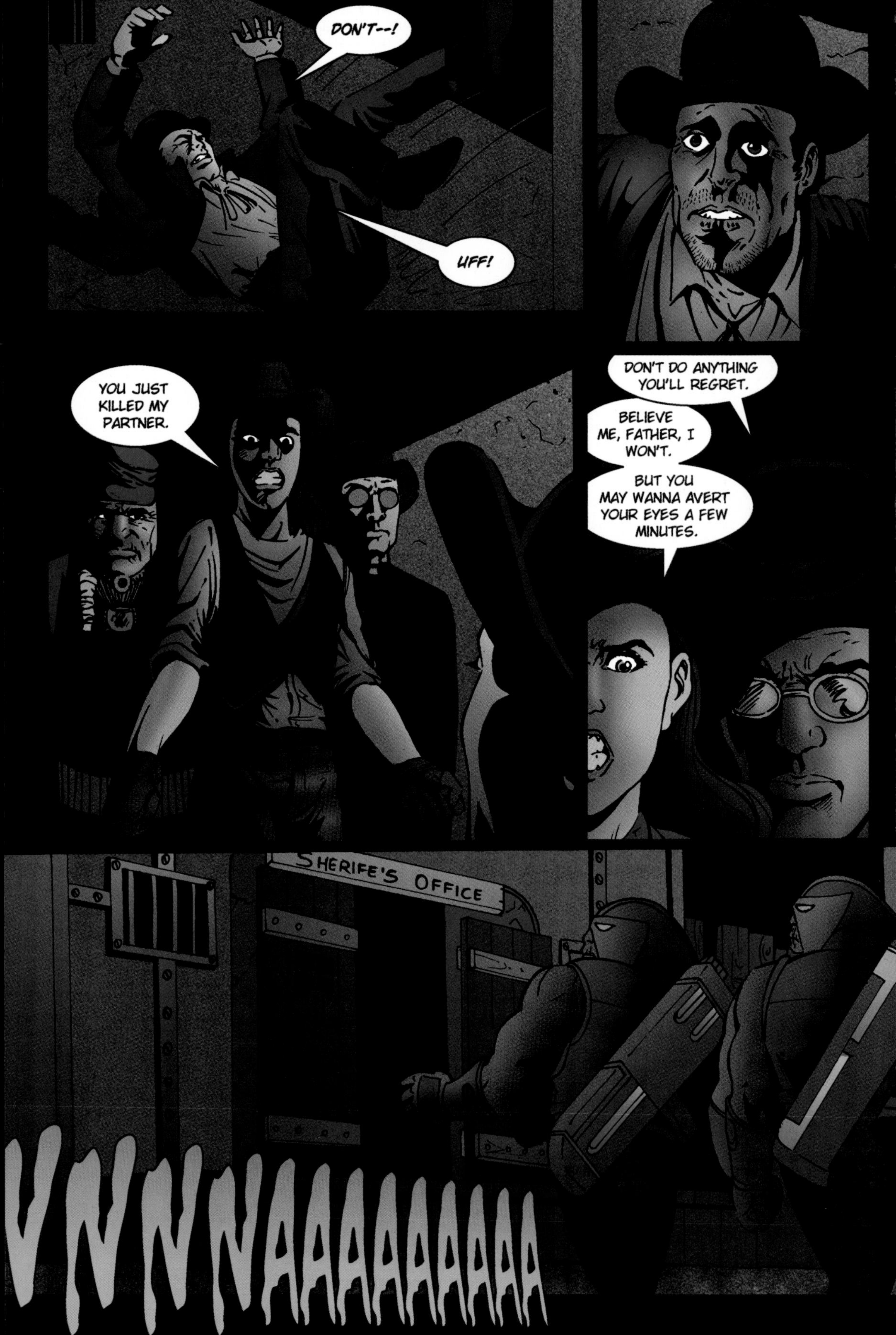
DON'T--!
UFF!
YOU JUST KILLED MY PARTNER.
DON'T DO ANYTHING YOU'LL REGRET.
BELIEVE ME, FATHER, I WON'T.
BUT YOU MAY WANNA AVERT YOUR EYES A FEW MINUTES.
SHERIFE'S OFFICE
VNNNAAAAAAAA

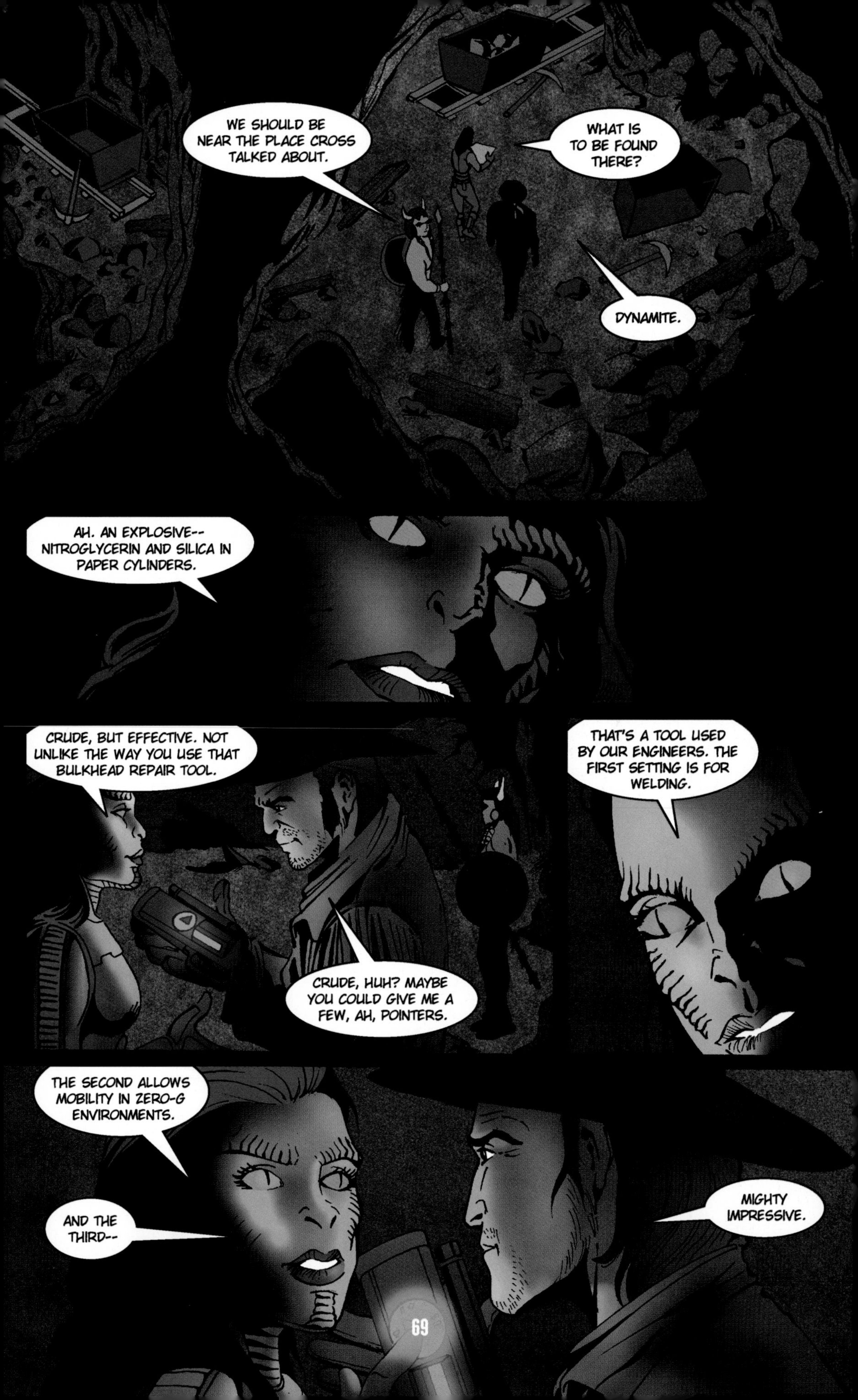
WE SHOULD BE NEAR THE PLACE CROSS TALKED ABOUT.
WHAT IS TO BE FOUND THERE?
DYNAMITE.
AH. AN EXPLOSIVE--NITROGLYCERIN AND SILICA IN PAPER CYLINDERS.
CRUDE, BUT EFFECTIVE. NOT UNLIKE THE WAY YOU USE THAT BULKHEAD REPAIR TOOL.
CRUDE, HUH? MAYBE YOU COULD GIVE ME A FEW, AH, POINTERS.
THAT'S A TOOL USED BY OUR ENGINEERS. THE FIRST SETTING IS FOR WELDING.
THE SECOND ALLOWS MOBILITY IN ZERO-G ENVIRONMENTS.
AND THE THIRD--
MIGHTY IMPRESSIVE.

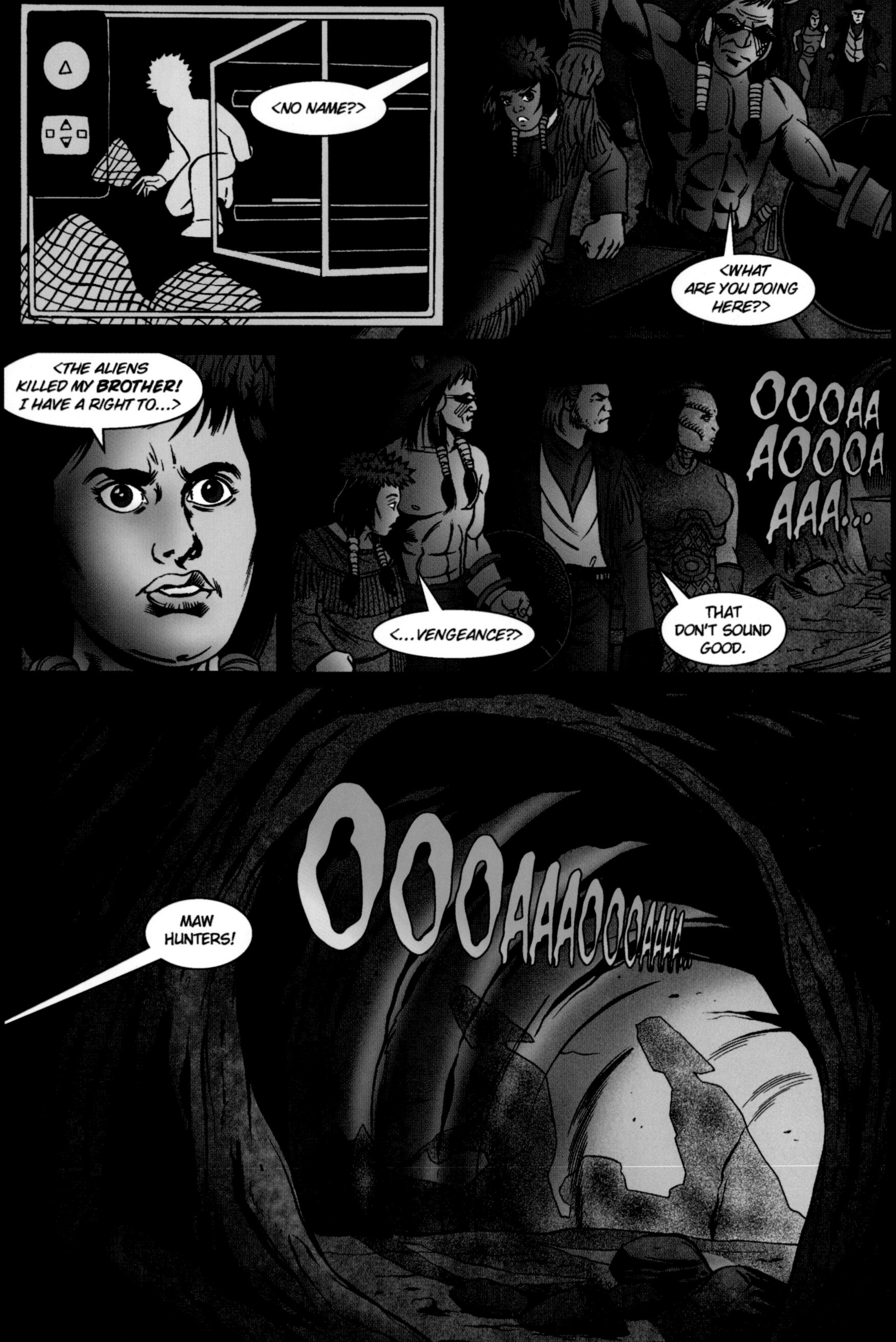

<NO NAME?>
<WHAT ARE YOU DOING HERE?>
<THE ALIENS KILLED MY BROTHER! I HAVE A RIGHT TO...>
<...VENGEANCE?>
THAT DON'T SOUND GOOD.
OOOAAAOOOAAAA...
OOOAAAOOOAAAA...
MAW HUNTERS!

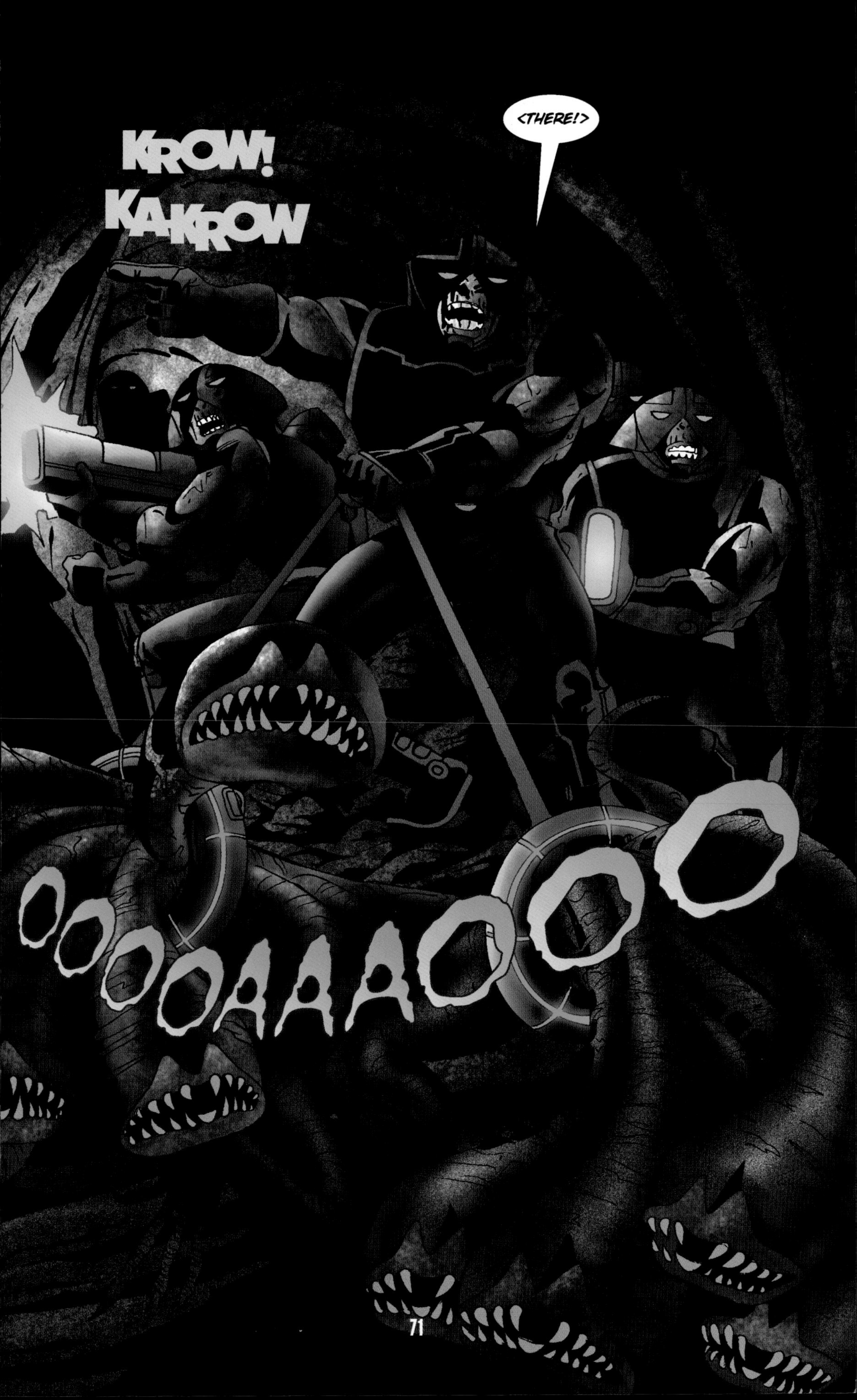
KROW!
KAKROW
<THERE!>
OOOOAAAOOOO

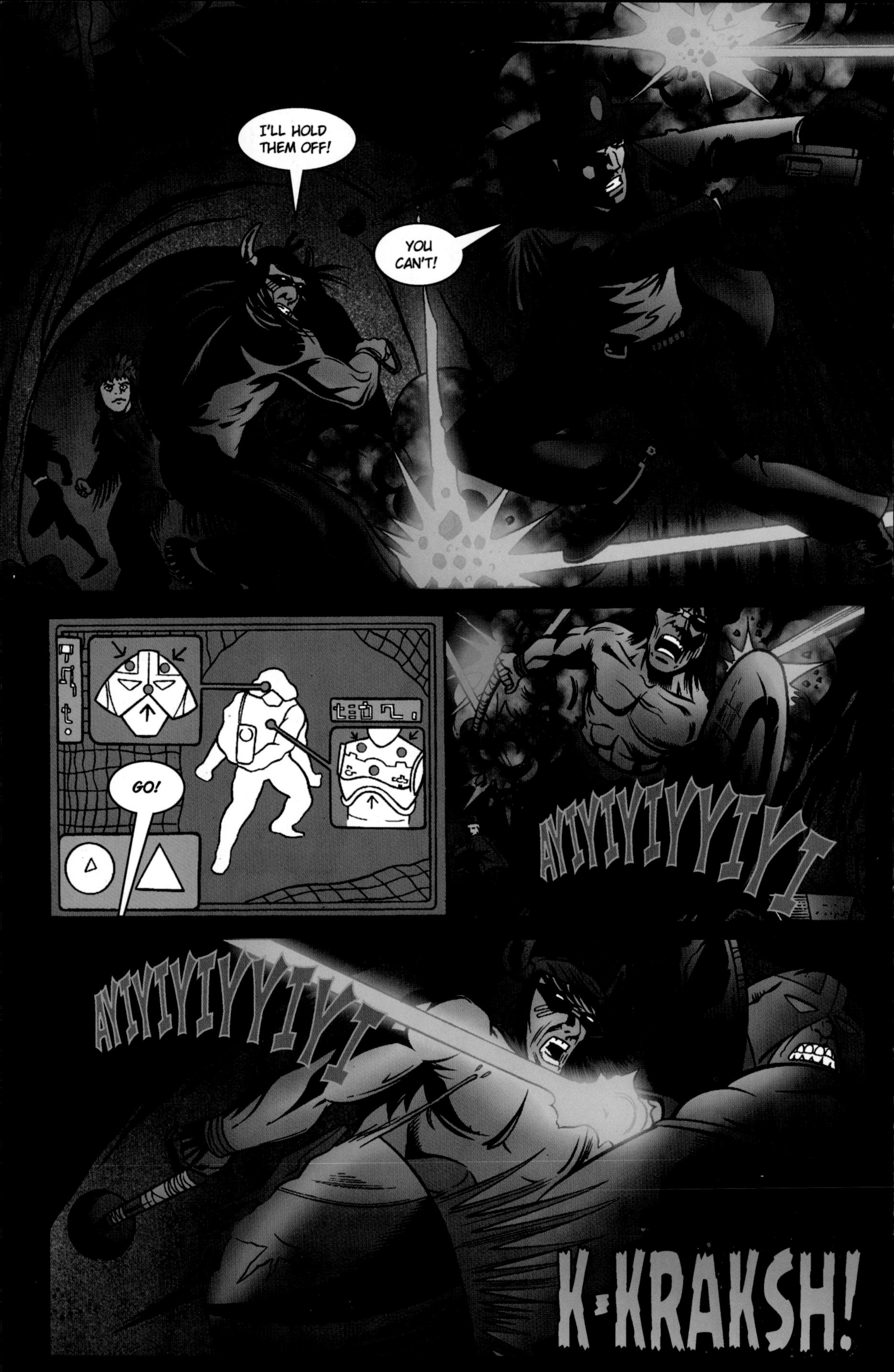
I'LL HOLD THEM OFF!
YOU CAN'T!
GO!
AYIYIYIYYIYI
AYIYIYIYYIYI
K-KRAKSH!

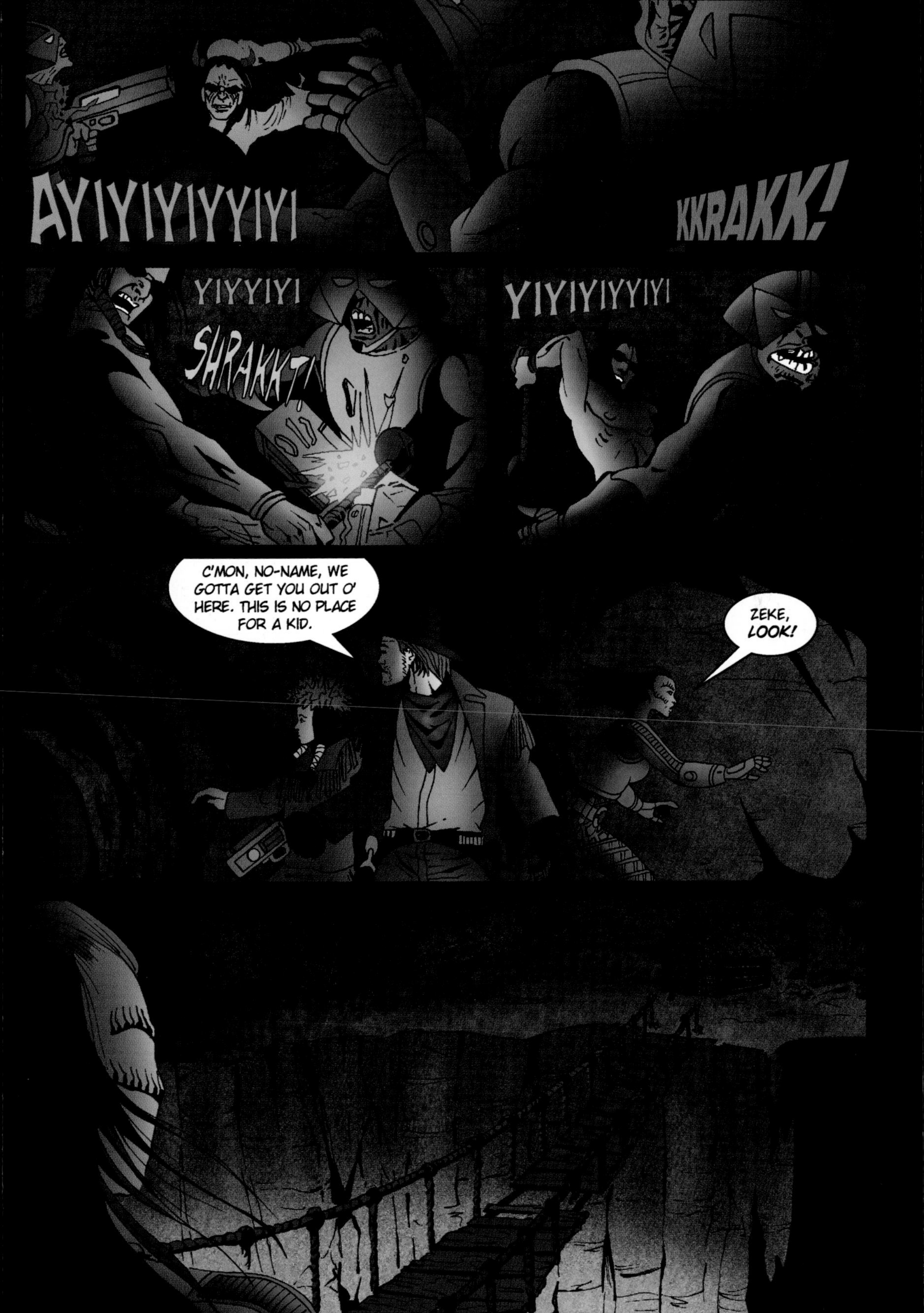
AYIYIYIYYIYI
KKRAKK!
YIYYIYI
SHRAKKT!
YIYIYIYYIYI
C'MON, NO-NAME, WE GOTTA GET YOU OUT O' HERE. THIS IS NO PLACE FOR A KID.
ZEKE, LOOK!

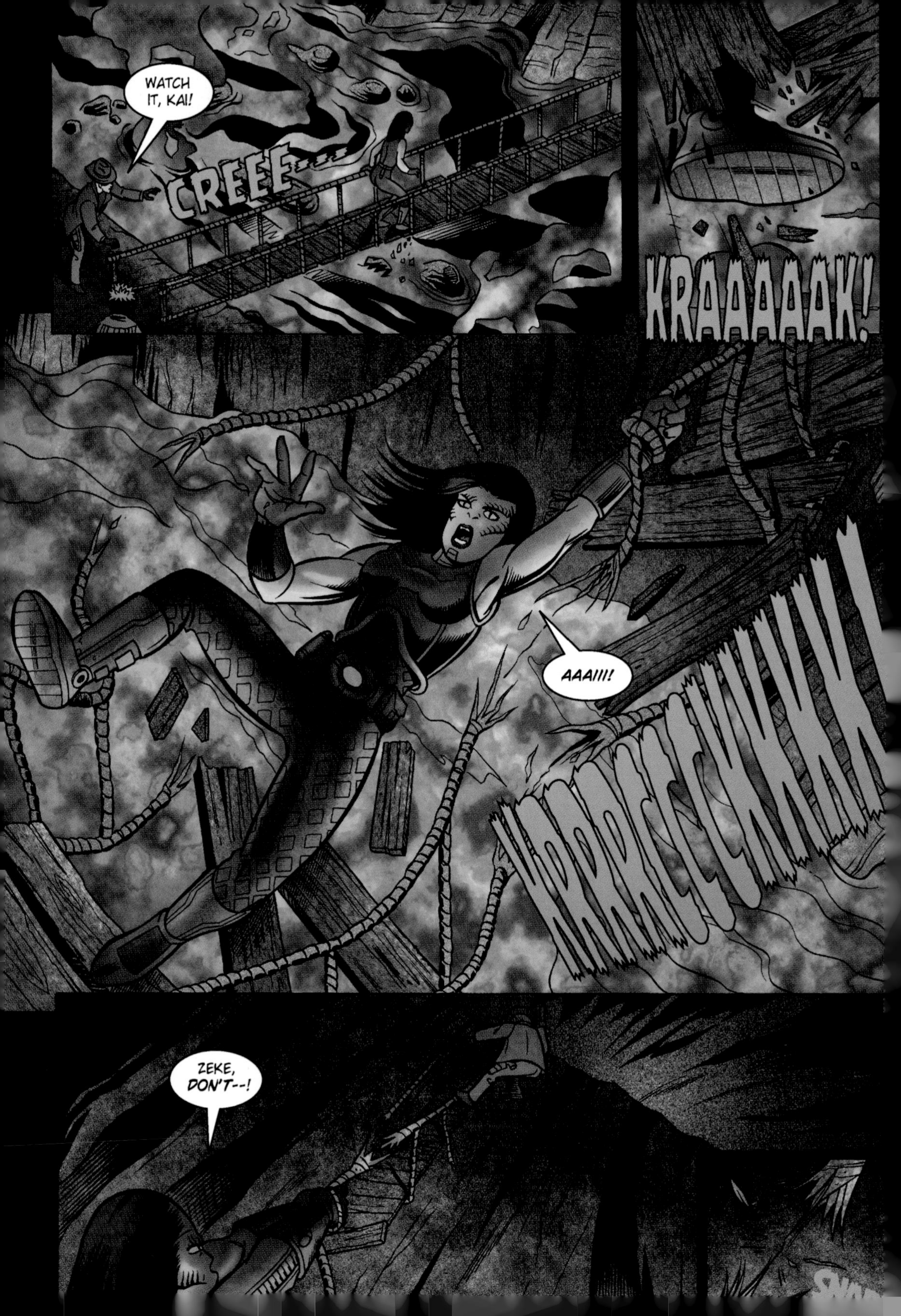
WATCH IT, KAI!
CREEE...
KRAAAAAK!
AAAIII!
ZEKE, DON'T--!

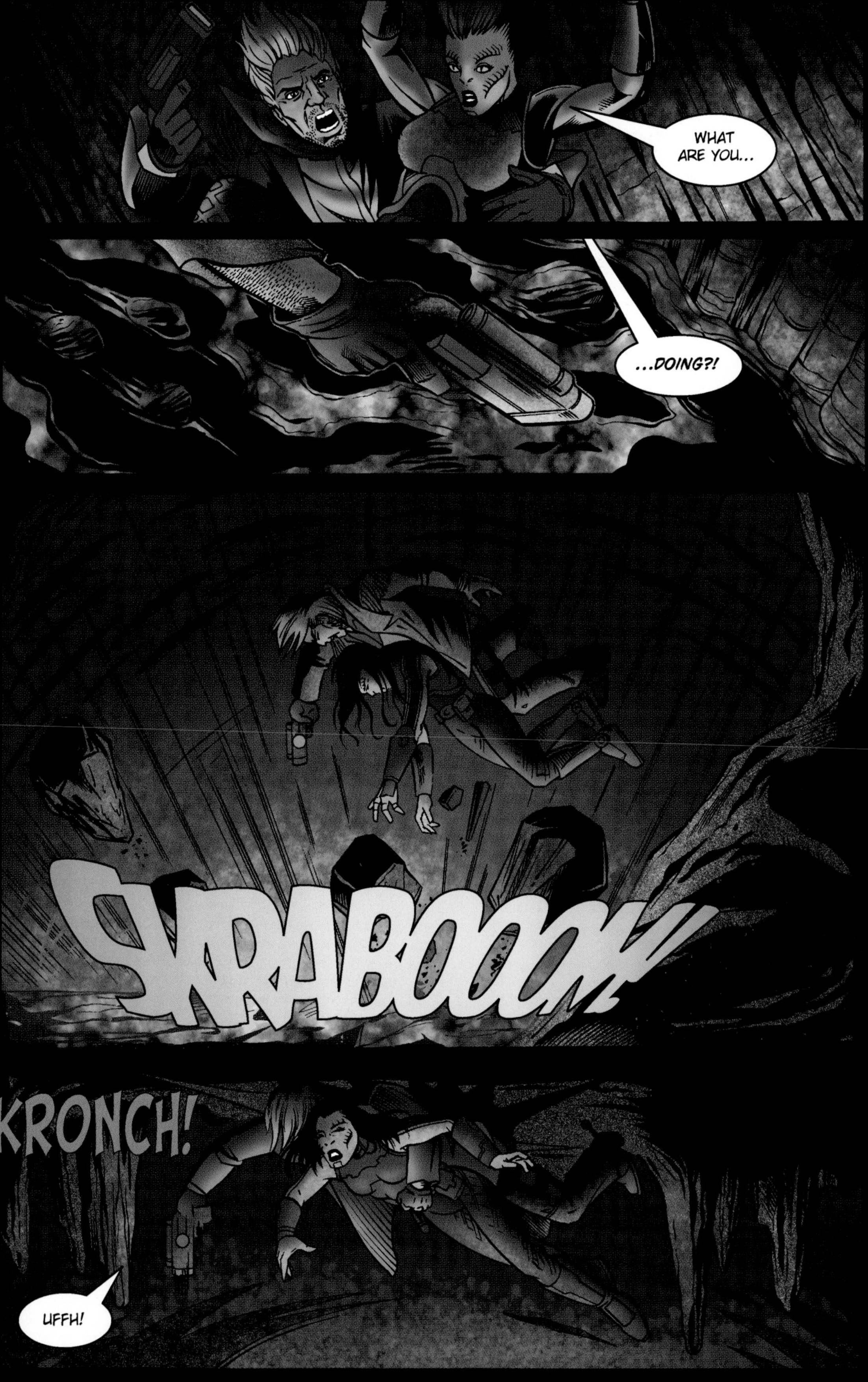
WHAT ARE YOU...
...DOING?!
SKRABOOOM!
KRONCH!
UFFH!

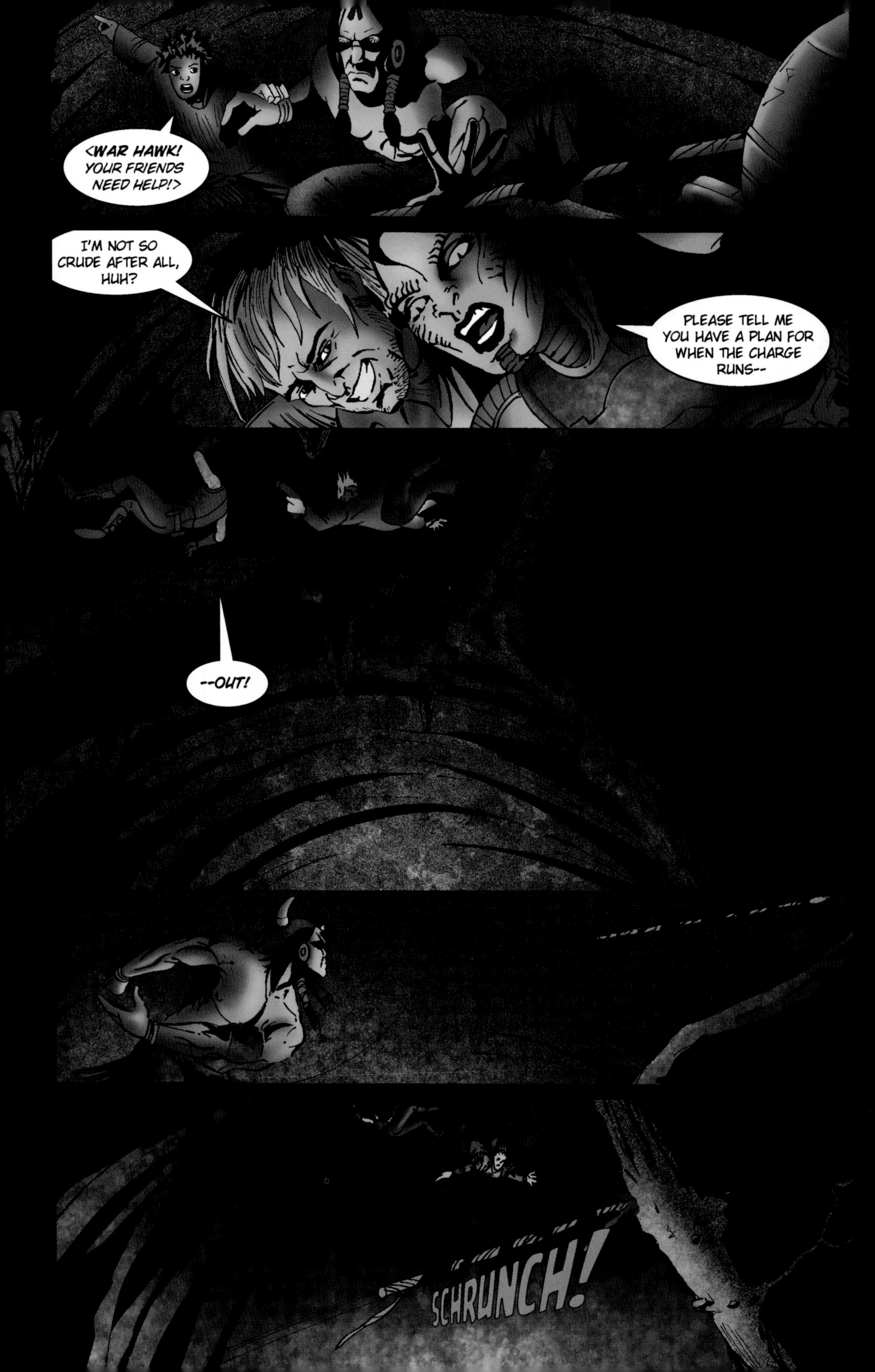

<WAR HAWK! YOUR FRIENDS NEED HELP!>
I'M NOT SO CRUDE AFTER ALL, HUH?
PLEASE TELL ME YOU HAVE A PLAN FOR WHEN THE CHARGE RUNS--
--OUT!
SCHRUNCH!

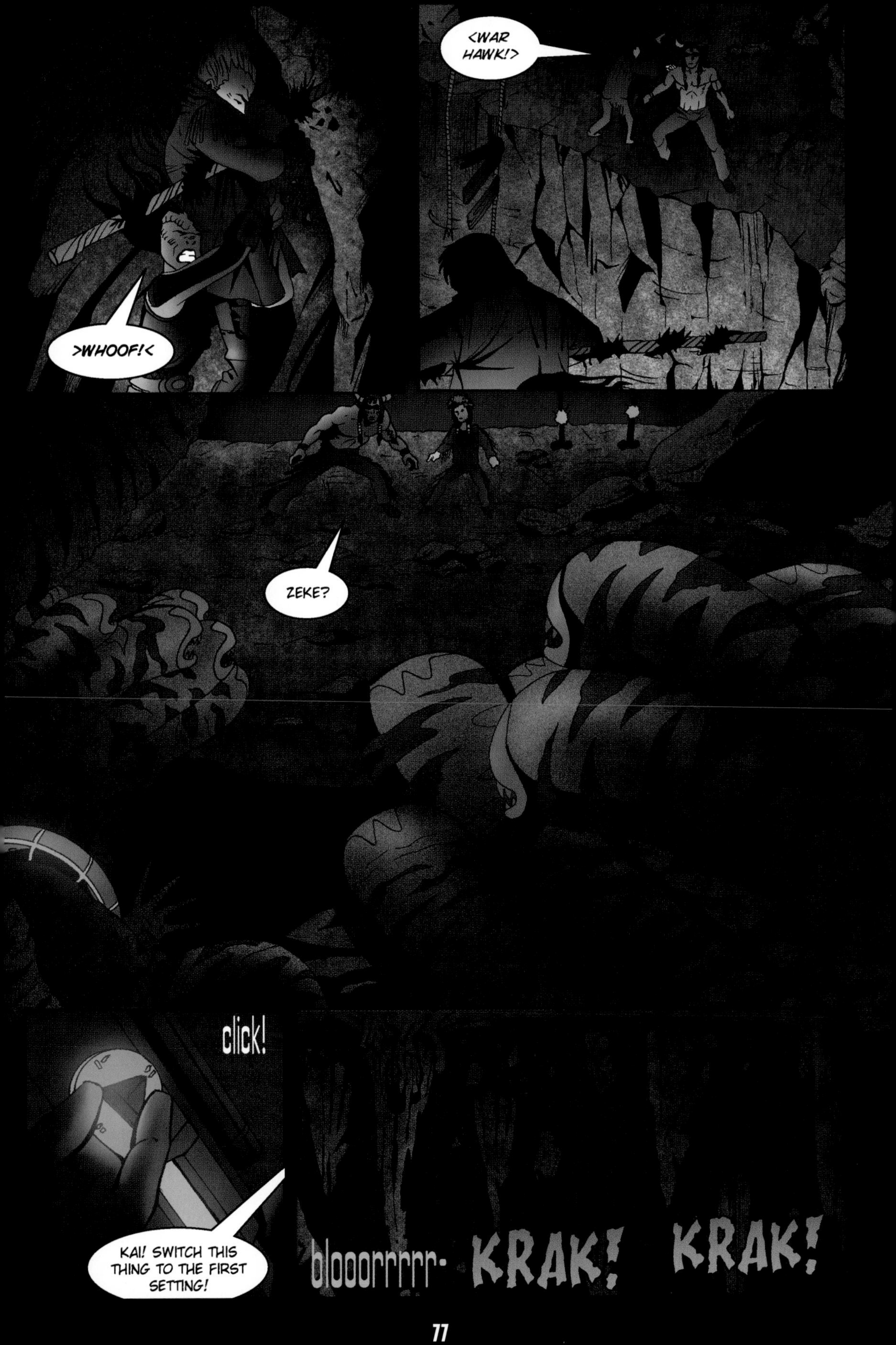
>WHOOF!<
<WAR HAWK!>
ZEKE?
click!
KAI! SWITCH THIS THING TO THE FIRST SETTING!
blooorrrrr-
KRAK!
KRAK!

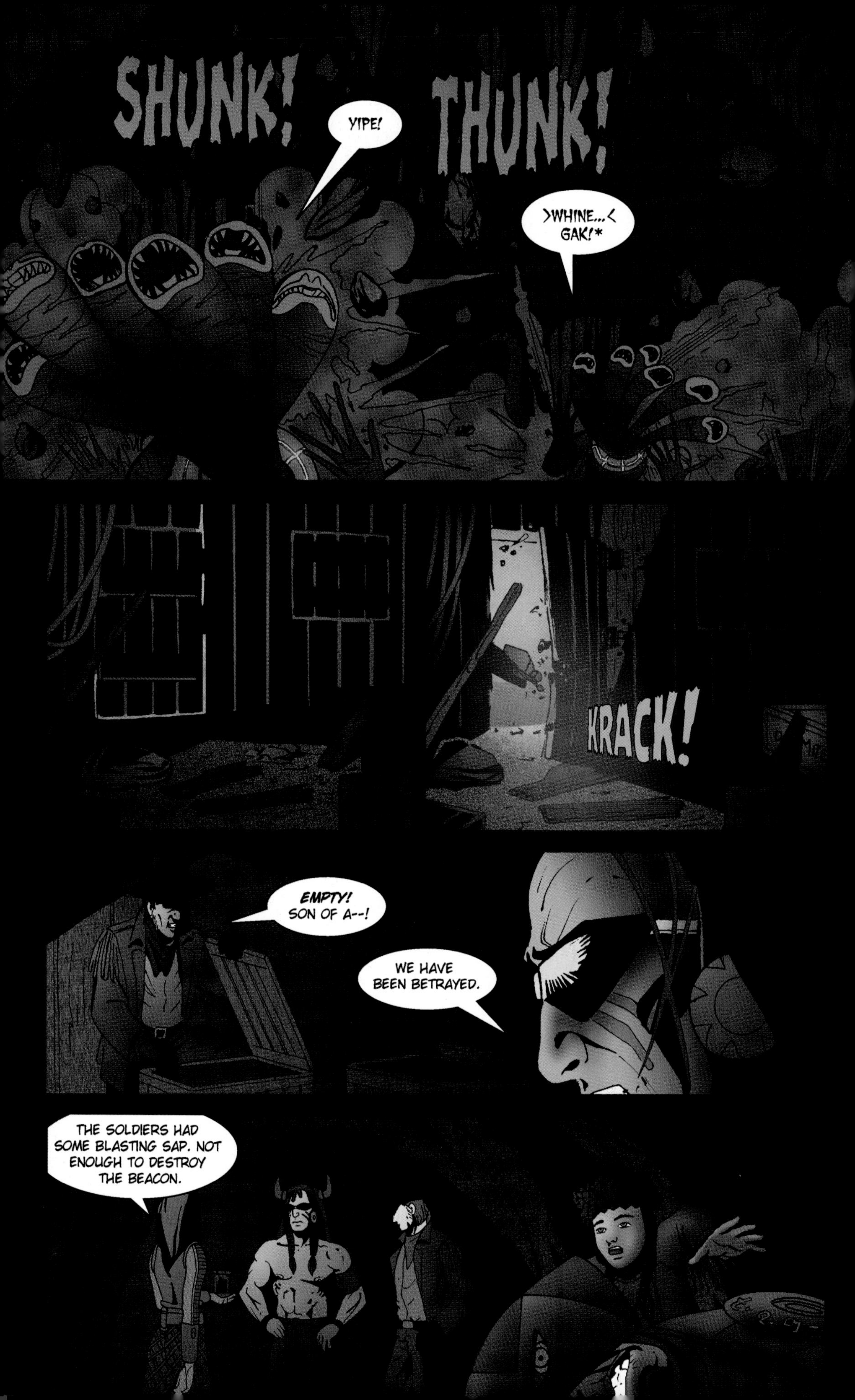
SHUNK!
YIPE!
THUNK!
>WHINE...<
GAK!*
KRACK!
EMPTY! SON OF A--!
WE HAVE BEEN BETRAYED.
THE SOLDIERS HAD SOME BLASTING SAP. NOT ENOUGH TO DESTROY THE BEACON.

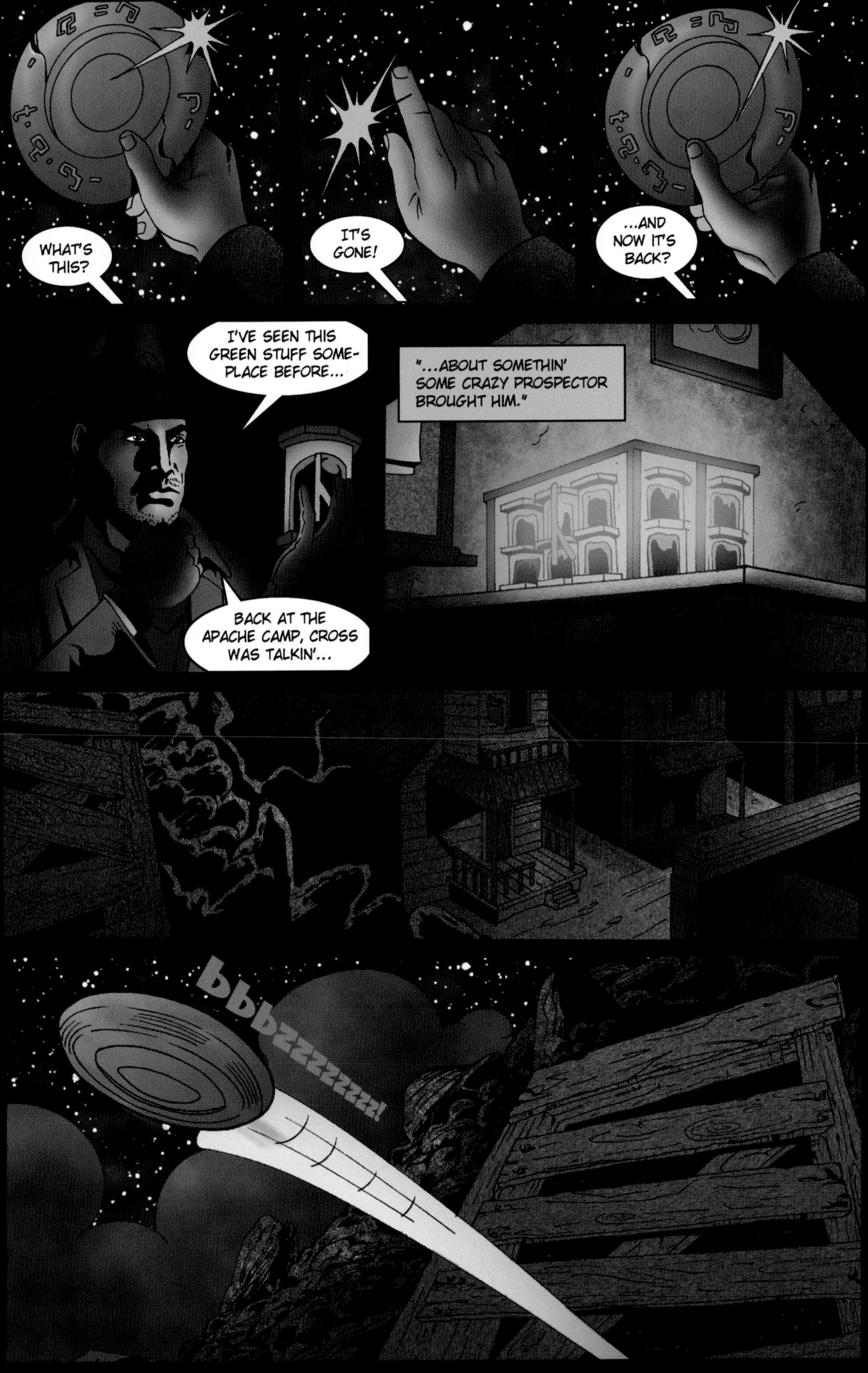
WHAT'S THIS?
IT'S GONE!
...AND NOW IT'S BACK?
I'VE SEEN THIS GREEN STUFF SOME-PLACE BEFORE...
BACK AT THE APACHE CAMP, CROSS WAS TALKIN'...
"...ABOUT SOMETHIN' SOME CRAZY PROSPECTOR BROUGHT HIM."
PPPZZZZZZZZ!

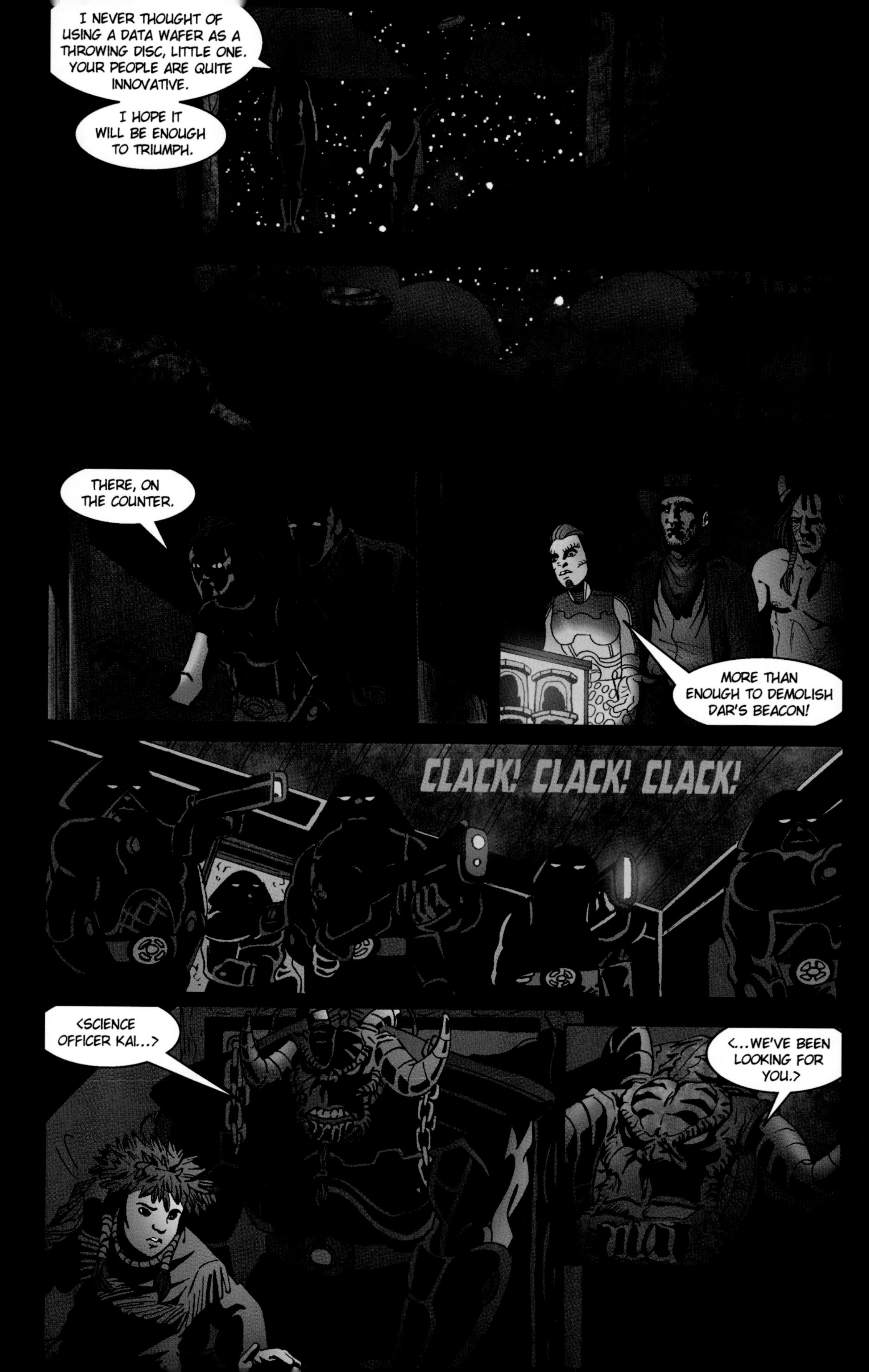
I NEVER THOUGHT OF USING A DATA WAFER AS A THROWING DISC, LITTLE ONE. YOUR PEOPLE ARE QUITE INNOVATIVE.
I HOPE IT WILL BE ENOUGH TO TRIUMPH.
THERE, ON THE COUNTER.
MORE THAN ENOUGH TO DEMOLISH DAR'S BEACON!
CLACK! CLACK! CLACK!
<SCIENCE OFFICER KAI...>
<...WE'VE BEEN LOOKING FOR YOU.>

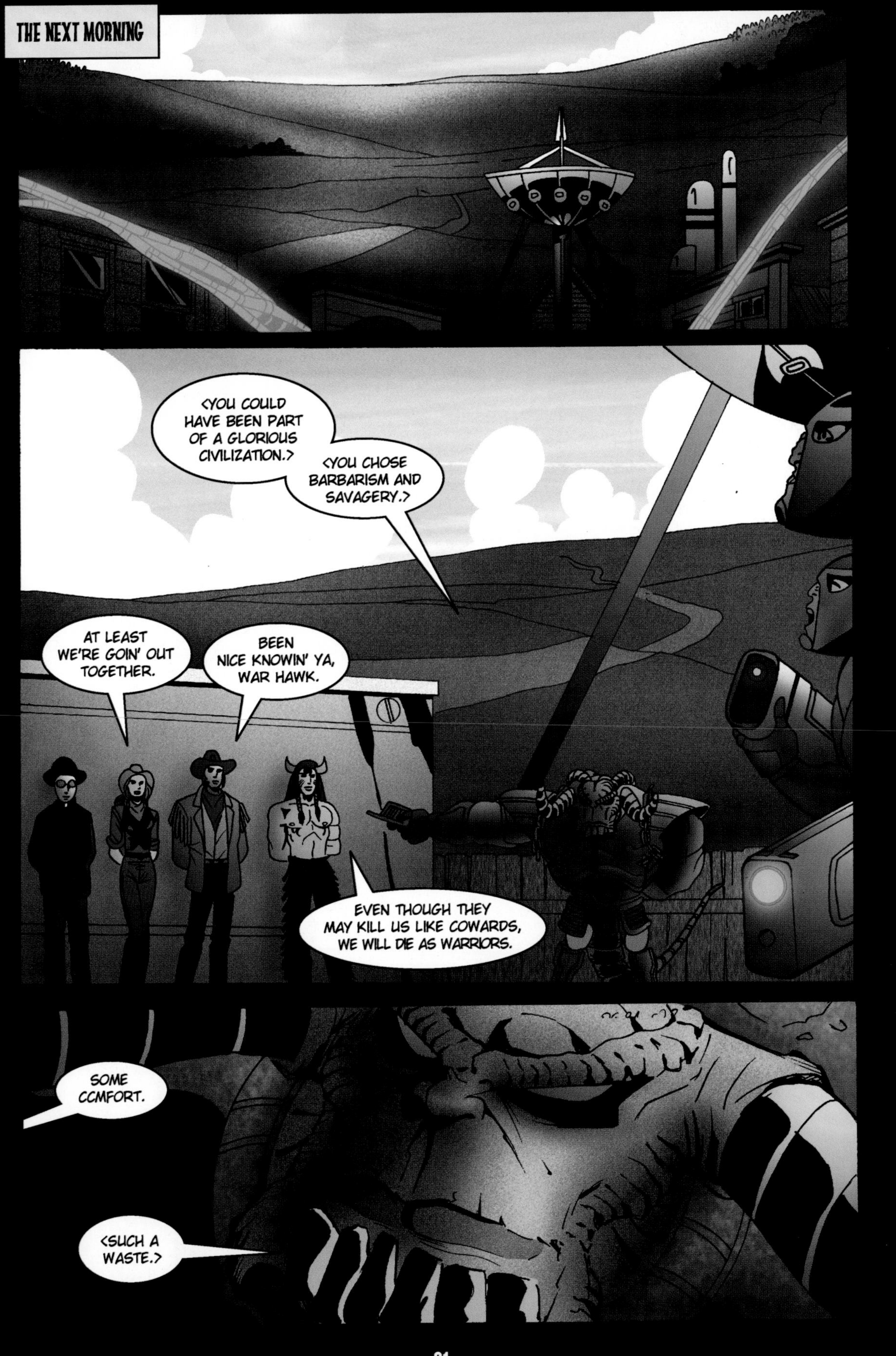
THE NEXT MORNING
<YOU COULD HAVE BEEN PART OF A GLORIOUS CIVILIZATION.>
<YOU CHOSE BARBARISM AND SAVAGERY.>
AT LEAST WE'RE GOIN' OUT TOGETHER.
BEEN NICE KNOWIN' YA, WAR HAWK.
EVEN THOUGH THEY MAY KILL US LIKE COWARDS, WE WILL DIE AS WARRIORS.
SOME CCMFORT.
<SUCH A WASTE.>

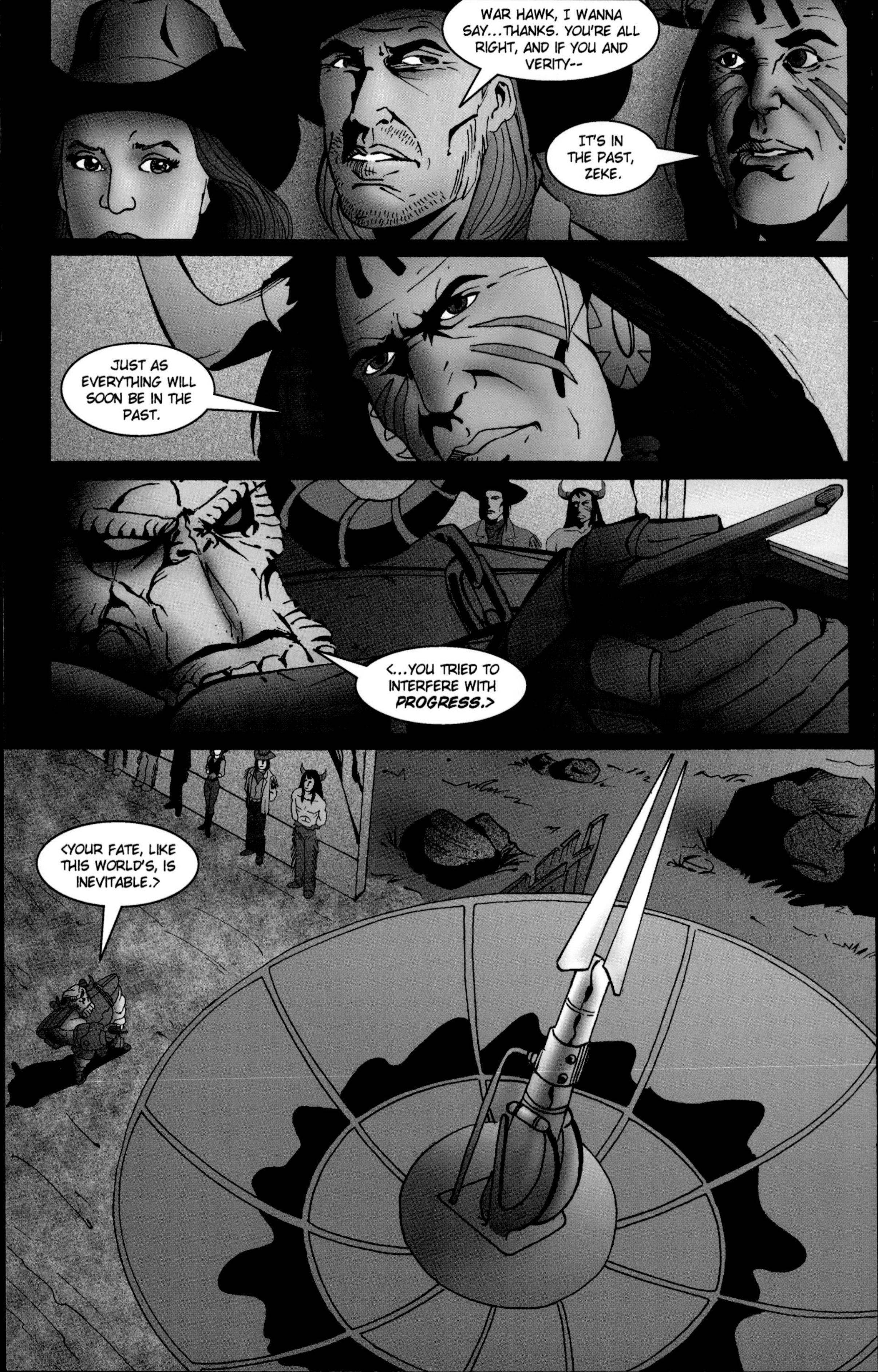
WAR HAWK, I WANNA SAY...THANKS. YOU'RE ALL RIGHT, AND IF YOU AND VERITY--
IT'S IN THE PAST, ZEKE.
JUST AS EVERYTHING WILL SOON BE IN THE PAST.
<...YOU TRIED TO INTERFERE WITH *PROGRESS.*>
<YOUR FATE, LIKE THIS WORLD'S, IS INEVITABLE.>

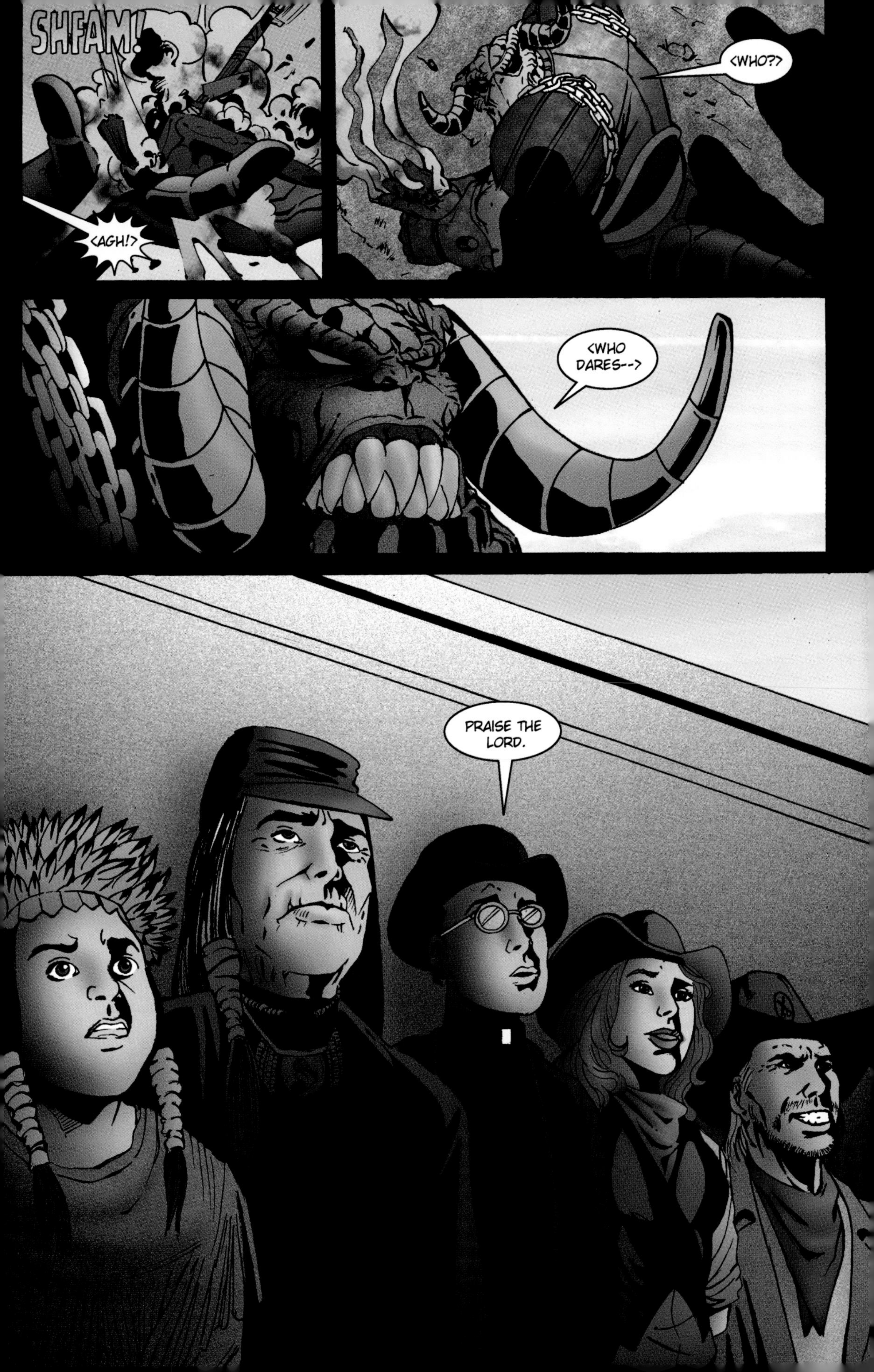
SHFAM!
<AGH!>
<WHO?>
<WHO DARES-->
PRAISE THE LORD.

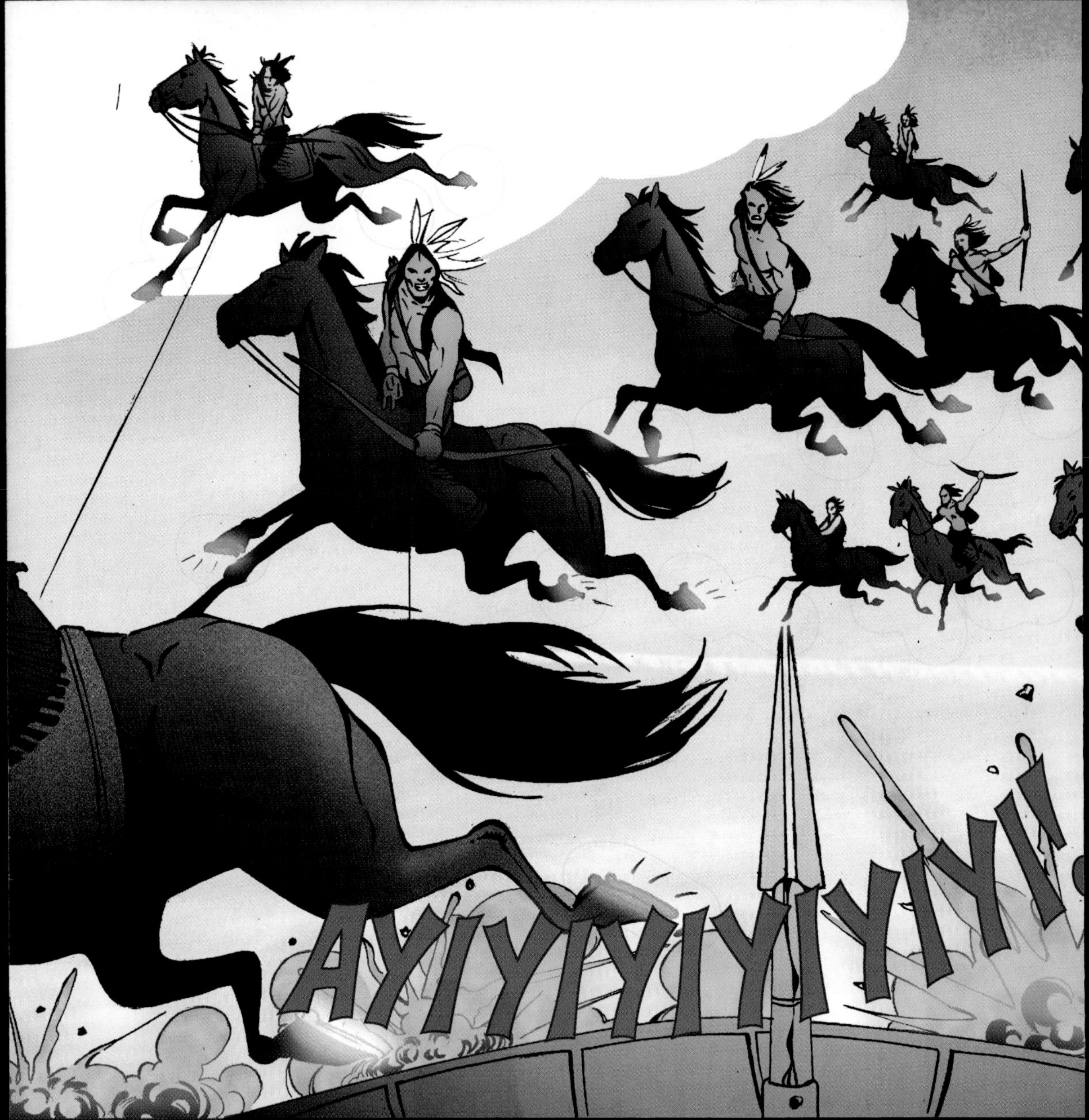
AYIYIYIYIYIYIYI!

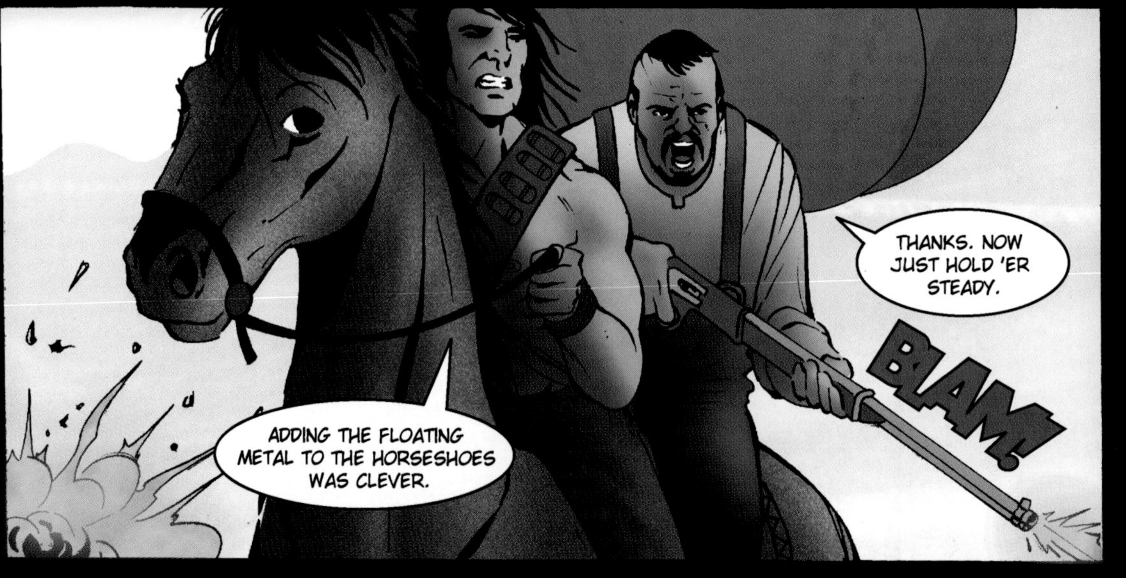
ADDING THE FLOATING METAL TO THE HORSESHOES WAS CLEVER.
THANKS. NOW JUST HOLD 'ER STEADY.
BLAM!

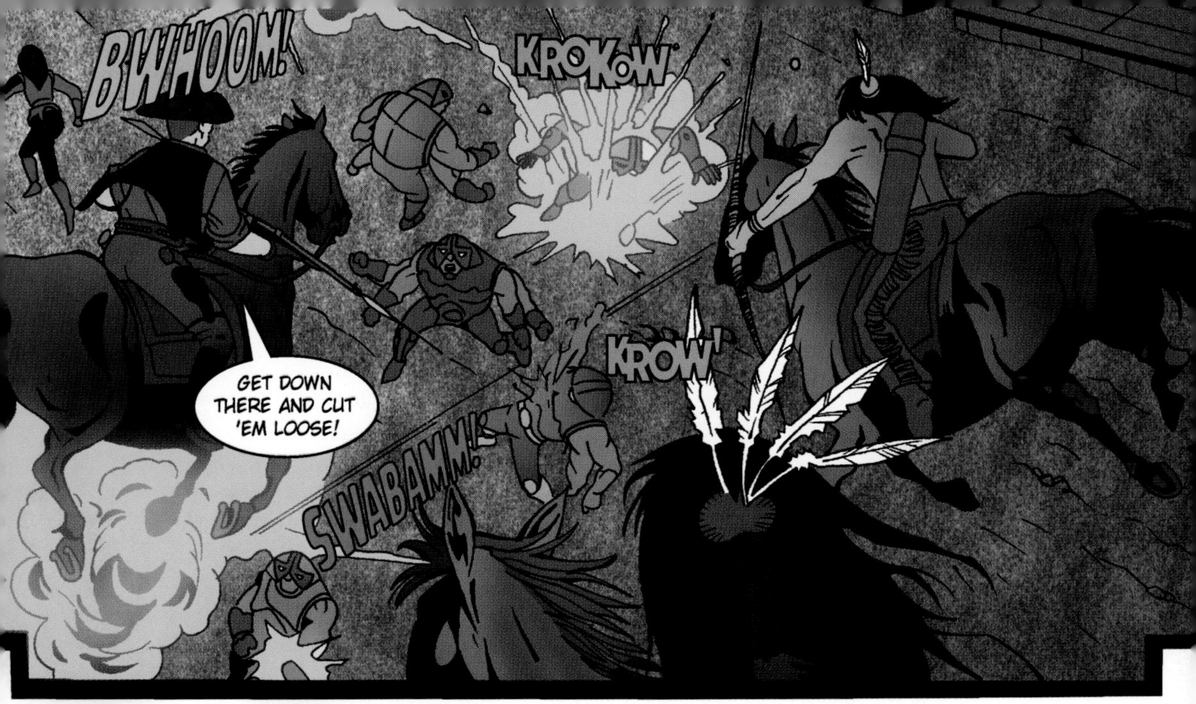
BWHOOM!
KROKOW
GET DOWN THERE AND CUT 'EM LOOSE!
KROW!
SWABAMM!

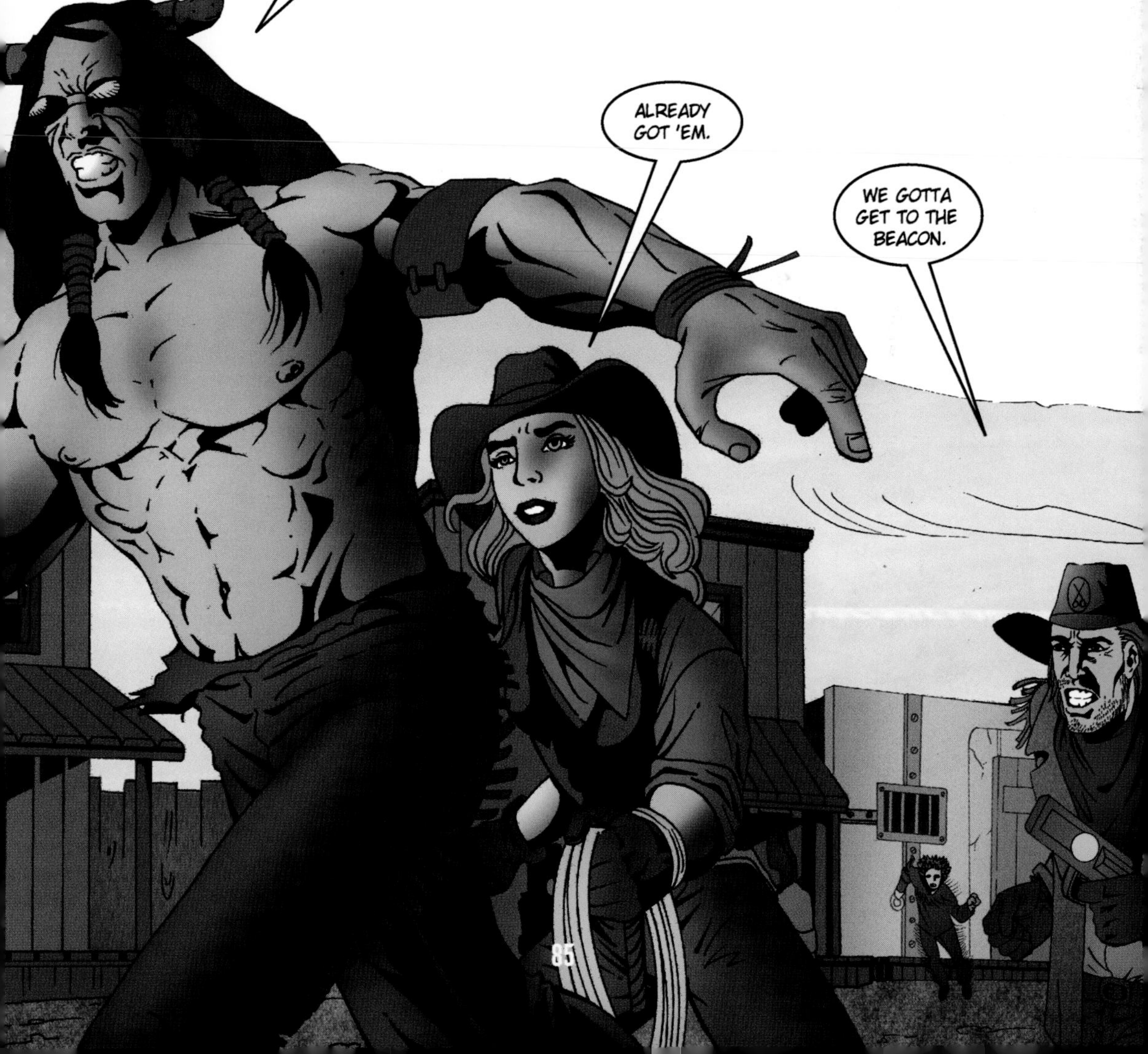
RETRIEVE YOUR WEAPONS FROM THE GUARDS.
ALREADY GOT 'EM.
WE GOTTA GET TO THE BEACON.

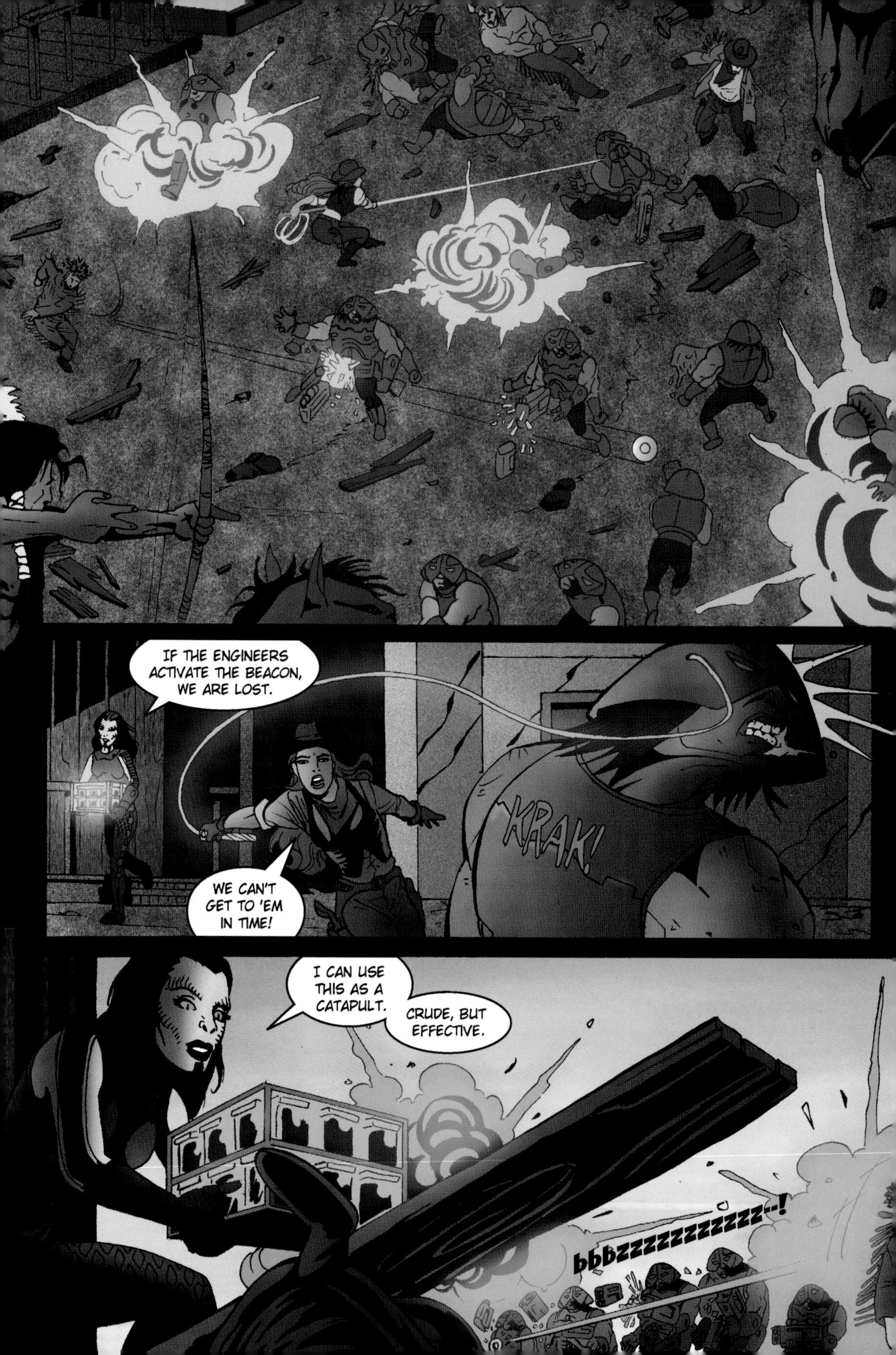
IF THE ENGINEERS ACTIVATE THE BEACON, WE ARE LOST.
KRAK!
WE CAN'T GET TO 'EM IN TIME!
I CAN USE THIS AS A CATAPULT.
CRUDE, BUT EFFECTIVE.
bbbzzzzzzzzzzzz--!

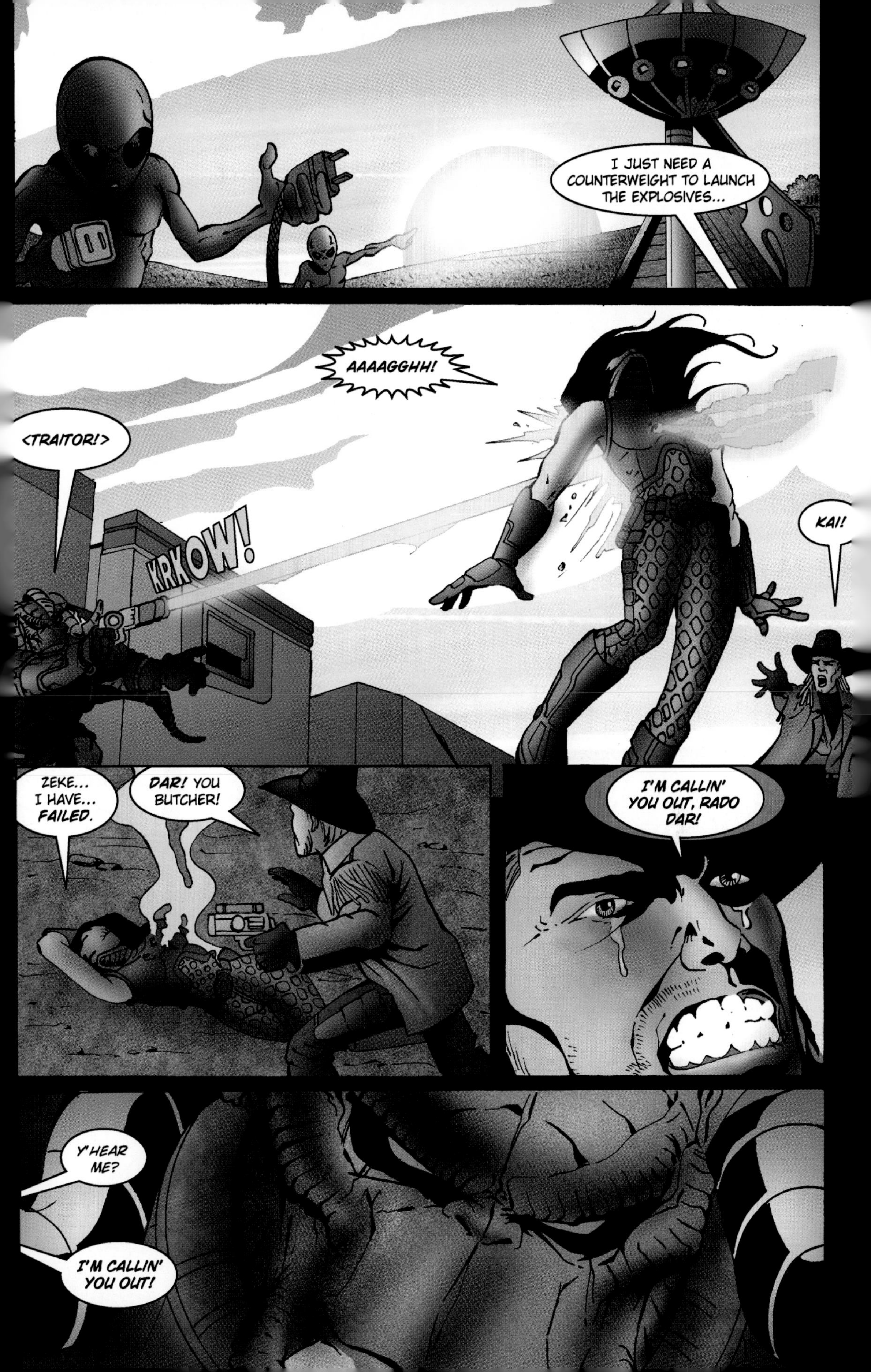
I JUST NEED A COUNTERWEIGHT TO LAUNCH THE EXPLOSIVES...
AAAAGGHH!
<TRAITOR!>
KRKOW!
KAI!
ZEKE... I HAVE... FAILED.
DAR! YOU BUTCHER!
I'M CALLIN' YOU OUT, RADO DAR!
Y'HEAR ME?
I'M CALLIN' YOU OUT!

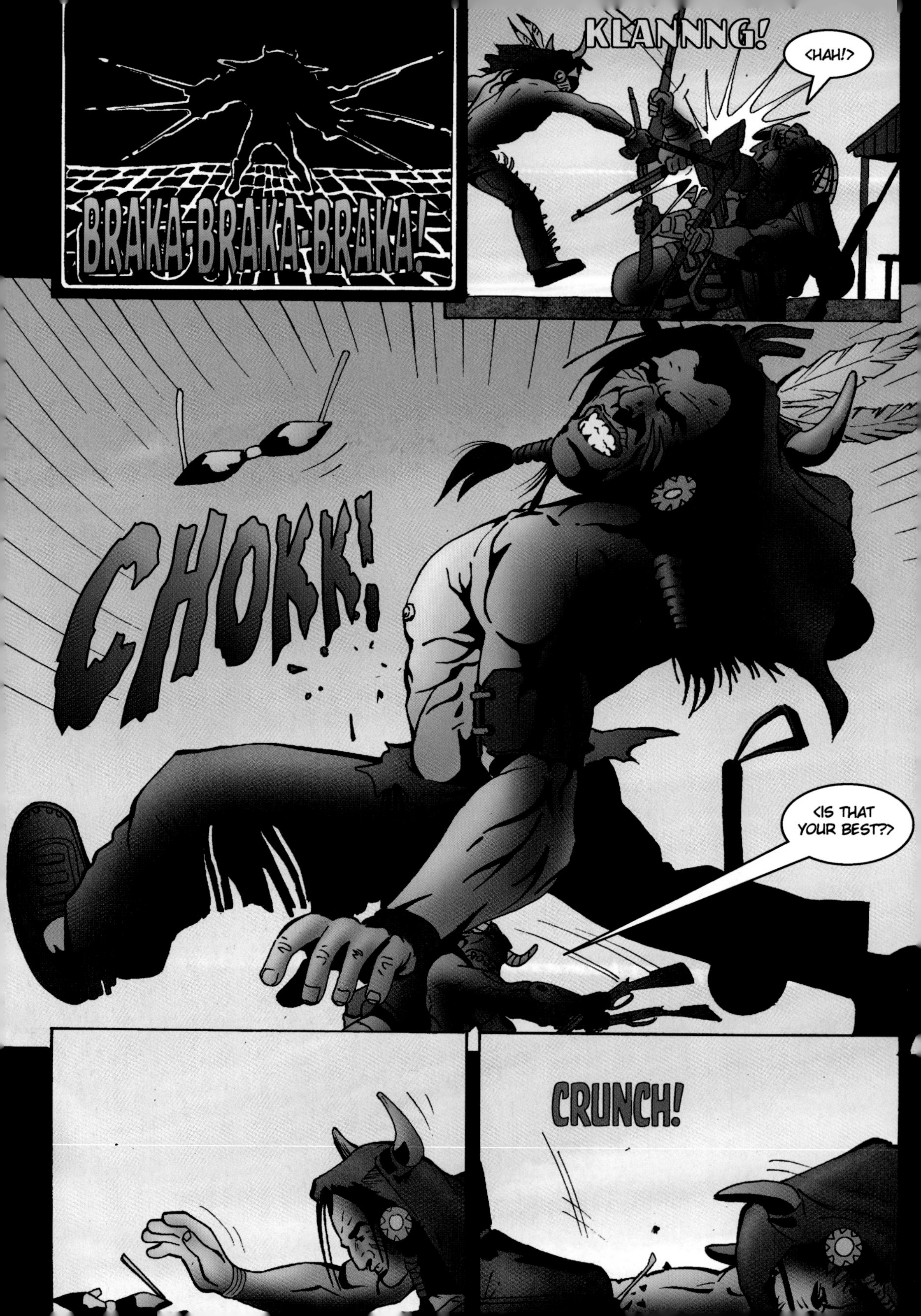

BRAKA-BRAKA-BRAKA!
KLANNNG!
<HAH!>
CHOKK!
<IS THAT YOUR BEST?>
CRUNCH!

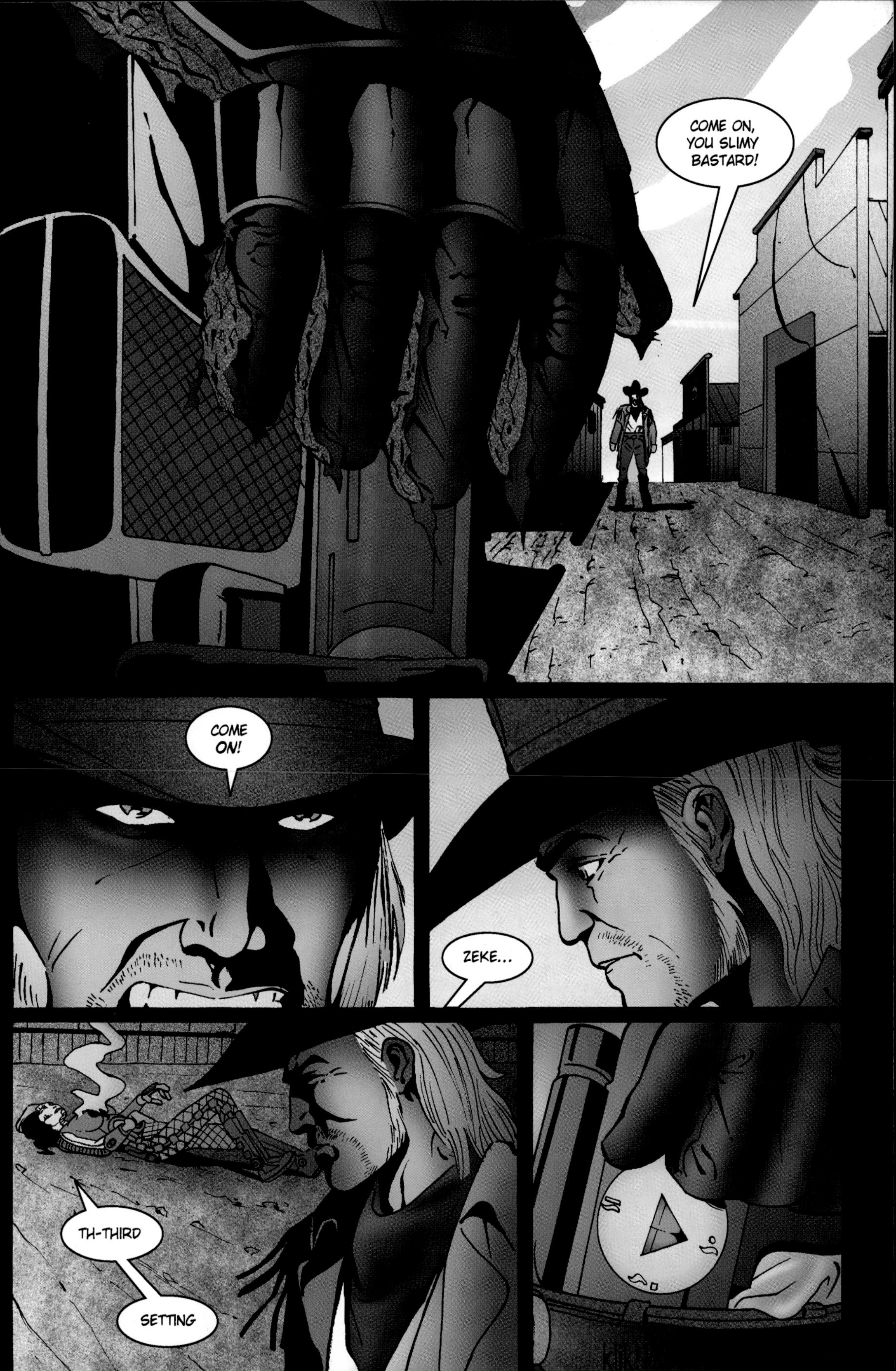
COME ON, YOU SLIMY BASTARD!
COME ON!
ZEKE...
TH-THIRD
SETTING
klik

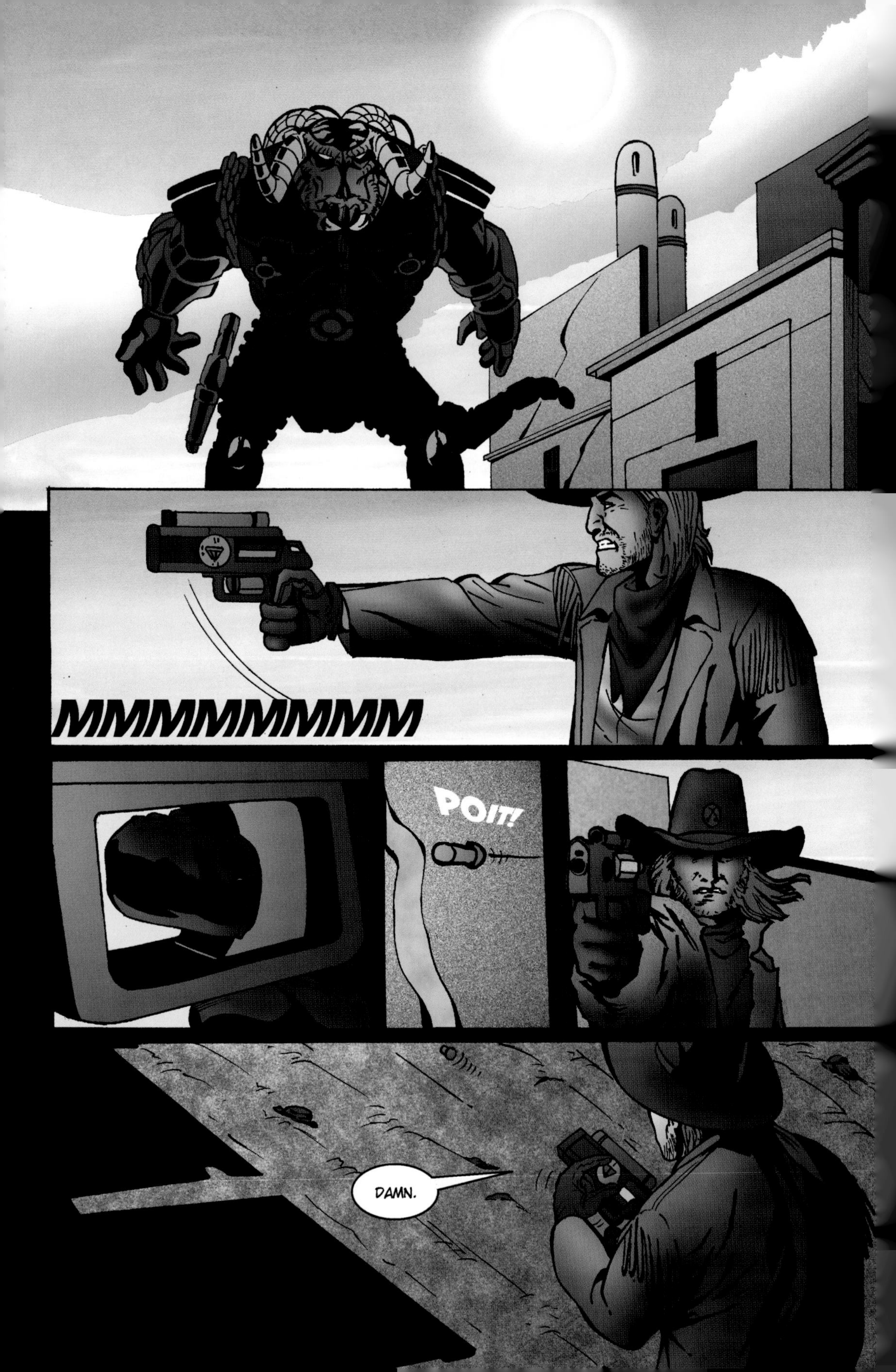
MMMMMMMMMM
POIT!
DAMN.

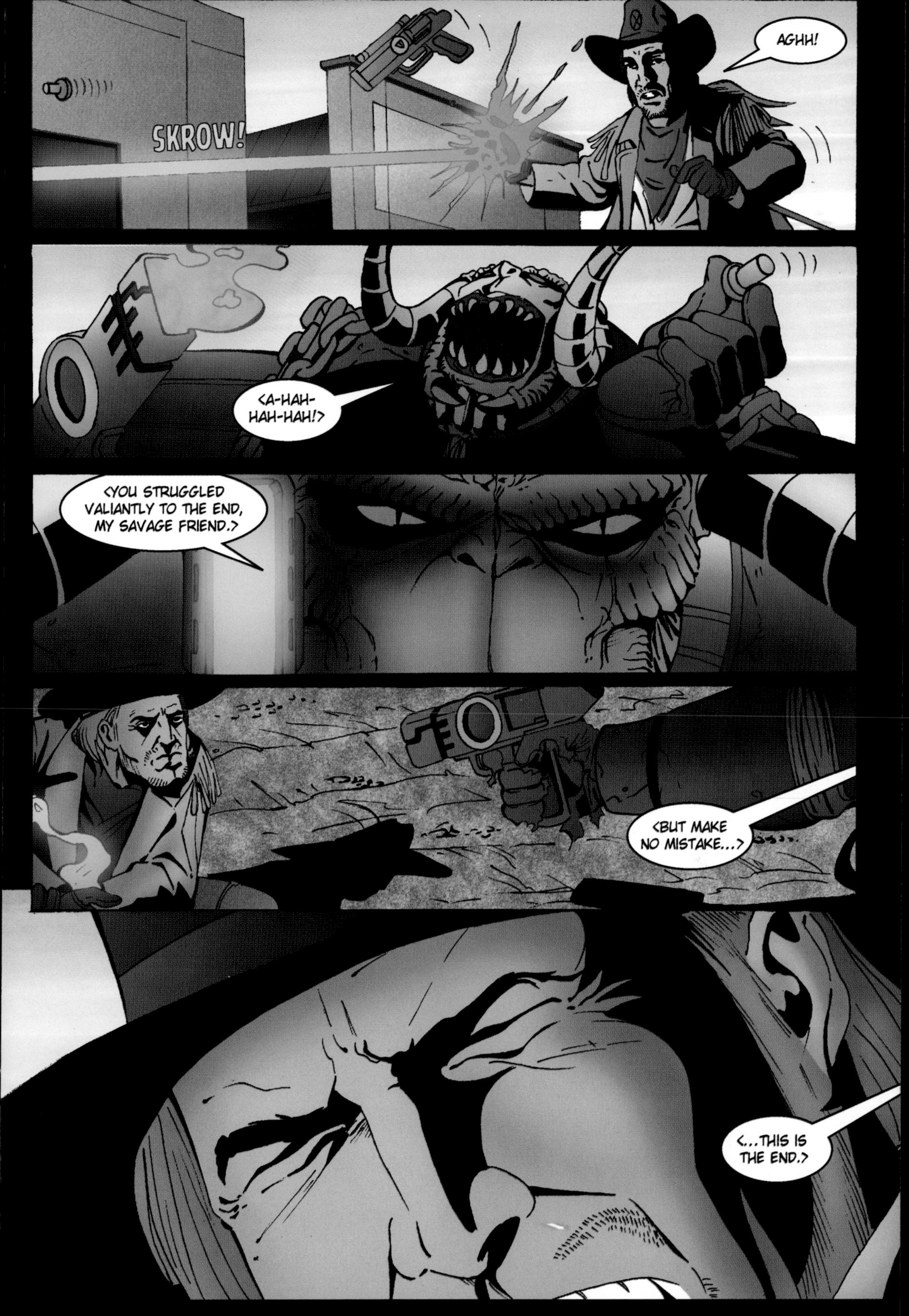
AGHH!
SKROW!
<A-HAH-HAH-HAH!>
<YOU STRUGGLED VALIANTLY TO THE END, MY SAVAGE FRIEND.>
<BUT MAKE NO MISTAKE...>
<...THIS IS THE END.>

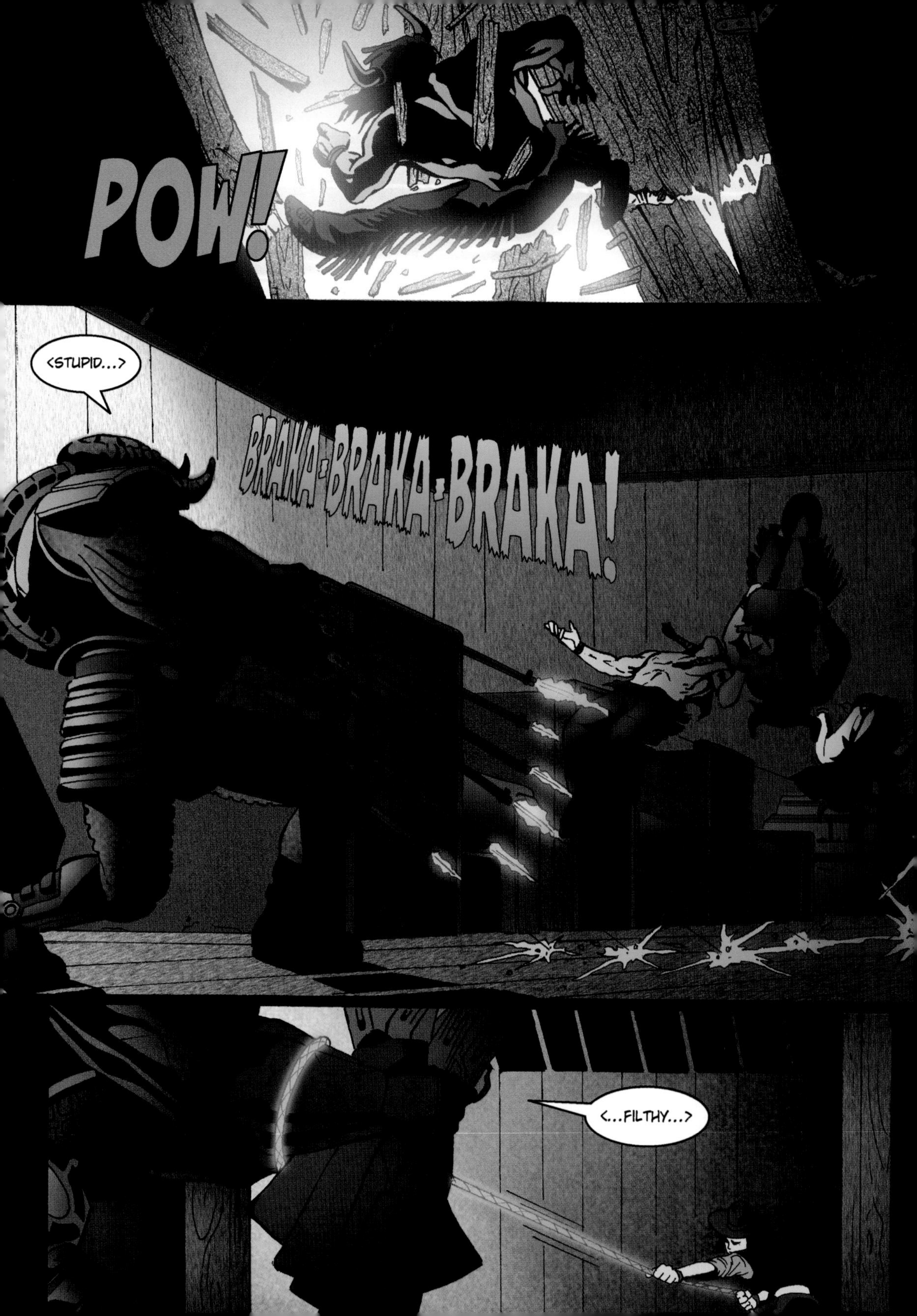
POW!
<STUPID...>
BRAKA-BRAKA-BRAKA!
<...FILTHY...>

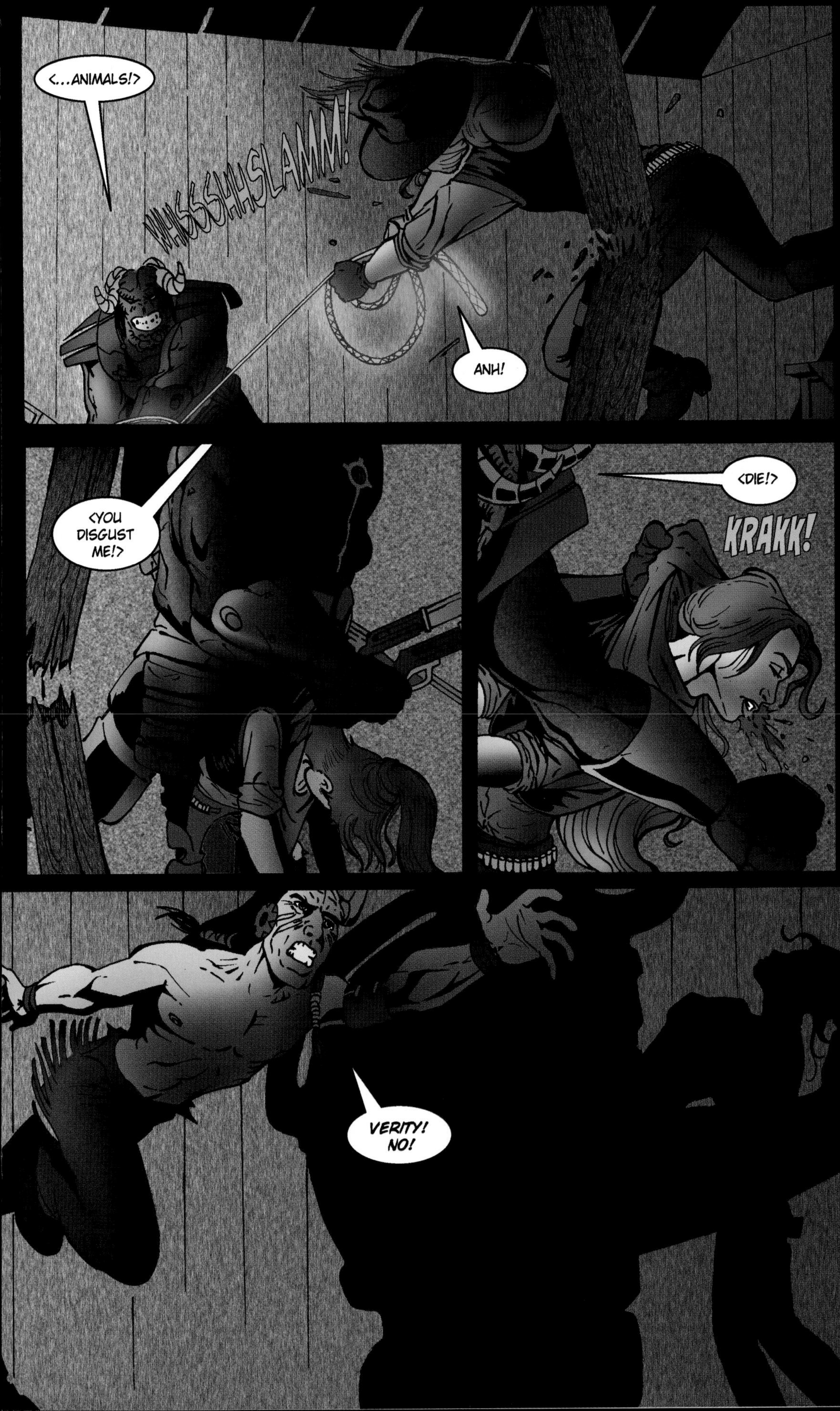
<...ANIMALS!>
WHSSSHHSLAMM!
ANH!
<YOU DISGUST ME!>
<DIE!>
KRAKK!
VERITY! NO!

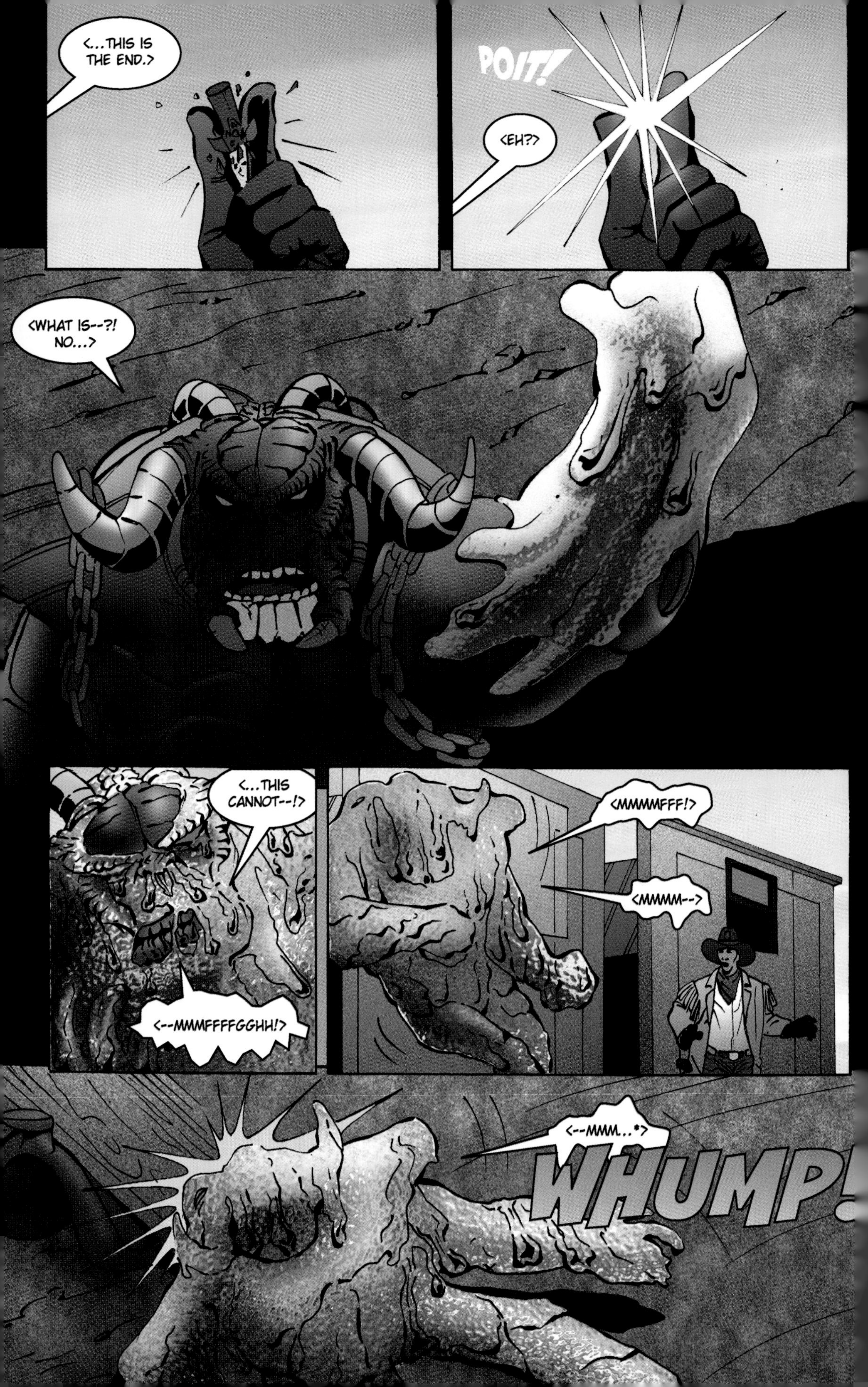
<...THIS IS THE END.>
POIT!
<EH?>
<WHAT IS--?! NO...>
<...THIS CANNOT--!>
<--MMMFFFFGGHH!>
<MMMMFFF!>
<MMMM-->
<--MMM...*>
WHUMP!

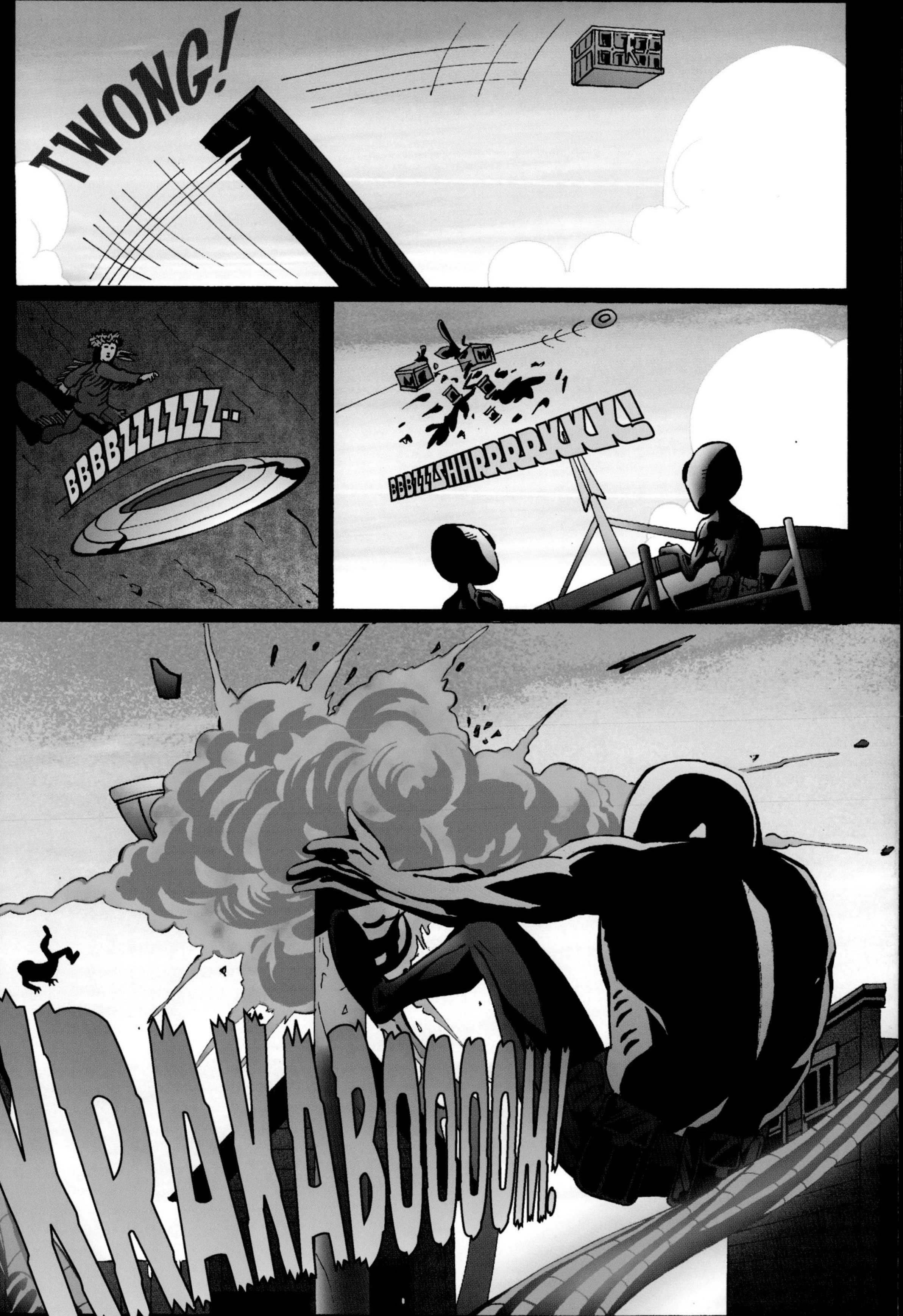
TWONG!
BBBBZZZZZZ..
BBBZZZSHHRRRRKKKK!
KRRAKABOOOOM!

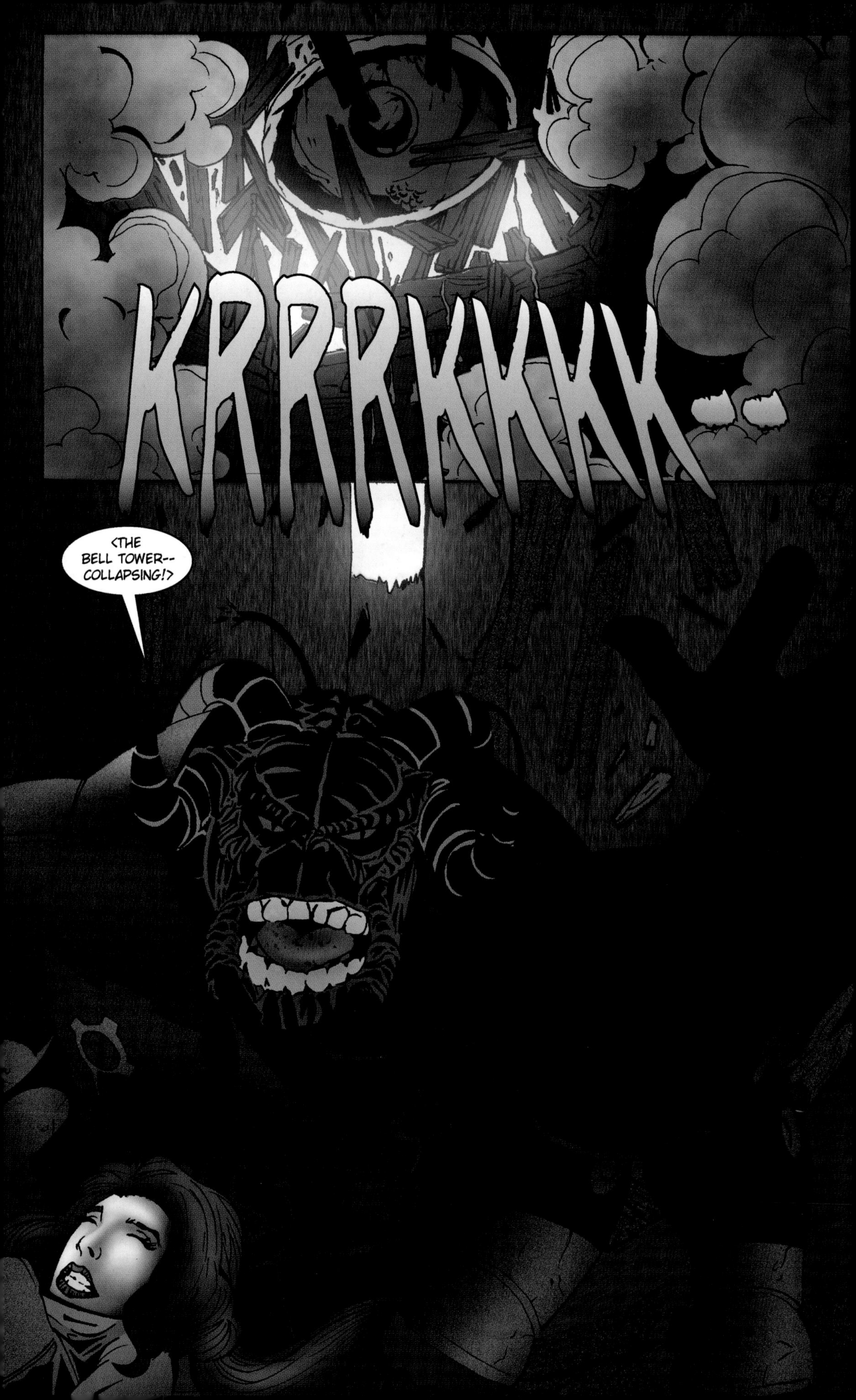
KRRRKKKK--
<THE BELL TOWER--COLLAPSING!>

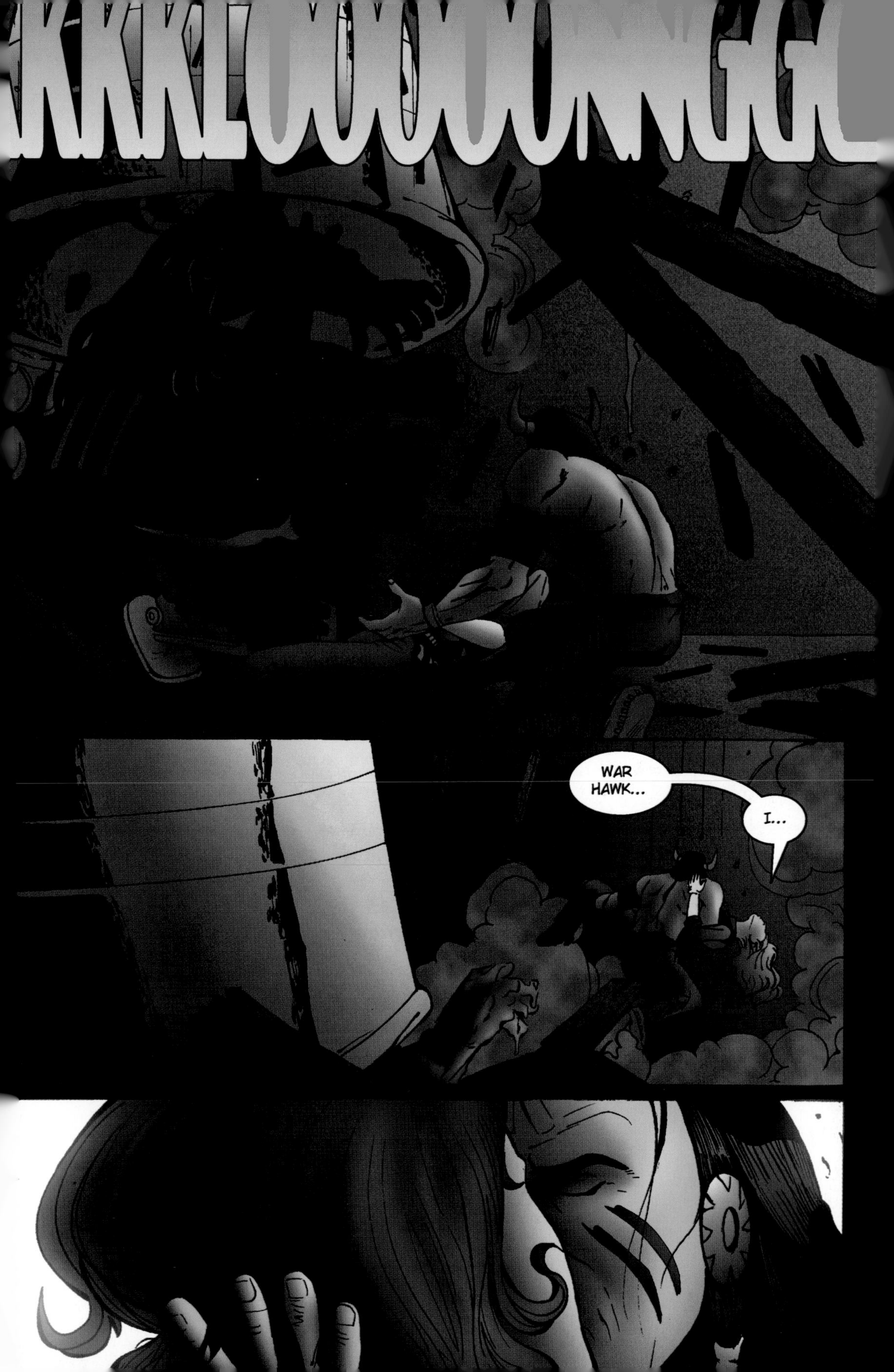
KKKLOOOOOONGG
WAR HAWK...
I...

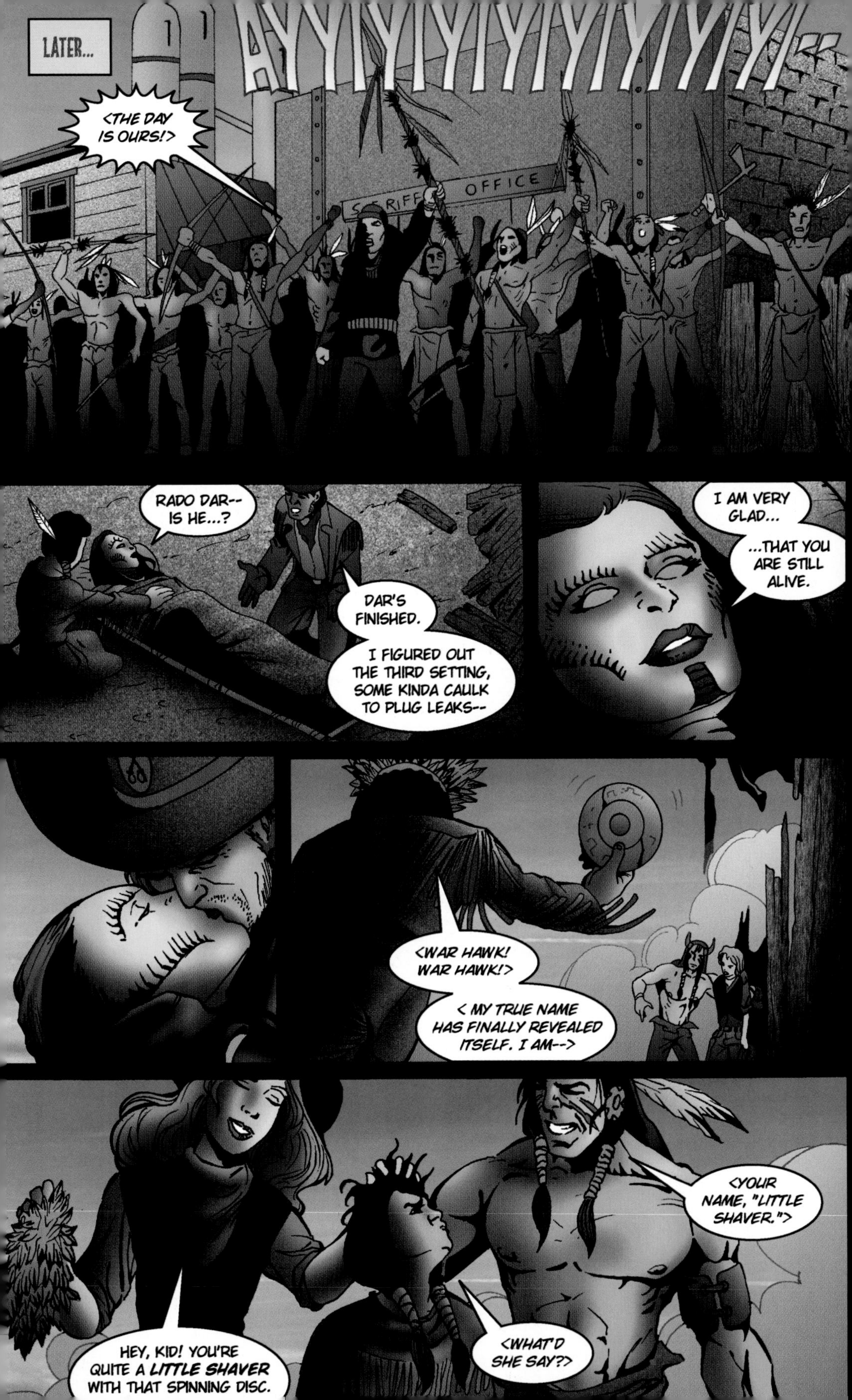
LATER...
AYYIYIYIYIYIYIYI--
<THE DAY IS OURS!>
SHERIFF OFFICE
RADO DAR-- IS HE...?
DAR'S FINISHED.
I FIGURED OUT THE THIRD SETTING, SOME KINDA CAULK TO PLUG LEAKS--
I AM VERY GLAD...
...THAT YOU ARE STILL ALIVE.
<WAR HAWK! WAR HAWK!>
< MY TRUE NAME HAS FINALLY REVEALED ITSELF. I AM-->
<YOUR NAME, "LITTLE SHAVER.">
HEY, KID! YOU'RE QUITE A LITTLE SHAVER WITH THAT SPINNING DISC.
<WHAT'D SHE SAY??>

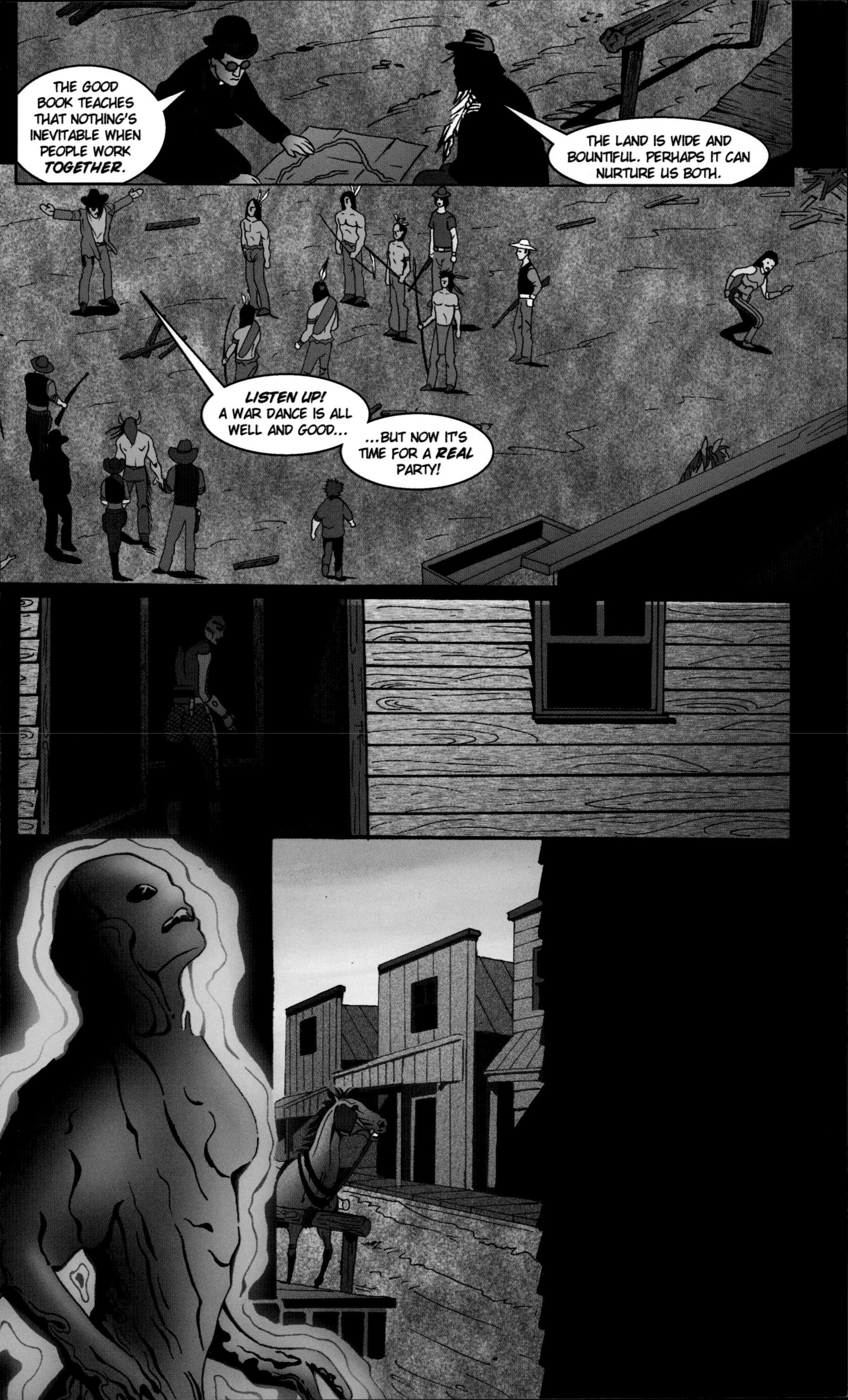
THE GOOD BOOK TEACHES THAT NOTHING'S INEVITABLE WHEN PEOPLE WORK **TOGETHER**.
THE LAND IS WIDE AND BOUNTIFUL. PERHAPS IT CAN NURTURE US BOTH.
LISTEN UP! A WAR DANCE IS ALL WELL AND GOOD...
...BUT NOW IT'S TIME FOR A **REAL** PARTY!

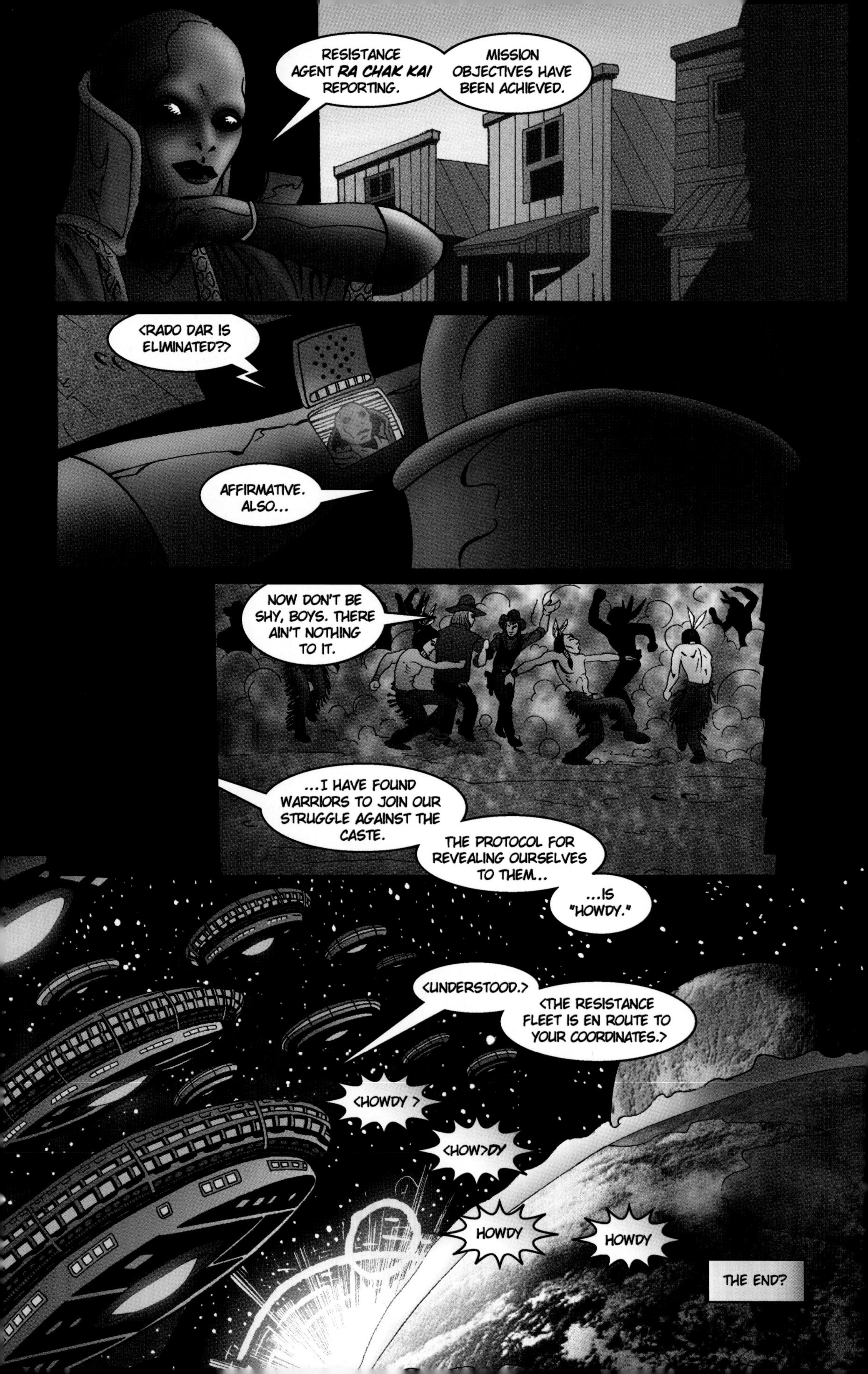
RESISTANCE AGENT RA CHAK KAI REPORTING.
MISSION OBJECTIVES HAVE BEEN ACHIEVED.
<RADO DAR IS ELIMINATED?>
AFFIRMATIVE. ALSO...
NOW DON'T BE SHY, BOYS. THERE AIN'T NOTHING TO IT.
...I HAVE FOUND WARRIORS TO JOIN OUR STRUGGLE AGAINST THE CASTE.
THE PROTOCOL FOR REVEALING OURSELVES TO THEM...
...IS "HOWDY."
<UNDERSTOOD.>
<THE RESISTANCE FLEET IS EN ROUTE TO YOUR COORDINATES.>
<HOWDY >
<HOW>DY
HOWDY
HOWDY
THE END?

COWBOYS & ALIENS

& ALIENS

Bonus Materials

Inks

Pencils

Page 11: Script

PAGE 11

PANEL 1: LONG, NARROW PANEL: DEEP FOCUS: NO-NAME GETS OFF HIS HO[RSE]
(FG) to join the trio of braves (BG), who have already dismounted and are ly[ing on]
their bellies on the edge of a cliff, propped up on their elbows and looking dow[n]
below them.

1. WHITE THUNDER (Apache): <What is it?>

PANEL 2: CU: SIDE TWOSHOT: MANY ARROWS ON THE LEFT, RED EAGLE LO[OKING]
OFF-PANEL TO THE RIGHT. Red Eagle's expression is nervous.

2. MANY ARROWS (Apache): <One of the white men's machines?>

PANEL 3: HUMONGOUS PANEL: LS: THE CRASHED SPACESHIP: Refer to Pla[tinum]
Studios concept art for guidance. Instead of the train of settlers pointing and
gawking at the craft, however, we have our three Indian braves and one appr[oaching]
overlooking it from a high cliff.

3. RED EAGLE (Apache): <This is beyond the whites.>

PAGE 12

PANEL 1: ANGLE DOWN: MS: THE BRAVES HEAD DOWN THE HILL. Red Eag[le and]
White Thunder are already way ahead of Many Arrows, holding his rifle, who [turns to]
the dejected No-Name, who stays put, hanging his head.

1. MANY ARROWS (Apache): <You stay here, No-Name.>

PANEL 2: CLOSE MEDIUM: TWOSHOT: A DISAPPOINTED NO-NAME FACES [MANY]
ARROWS. Many Arrows has a reassuring hand on No-Name's shoulder.

2. NO-NAME (Apache, sl): <But-->

3. MANY ARROWS (Apache): <PATIENCE, little brother. Your time will [come]
soon enough.>

PANEL 3: LS: CRASH SITE: TRIO OF BRAVES CREEP UP ON SHIP AS A HATC[H]
OPENS like a gangplank leading to the ground, disgorging an incredible amo[unt of]
MIST and a large number of HUMANOID FIGURES. The ground in the desert [area]
where the saucer crashed is littered with debris and wreckage from a gapin[g hole in]
the ships hold. The Indians approach low, weapons in hand.

4. WHITE THUNDER (Ap., dot): <There are PEOPLE in there...>

Page 12: Script

Pencils

Inks

Words:
Van Lente & Foley

Colors

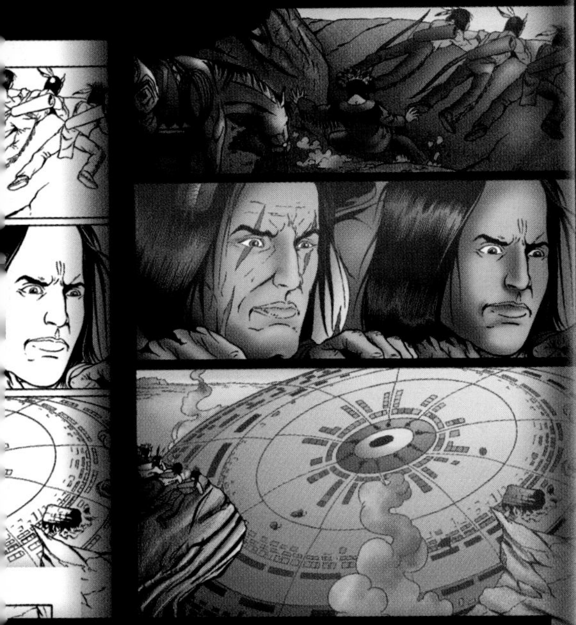

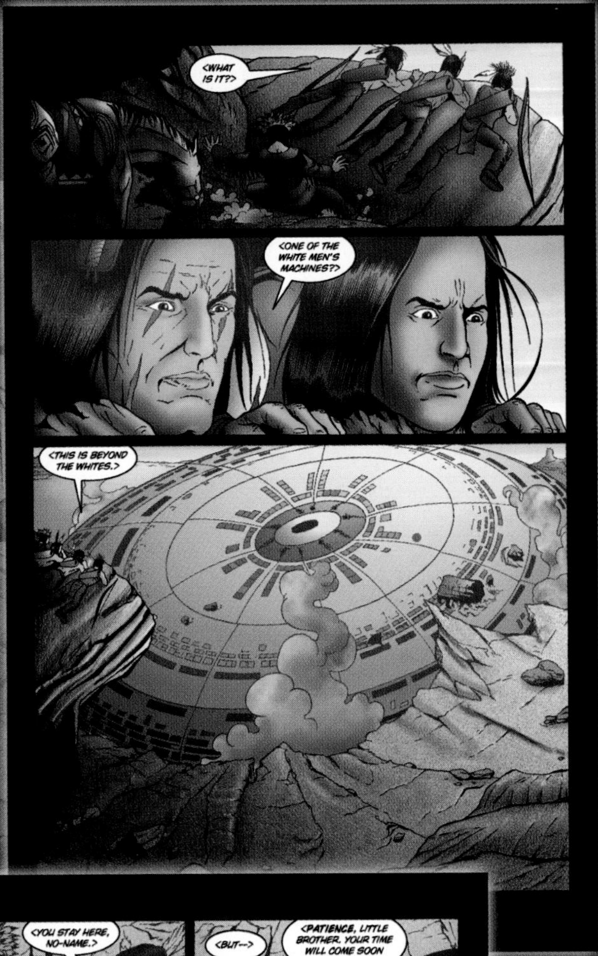
<WHAT IS IT?>
<ONE OF THE WHITE MEN'S MACHINES?>
<THIS IS BEYOND THE WHITES.>

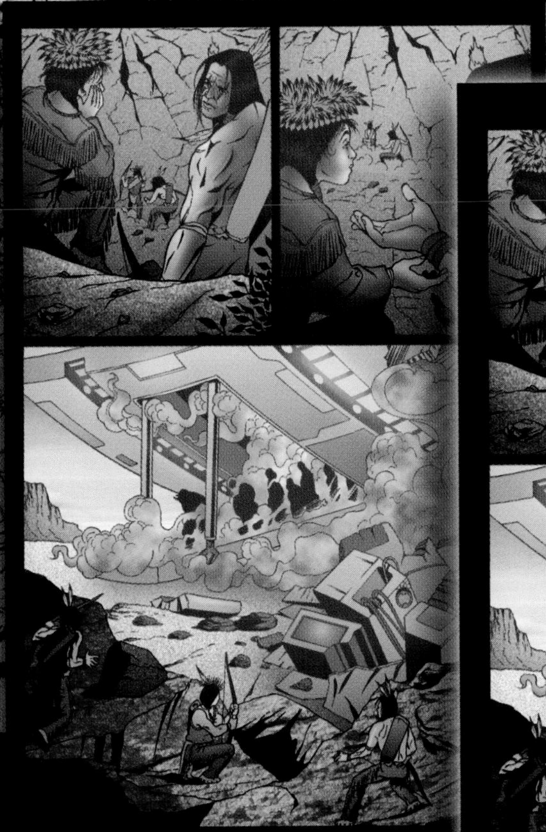

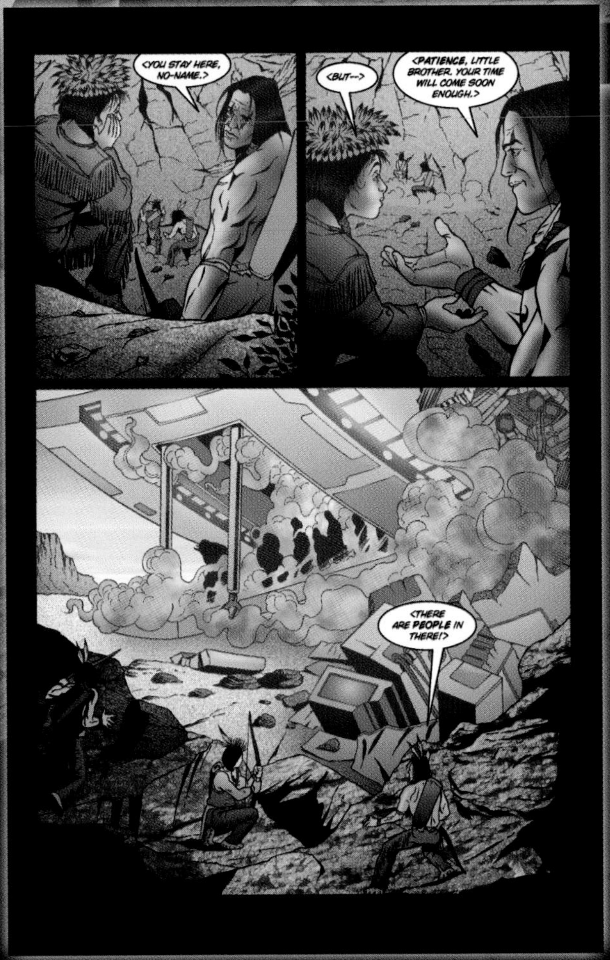
<YOU STAY HERE, NO-NAME.>
<BUT-->
<PATIENCE, LITTLE BROTHER. YOUR TIME WILL COME SOON ENOUGH.>
<THERE ARE PEOPLE IN THERE!>

Colors

Creator Bios

Writer: Fred Van Lente

In comics, Fred Van Lente is the writer and co-creator, along with artist Steve Ellis, of the SF thriller Tranquility (winner of a 1998 Spectrum Award for Best Science Fiction Art) and the critically acclaimed "super-crime" series The Silencers from Moonstone Books. He designed the hilarious "First-Class Roleplaying Game for Third-Rate Heroes," Stuper Powers!, currently in its second edition.

In 2002 the Academy of Motion Picture Arts and Sciences named Van Lente a quarter-finalist for the Don & Marie Nicholl Screenplay Fellowship for his comedy/adventure Knightlife. His short comedy The Fan Club took Honorable Mention at the Society of Film and Television Engineers Student Film Festival.

Currently, Van Lente is penning the romantic comedy When You Dance for Mainline Films and the horror thriller Phobia for Sub-Rosa Entertainment.

Writer: Andrew Foley

Andrew Foley drew his first comic book in crayon, on the wall of his family's living room. Rather than doing something sensible, like spanking him, sending him to bed without his supper, or throwing him out with the bathwater, his parents instead supported him in his artistic endeavors. This support enabled him to attend the Alberta College of Art (which he eventually got out of) in Calgary, Alberta (from which he's yet to escape).

To this day, Andrew isn't sure why he decided to try his hand at writing comic books, but he's pretty sure the flushing sound he heard as he made the decision was the comics industry going down the toilet. Andrew is writing a variety of other comics and graphic novels for Platinum Studios, including Conviction, Age of Kings, Threads (with Scott O. Brown), Return of the Wraith, and Jeremiah: The Last Empire, the authorized sequel to the Showtime television series. His other comics work includes Parting Ways, a 142-page graphic novel illustrated by Scott Mooney and Nick Craine, and the recently released Done to Death, with Fiona Staples. Buying any of these books will have an appreciable effect on lowering the crime rate in Andrew's neighborhood.

Pencils: Luciano Lima

Luciano Lima is a comics artist living in São Paolo, Brazil, where he is part of Fabricio Grellet's Magic Eye Studios. He has worked for Dark Horse on Grifter and The Mask, for Marvel on Wolverine and X-Force, and for the French publisher Semic.

Inks: Luciano Kars & J. Wilson

Kars and Wilson are both staff artists at Brazil's Magic Eye Studios, a comics art and script studio managed by Fabrício Grellet that has produced work for comic book and graphic novel publishers around the world.

Inks: Silvio Spotti

Silvio Spotti was born in São Paulo, where he still lives and works. He has a degree in arts from the FMU/FAAM university, and began his career in 1992 as a penciller for the small press in Brazil. In 1996 he started working as an inker, working on a Brazilian version of the Street Fighter comic book, through the Arthur Garcia Studio. In 2003 he did his first U.S. work through Magic Eye Studios, inking IDW's Wynonna Earp. Since then, he has inked Stargate SG1, Robocop, and Stargate Atlantis for Avatar Press, as well as Daniel Prophet of Dreams for Alias Comics. As a penciller/inker, Spotti has also done work for Disney (USA/Europe), drawing stories for Donald Duck, Kim Possible, Toy Story, Little Mermaid, and others.

Colour: Andy Elder

Andy Elder began working professionally in comics in 2005. His other credits include inking and coloring Warhead from AIT/Planet Lar, assisting colourists Jamie Grant and Jim Devlin on Testament for DC, and assisting Ian Richardson on 2000A.D.'s Sinister Dexter. His inks and colours will also be featured in Platinum's upcoming graphic novel Final Orbit. He's currently writing three creator-owned series, to be unveiled in 2007.

He lives on the west coast of Scotland.

Created by: Scott Mitchell Rosenberg

Scott Mitchell Rosenberg is chairman of Platinum Studios, an entertainment company that controls the world's largest independent library of comic book characters and adapts them for film, television and all other media. As chairman, Scott has played an integral role in creating the largest independent library of titles in comic book history. The Platinum Studios Library includes thousands of characters that have been published in millions of books all over the world, including anchor titles such as Cowboys & Aliens and Unique.

Scott established Platinum Studios in 1997, following a successful, high-profile career as the founder of Malibu Comics, a leading independent comic book company that was sold to Marvel Comics in 1994. During his time at Malibu, Scott led many successful comic spin offs into toys, television, and feature films, including the billion-dollar film and television phenomenon Men in Black.

Scott began his career in the comic book industry at age 13 when he started a mail order company. Scott became known for picking early hits, as many of the writers, stories and characters he selected were not originally chart toppers. Based on his retail success, Scott began publishing his own independent comic book titles, which led to the creation of Malibu Comics in 1986. His first launch, Ex-Mutants, was an instant hit.

Since that time, Scott has been recognized as a pioneer and a leader in the comic book industry. He recognized that comics were on the verge of one of many revolutions that would allow openings for new, smaller publishers, and that the advent of the Macintosh computer (circa 1986) and other technological advances of that time would soon allow those smaller companies to look bigger, minimizing their costs and maximizing the quality of their output. He then brokered an industry-changing deal in 1992, when the seven top-selling artists defected from Marvel Comics to form Image Studios. Scott signed the artists to a label deal at Malibu to distribute Image Studios comics until their new company was up and running. In addition, Scott worked with Adobe and their Photoshop software to develop the leading standard system for the computer coloring of comic books.

Today, Scott produces and develops comic book properties for all media, including a slate of high-profile, live-action feature films, television series for major networks, direct to DVD features, direct to web content and many, many other avenues. His vision has allowed Platinum to develop the business model of the future where properties are developed simultaneously for multiple distribution models, maximizing profitability, visibility and availability for everyone involved, from the creator to the consumer.

Scott has been happily married since 1992, and lives in California with his wife and two daughters.

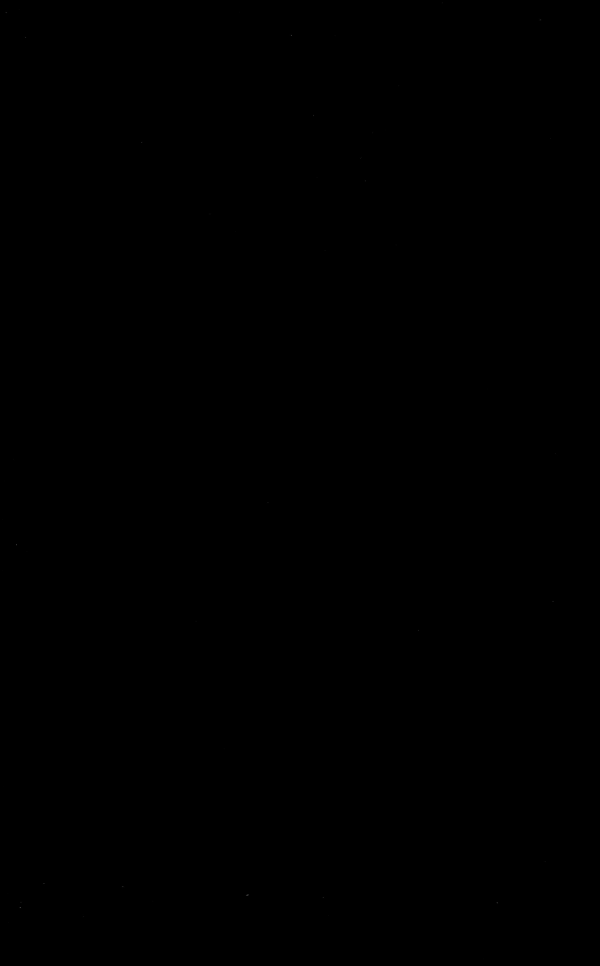

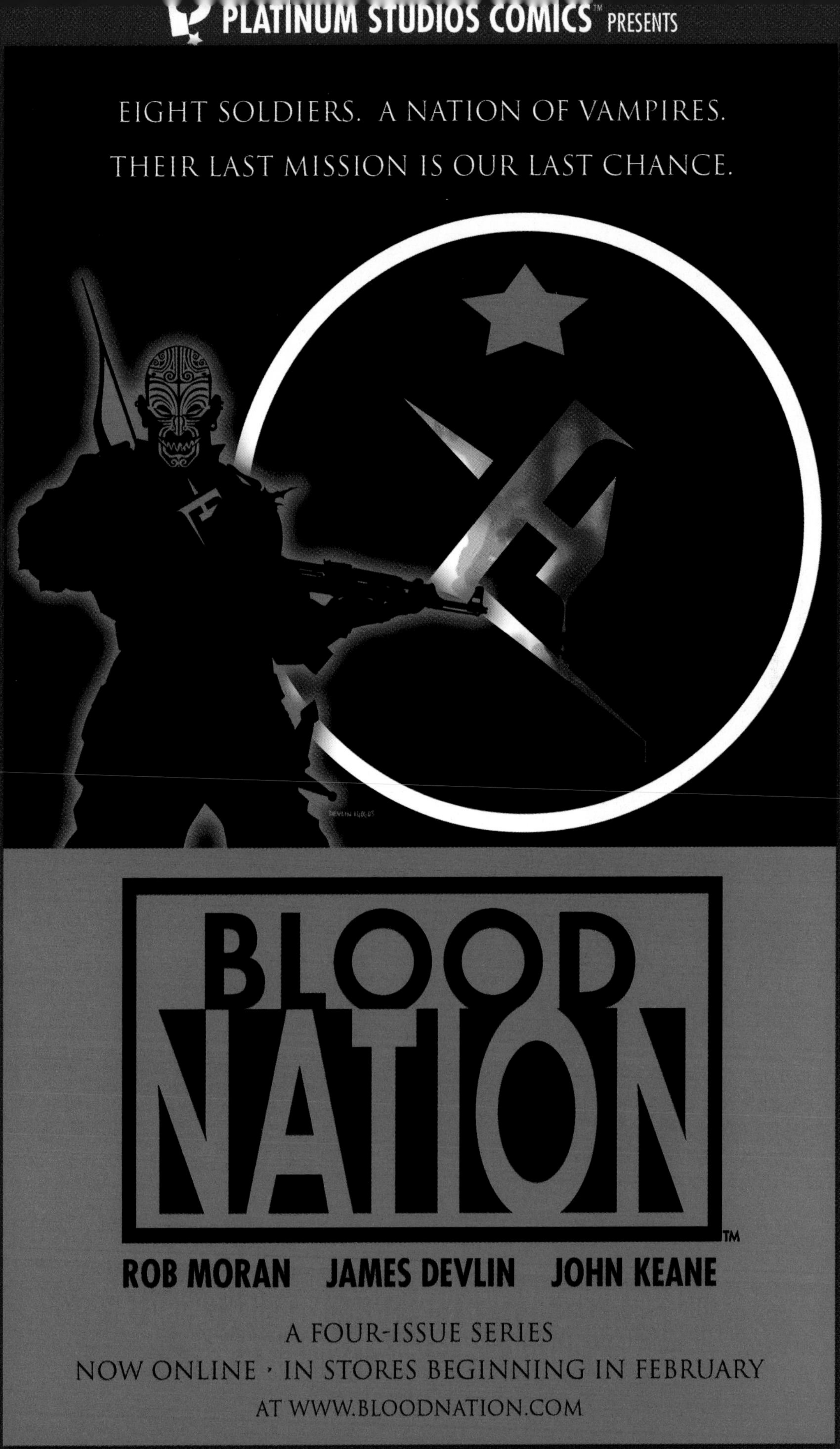
PLATINUM STUDIOS COMICS™ PRESENTS
EIGHT SOLDIERS. A NATION OF VAMPIRES.
THEIR LAST MISSION IS OUR LAST CHANCE.
BLOOD NATION™
ROB MORAN JAMES DEVLIN JOHN KEANE
A FOUR-ISSUE SERIES
NOW ONLINE · IN STORES BEGINNING IN FEBRUARY
AT WWW.BLOODNATION.COM

"Wrestle not with monsters, lest ye become a monster."
— Friedrich Nietzsche

WATCHDOGS

GRAPHIC NOVEL BY FRED VAN LENTE AND BRIAN CHURILLA
NOW ONLINE • IN STORES FEBRUARY 2007
www.drunkduck.com/watchdogs

PLATINUM STUDIOS COMICS™ PRESENTS

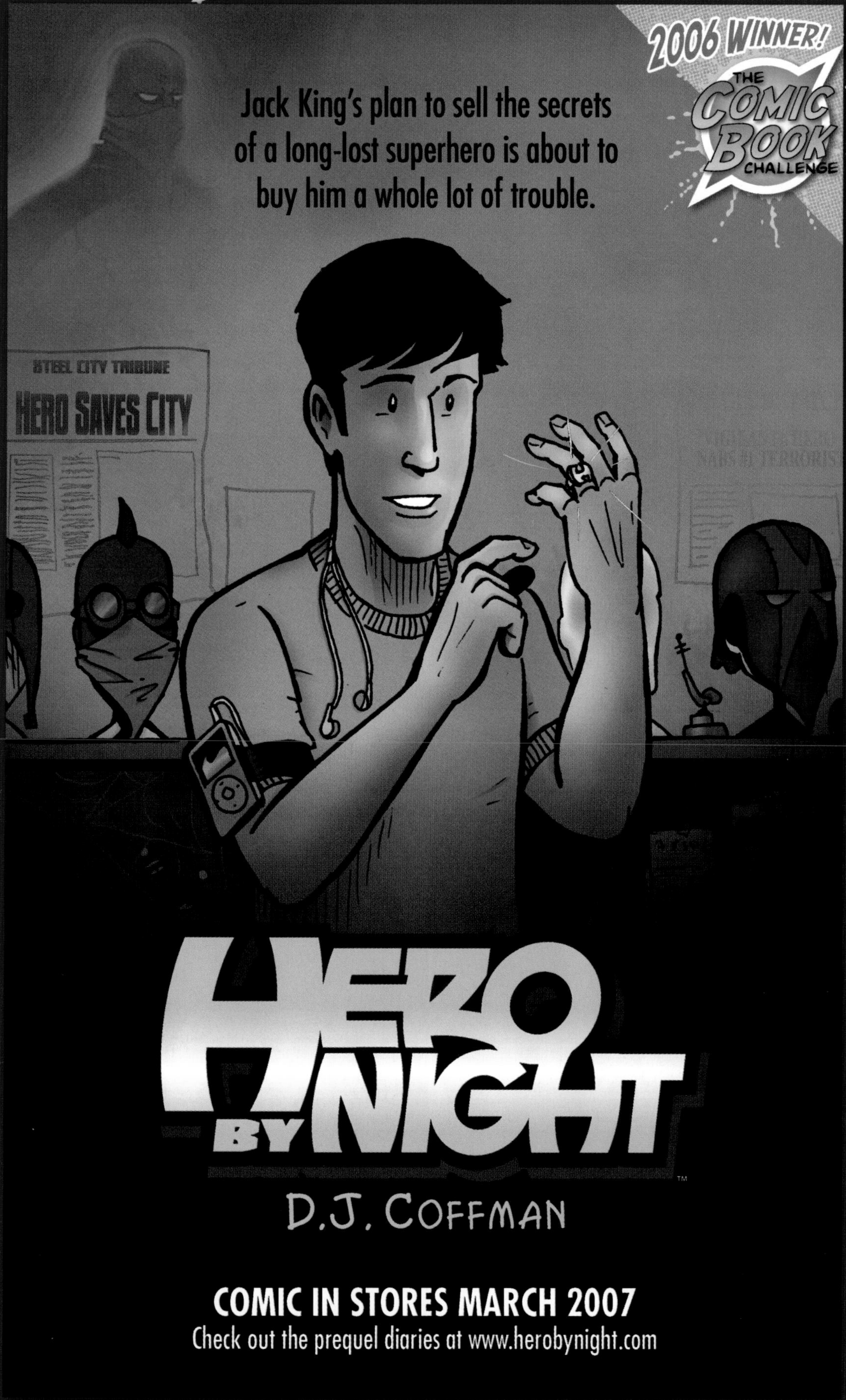

2006 WINNER!
THE COMIC BOOK CHALLENGE
Jack King's plan to sell the secrets of a long-lost superhero is about to buy him a whole lot of trouble.
STEEL CITY TRIBUNE
HERO SAVES CITY
HERO BY NIGHT™
D.J. COFFMAN
COMIC IN STORES MARCH 2007
Check out the prequel diaries at www.herobynight.com

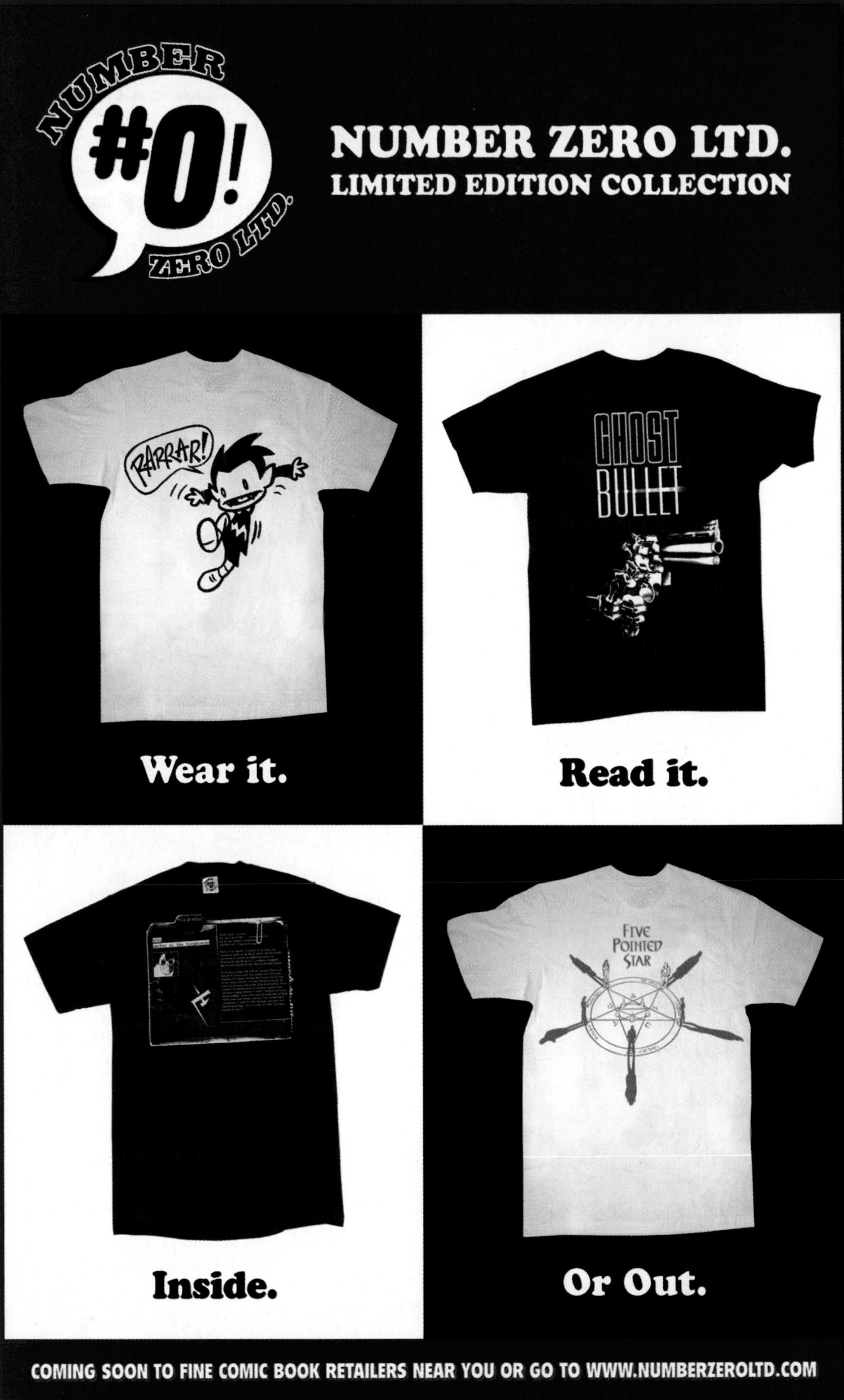
NUMBER #0! ZERO LTD.
NUMBER ZERO LTD.
LIMITED EDITION COLLECTION
RARRAR!
Wear it.
GHOST BULLET
Read it.
Inside.
FIVE POINTED STAR
Or Out.
COMING SOON TO FINE COMIC BOOK RETAILERS NEAR YOU OR GO TO WWW.NUMBERZEROLTD.COM

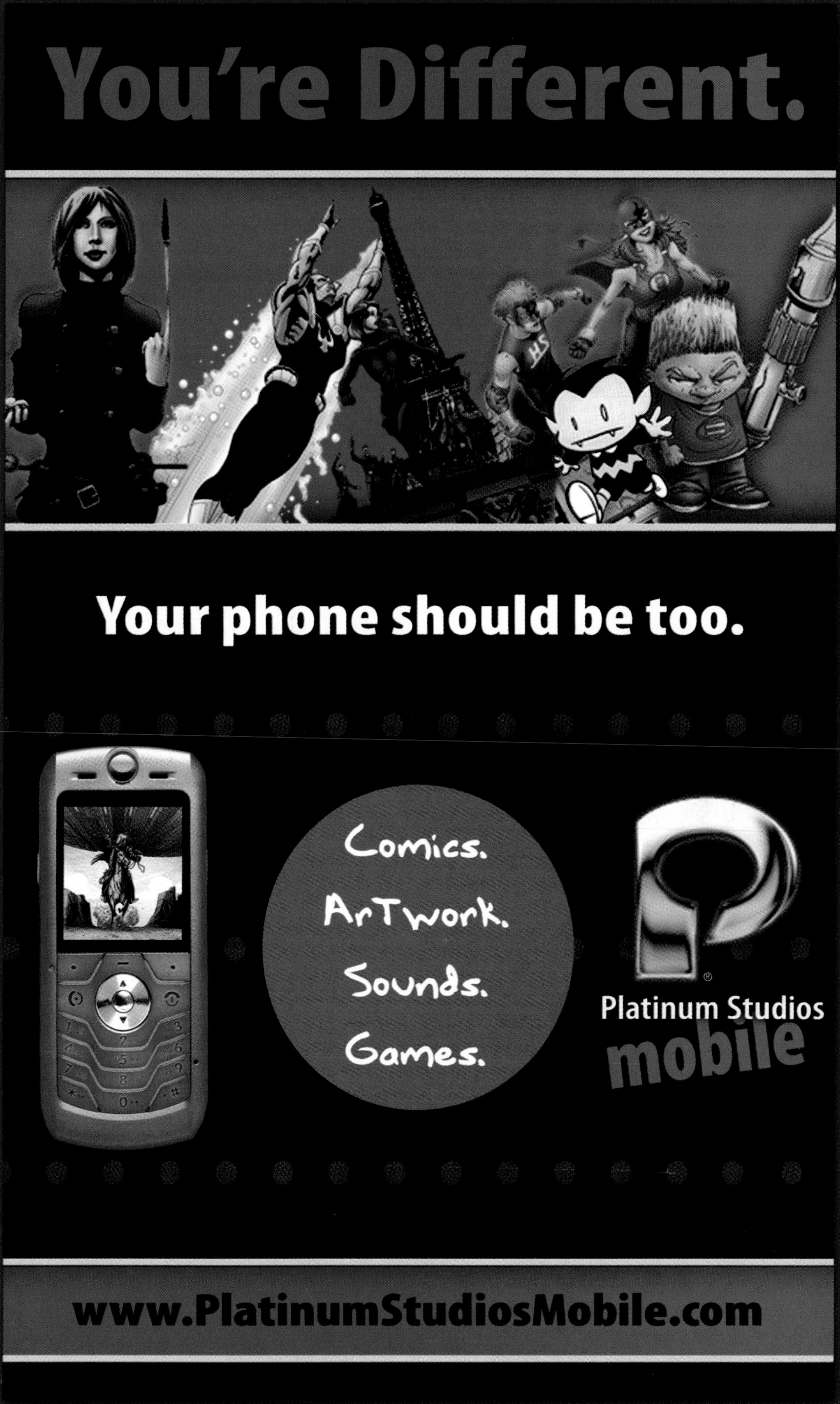
You're Different.
Your phone should be too.
Comics.
ArTwork.
Sounds.
Games.
Platinum Studios
mobile
www.PlatinumStudiosMobile.com

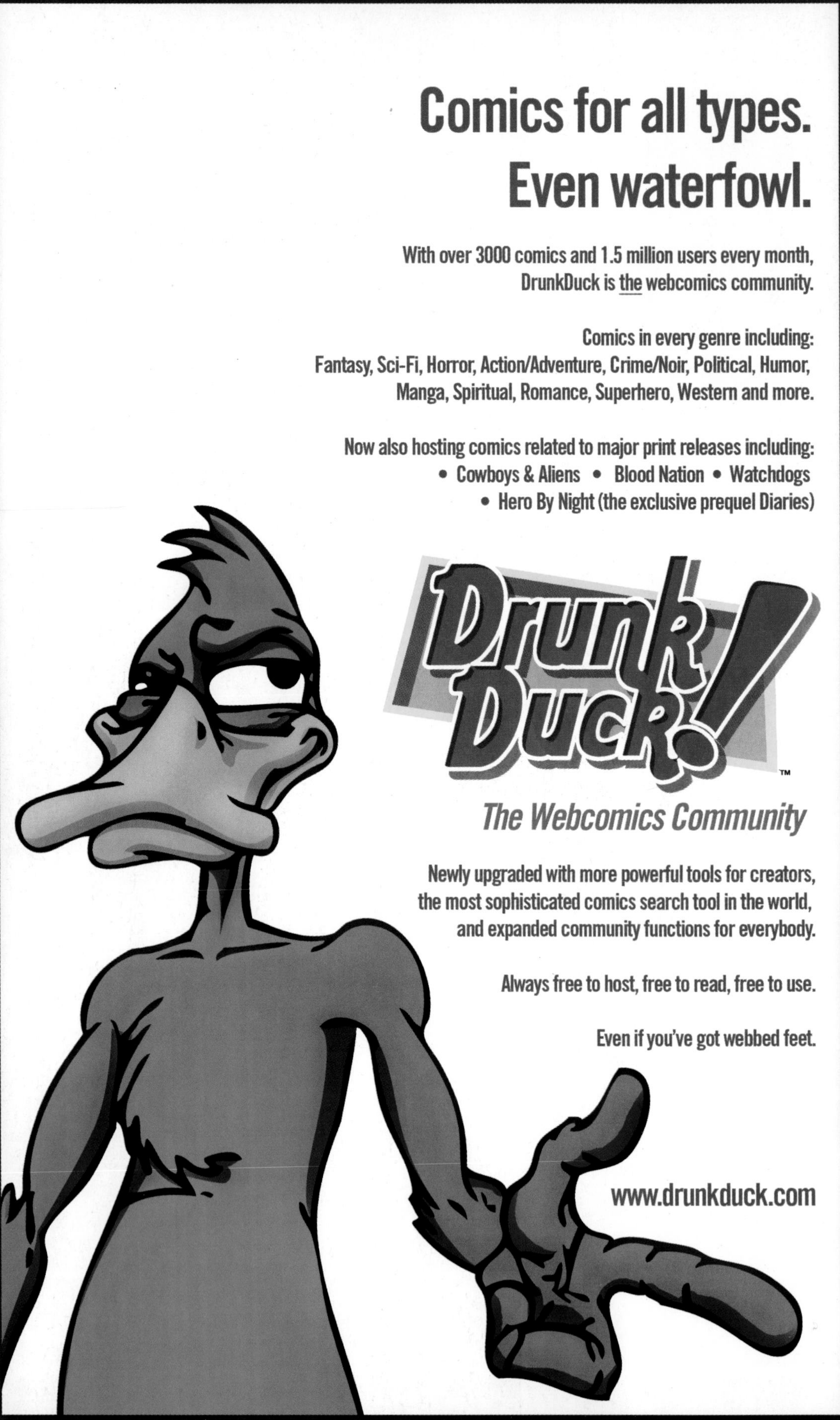
Comics for all types.
Even waterfowl.
With over 3000 comics and 1.5 million users every month,
DrunkDuck is the webcomics community.
Comics in every genre including:
Fantasy, Sci-Fi, Horror, Action/Adventure, Crime/Noir, Political, Humor,
Manga, Spiritual, Romance, Superhero, Western and more.
Now also hosting comics related to major print releases including:
• Cowboys & Aliens • Blood Nation • Watchdogs
• Hero By Night (the exclusive prequel Diaries)
Drunk Duck!™
The Webcomics Community
Newly upgraded with more powerful tools for creators,
the most sophisticated comics search tool in the world,
and expanded community functions for everybody.
Always free to host, free to read, free to use.
Even if you've got webbed feet.
www.drunkduck.com